U.S. Leadership, History, and Bilateral Relations in Northeast Asia

Whereas most discussions of history have centered on the rift between China and Japan, this book focuses on three other divisions stemming from deep-seated memories within Northern Asia, which increasingly will test U.S. diplomacy and academic analysis. The first division involves long-suppressed Japanese and South Korean memories that are critical of U.S. behavior – concerning issues such as the atomic bombings, the Tokyo Tribunal, and the Korean War. How should the United States respond as these memories come out into the open, complicating vital bilateral alliances? The second division is the enduring disagreement between Japan and South Korea over history. What can the United States do to invigorate urgently needed trilateral ties? The third and most important division is the revival of a sinocentric worldview, which foretells a struggle between China and other countries concerning history, one that has already begun in China's dispute with South Korea and is likely to implicate the United States above all. Presenting three perspectives on each theme, the book launches a multisided discussion of the importance of history in international relations.

Gilbert Rozman received his Ph.D. from Princeton University in 1971, where he has taught since that time. His books and articles concern four countries in Northeast Asia: China, Japan, Russia, and South Korea.

U.S. Leadership, History, and Bilateral Relations in Northeast Asia

Edited by

GILBERT ROZMAN

Princeton University

CAMBRIDGE UNIVERSITY PRESS
Cambridge, New York, Melbourne, Madrid, Cape Town, Singapore,
São Paulo, Delhi, Dubai, Tokyo, Mexico City

Cambridge University Press
32 Avenue of the Americas, New York, NY 10013-2473, USA

www.cambridge.org
Information on this title: www.cambridge.org/9780521190565

First published 2011

Printed in the United States of America

A catalog record for this publication is available from the British Library.

Library of Congress Cataloging in Publication data

U.S. leadership, history, and bilateral relations in Northeast Asia / edited by
Gilbert Rozman.
   p. cm.
Includes bibliographical references and index.
ISBN 978-0-521-19056-5 Hardback
  1. United States – Foreign relations – East Asia.   2. East Asia – Foreign relations –
United States.   3. Collective memory – Political aspects – East Asia.   4. East Asia –
Foreign relations – 20th century.   5. East Asia – Politics and government – 20th
century.   I. Rozman, Gilbert.   II. Title: United States leadership, history, and bilateral
relations in Northeast Asia.   III. Title: US leadership, history, and bilateral relations in
Northeast Asia.
DS518.8.U16   2010
327.7305 – dc22   2010012381

ISBN 978-0-521-19056-5 Hardback

Contents

List of Contributors   *page* vii

Acknowledgments   ix

    Introduction   1
    Gilbert Rozman

PART I. HISTORICAL MEMORIES AND BILATERAL TIES
WITH ALLIES

1. Japan's Historical Memory toward the United States   17
    Kazuhiko Togo

2. Values and History in U.S.–South Korean Relations   45
    Gi-Wook Shin

3. U.S. Leadership, History, and Relations with Allies   72
    Gilbert Rozman

PART II. HISTORICAL MEMORIES, JAPANESE–SOUTH KOREAN
RELATIONS, AND U.S. VALUES

4. Japan–South Korea Relations and the Role of the United
    States on History   97
    Kazuhiko Togo

5. Getting Away or Getting In: U.S. Strategic Options in the
    Historical Controversy between Its Allies   124
    Cheol Hee Park

6. U.S. Strategic Thinking on the Japanese–South Korean
    Historical Dispute   143
    Gilbert Rozman

PART III. HISTORICAL MEMORIES, SINO–SOUTH KOREAN
RELATIONS, AND U.S. VALUES

7. Sino–South Korean Differences over Koguryo and the
   U.S. Role   171
   Jin Linbo

8. New Grounds for Contestation: South Korea's Koguryo-Era
   Historical Dramas and Sino-Korean Relations   190
   Scott Snyder

9. U.S. Strategic Thinking on Sino–South Korean Differences
   over History   208
   Gilbert Rozman

Index   227

List of Contributors

Jin Linbo is a Senior Research Fellow at the China Institute of International Studies.

Cheol Hee Park is an associate professor at the Graduate School of International Studies at Seoul National University.

Gilbert Rozman is Musgrave Professor of Sociology at Princeton University.

Gi-Wook Shin is Tong Yang, Korea Foundation, and Korea Stanford Alumni Chair of Korean Studies; Professor of Sociology; and Director of the Walter H. Shorenstein Asia-Pacific Research Center at Stanford University.

Scott Snyder is a senior associate at the Asia Foundation and Pacific Forum Center for Strategic and International Studies (CSIS).

Kazuhiko Togo is a visiting professor at Kyoto Sangyo University and former Japanese ambassador to the Netherlands.

Acknowledgments

This book was made possible through the encouragement and generous support of the Northeast Asia History Foundation. The Foundation sponsored projects covering the separate parts of the book, which have been consolidated in this single tome. Through its assistance, a conference was also held to coordinate and update the contributions. Each of the authors has appreciated the opportunity to bring into the open differences in thinking about the U.S. role in addressing values and historical memory with the goal of moving forward toward bridging them. Taking into account both academic and policy perspectives, the chapters that follow offer a series of exchanges of views, which are best read together to benefit from the joint effort sought by the Foundation to address our common challenges.

We are grateful also to various former officials in the countries covered, notably the United States, for sharing the lessons of their past experiences. Among the authors, the editor owes a special debt to Kazuhiko Togo, who agreed to write two chapters and took great care to present his views of the links between historical memory, values, and diplomacy in a forward-looking manner. Additional thanks are due to two anonymous readers, whose constructive queries helped to reframe the discussion. Finally, we should acknowledge the attentive efforts of Lew Bateman and others at Cambridge University Press in seeing this work through to publication.

Gilbert Rozman

U.S. Leadership, History, and Bilateral Relations in
Northeast Asia

Introduction

Gilbert Rozman

In 1950, history seemed all but forgotten as the specter of communism hung ominously over Northeast Asia. The Chinese Communist Party had just fought its way to power in a revolution aimed at sweeping aside history, especially Confucianism, which was seen as leaving China backward and ill prepared to rise up and modernize. The Korean War had turned Koreans away from memories of the past that united them to a fateful choice about their future as part either of the wave of communism or of the U.S.-led "free world" bloc. In Japan, preparations were under way for the San Francisco Peace Treaty, which focused on putting aside the legacy of Japan's colonialism and wars in order to rebuild as part of the U.S.-led bloc. Large numbers of Chinese, Japanese, and South Koreans were inclined to condemn their past for the sorrows and weakness it had brought; few defended it. With their eyes on modernity, which leaves the past behind, Americans were eager to embrace a democratic Japan and South Korea while condemning communist states that were seen as rejecting both their own traditions and the promise of the free market and free world.

In 2010, the specter of history is hanging over Northeast Asia, but a struggle lies ahead. Confusion reigns as to what is the true threat from historical legacies and memory. Over the previous decade, concern centered on Japanese revisionism, defending the conduct of Japan in 1895–1945 in a manner that offends its neighbors. Yet, that issue was framed too narrowly, missing the problem of Japanese-U.S. historical differences, which is no less explosive. Attention turned to South Korean refocusing on history, galvanized by progressives led by President Roh Moo-hyun, who were incensed by Japan's view of history. Yet, the broader sweep of

South Korea's rediscovery of history was overlooked, both the incendiary problem of historical differences with the United States and an abrupt awakening to the prospect of clashing Chinese historical views. Indeed, of all historical memory challenges, the least noted but potentially most serious may be sinocentrism, with China influenced by old ways of thinking about its place in Asia both threatening the U.S. role in the region as if it signifies hegemonism – heir to imperialism – and arousing fears in neighboring states that this outlook could serve as a rationale for Chinese hegemonism. In a span of two decades, successive reinterpretations of history in Japan, South Korea, and China have alarmed neighbors and posed an unexpected challenge to U.S. thinking.

During the cold war, narrowing differences over historical issues was postponed. The Yoshida Doctrine called on Japan to rely on U.S. leadership in order to give priority to economic development without becoming sidetracked with historical differences. The anticommunism of leaders such as President Park Chung-hee also led to setting aside differences with the United States over history while agreeing to normalization with Japan without any resolution of the aroused grievances of the Korean people. In China too, history had little place except as part of anti-imperialist rhetoric in pursuit of revolutionary causes favored by Mao Zedong's brand of communism. When Deng Xiaoping redirected China onto the path of reform socialism, he was also loath to dwell on historical memories. It mostly sufficed to highlight "friendship" relations with Japan and pragmatic U.S. ties. In Jiang Zemin, Abe Shinzo, and Roh Moo-hyun, we find leaders emboldened to raise the profile of history disputes, but even they hesitated to widen the scope in order to reflect the full extent and intensity of simmering historical memories. Despite new leadership committed to managing some of the most combustible memories – President Hu Jintao in facing Japanese revisionism after Prime Minister Koizumi Junichiro's annual Yasukuni Shrine visits, President Lee Myung-bak in facing the same challenge, and Prime Minister Hatoyama Yukio's promise to avoid similar provocations – emotions centered on history issues could erupt anew, expressing long-suppressed grievances against the United States and rekindled grievances against China. In the 1990s and 2000s, preoccupation with Japan served as a ready outlet for a range of views about historical injustice that may take different forms in the coming decades.

Visiting China, President Barack Obama in November 2009 stressed common interests, while affirming U.S. values. Although history was not in the forefront during his visit, many issues had a historical component.

On climate change, the Chinese insisted that the Western industrialized states were responsible for the problem due to past neglect, and therefore must bear the costs of new global environmental initiatives. On Tibet and Xinjiang, China blamed outside interference, following a longstanding pattern, for threats to their sovereignty, appealing for new commitments at odds with human rights concerns. While the Taiwan issue seemed to be under control, given the cooperative approach of President Ma Ying-jeou, this remained the foremost difference in historical thinking, and the prospect of a major U.S. arms sale to Taiwan as well as a calculation in China that Ma would not move beyond trade talks to political talks could enflame the atmosphere. More immediate were differences over how to deal with North Korea's nuclear weapons threat, as the Chinese put this in a different historical context and sought a softer approach that some regarded as sinocentric in spirit, solidifying Chinese influence over the peninsula. Japan and South Korea perceived a growing challenge from sinocentrism, and the United States needed to recognize it as well in pursuit of a cohesive strategy that would prevent a rising China from forging exclusive regionalism in an East Asian community. History was now an unmistakable battleground for arguments directed toward the reorganization of Asia.

Various historical grievances are coming to the forefront. Claiming to speak for developing countries, China accuses the industrialized states of irresponsible ravaging of our common heritage. Returning to the theme of anti-imperialism, reinforced by critiques of antihegemonism, China is also renewing its denunciation of the unjust world order that evolved in modern times. With calls for Obama to visit Hiroshima gaining ground in Japanese diplomatic circles, the debate over World War II is heating up too. Unlike the rancorous recent charges about history centered on Japan, notably in 2005, the scope has widened and the United States is deeply implicated. History has returned to the spotlight.

U.S. officials and academics have often steered clear of history issues as someone else's problem. They have counseled Japanese and South Koreans to set such issues aside, while associating historical concerns in China, and Russia too, with ideological holdovers that are overcome as countries become more realist in orientation. Unaware of how much the United States is implicated in the historical controversies of this region, Americans are ill prepared to take positive steps to managing these issues. This is not just a problem of unilateralist insensitivity to the perceptions of other states. Even multilateral leadership faces the challenge of widening the scope of mutual understanding to include historical sensitivities long

ignored. This is important for bilateral alliances with Japan and South
Korea, for trilateral coordination in which the United States works closely
with both of these allies, and for solidarity in the face of the revival of
sinocentrism, one manifestation of which can be seen in the Koguryo
historical issue between China and South Korea.

Since 1945, U.S. leadership in Northeast Asia has rested on shared
values as well as military power. On the one hand, these were values of
allied resistance to the spread of communism by force from the Soviet
Union, "Red China," or North Korea. An image of the "free world"
loomed large in forging Japanese and South Korean dependency on the
United States. With time, this image lost its appeal, as images of "anti-
Soviet," "reform," and "friendship" China gained popularity in Japan
and later South Korea; then the Soviet Union faded as a concern as the
cold war ended and that country collapsed; and finally an isolated North
Korea beset with severe problems made an invasion inconceivable, even
if new dangers arose from its nuclear weapons and missiles. On the other
hand, leadership of the two alliances also became rooted in a shared view
of history as a struggle for self-determination and democracy. This meant
rejection of colonialism and dictatorship. If some revisionists in Japan
were equivocal about condemning past control of Korea and China at the
same time as military rulers in South Korea kept insisting that democracy
had to be postponed to achieve rapid development, it was widely assumed
that these were temporary differences that would fade with time. After
all, the value consensus during the cold war was deemed so solid that a
shared sense of history could only steadily deepen. The post–cold war era
has revealed, however, that, even between allies, differences over history
in this region have explosive potential, while China's evolving views of
history pose new, unanticipated challenges to its neighbors as well as to
the United States.

Apart from taking pride in their Constitution, Americans do not look
very far back when incorporating values into their national identity. The
two defining twentieth-century events that retain their impact are the prolonged struggles against Hitler's *genocidal* Nazi aggression and Stalin's
great terror communist machine bent on world revolution. Yet, two different struggles for a time eclipsed all others and still remain part of
the lexicon of evil: Japan's militarist aggression, despite the fact that
Emperor Hirohito (under whom Japan attacked Pearl Harbor and committed war crimes) emerged as a partner in the postwar occupation;
and Mao Zedong's support for North Korean aggression and fanatical
class struggle, despite his reemergence as the U.S. partner in normalizing

relations. These two examples reveal that history in East Asia is more complex. If it is not easy to continue to vilify those who have become your partners, the U.S. view of history still takes note of current attitudes toward the two defining struggles of "allies versus axis" and "free world versus totalitarianism." Were Japan (or Germany) to revive the offending symbols by defending its past behavior, Americans might be aroused from their usual historical amnesia. To a lesser extent, revived Chinese pride in the history of socialism may appear provocative.

The Role of History in East Asian Bilateral Relations

East Asian national identities rely heavily on interpretations of history. In 2003, Roh was elected president, bringing to power a South Korean progressive steeped in a milieu of criticism of the United States for its historical behavior. In 2004, the "battle over Koguryo" erupted between China and South Korea, disputing how to depict the history of an ancient kingdom. In 2005, ties between Japan and South Korea suffered a sharp setback over history linked to the Dokdo/Takeshima territorial dispute. In 2007, Abe Shinzo was chosen as the prime minister of Japan, representing revisionists whose views of history directly clash not only with those of South Korea and China but also with those of the United States. There is ample evidence of new historical challenges also if one looks closely at the messages of the opening ceremonies of the Beijing Olympics of 2008 and at the speeches at the sixtieth anniversary celebration of the founding of the People's Republic of China (PRC) in 2009 amid history projects stressing a sinocentric approach toward nations inside China's current borders and in neighboring states. In the background, North Korea kept asserting its angry historical grievances and Russia was reverting to aspects of the Soviet worldview favorable to much of Stalin's legacy. None of the states in Northeast Asia has so far been inclined to downplay history in its identity.

By 2010, clashes over history had calmed down. Abe and his successors stepped back from visits to the Yasukuni Shrine in hopes of stabilizing relations and then the Democratic Party of Japan (DPJ) defeated the Liberal Democratic Party (LDP) in the Lower House elections of August 30, 2009, promising to defuse tensions over history. After Lee assumed the presidency of South Korea on February 25, 2008, he repudiated the historical views of his predecessor, stressing the need to improve ties to the United States and Japan. Obama's more measured approach to values than that of George W. Bush also exerted a calming influence from 2009. When the leaders of China, Japan, and South Korea met in October, they expressed interest in cooperating in the creation of an East Asian community, while discussions were started about writing a trilateral history textbook with government cooperation as a means of narrowing differences and raising consciousness of shared history on which the nations agree. Yet, just as the downward spiral over history earlier in the decade exaggerated the danger of this focus undermining regional stability, improvements at the end of the decade do not signify a breakthrough. The lesson to be drawn is not that the more analysts ignore history, the less relevant it will seem, but that a deeper appreciation of the impact of history is required to increase trust.

If the salience of history in current bilateral relations waxes and wanes for East Asian states, its overall significance for national identity remains high. This is consistent with the Confucian tradition, which rests legitimacy heavily on interpreting history in the correct manner. It is evident in writings about history, which reveal an intensity seldom found elsewhere in states with sustained economic development. The role of history in bilateral relations with the United States may not always be at the center of public debate, given the U.S. role in regime success or national security in these states, but that does not mean that history does not have great sensitivity. History has sparked strong emotions in regard to ties within the region and could do so for ties with the United States. Topics such as the atomic bombs dropped on Hiroshima and Nagasaki and the division of Korea into two opposing states are fraught with tremendous emotional potential for U.S. allies, and after 1949 Chinese history has repeatedly centered on rebuking U.S. imperialism/hegemonism.

The biggest test of Sino-Japanese mutual understanding over history came to a head when the joint committee issued the conclusion to its final report at the end of 2009. At China's request, contemporary history after 1945 was dropped. Many differences were exposed in covering the essence of the war and responsibility for it. Although the Japanese chair Kitaoka Shinichi reported some progress, this project had brought little reconciliation.[1] The history gap was a reflection of conflicting national identities: the 1930s and 1940s test pride in the struggle against imperialism and the rise of communism; the cold war tests similar issues in China and the meaning of Japan's abrupt shift; and even the post–cold war era poses a test centered on what future is sought for regionalism

---

[1] "Senso rikai ni konan aru: Nitchu rekishi kenkyui ga soron kohyo," *Yomiuri shimbun*, December 25, 2009.

and globalization. At the center in all of the tests is how to assess the role of the United States as a historical force. China's failure to address sinocentrism and obsession with U.S. hegemonism, Japan's failure to be forthright about its imperialism and confusion over Asianism, and South Korea's difficulty in finding consensus on its history of division and dependence leave a tangle of historical confusion that cannot be overcome or even mitigated without new leadership.

The Impact of Historical Issues on U.S. Regional Leadership

U.S. priorities in relations with China, Japan, and South Korea are numerous. Some may reason that, as during the cold war or even in the two decades of transition that followed, spending energy on history issues is a diversion that would heighten emotions and interfere with more urgent objectives. In particular, becoming sidetracked in resolving historical differences with U.S. allies has little appeal when bilateral and even trilateral coordination is increasingly needed to face the brinkmanship of North Korea, the rise of China, and the renewed assertiveness of Russia as well as challenges in other regions from South Asia's Afghan-Pakistan front to Southwest Asia's destabilizing Iraq-Iran region. There is great merit at a time when states are grappling with the world financial crisis and climate change in avoiding lesser issues with great divisive potential. Yet, the case for acknowledging that history matters and working with leaders inclined to narrow existing differences also has merit. This applies to Japan and South Korea as well as China. U.S. leadership in the region can suffer if unresolved differences in perceptions of historical events and the values that are readily associated with them linger in these two key allies.

In 1998, in the wake of the Asian financial crisis, South Korean President Kim Dae-jung, whose election victory brought a transfer of power that confirmed the maturity of South Korea's democracy, strongly endorsed globalization guided by universal values. If it had seemed that the spread of U.S. values since the end of the cold war had stumbled only against the tenacity of "Asian values," now even those seemed to be succumbing to the triumphalism of "universal values." Yet, no sooner had Americans been reassured by Kim's dismissal of "Asian values" and endorsement of alliance ties based on a shared worldview then a wave of "anti-Americanism" swept South Korea, punctuated by the election of Roh as a president intent on distancing his country from the United States. Similarly, in 2006, in the face of growing concern about threats to the status quo from North Korea and China, Japanese Foreign Minister

Aso Taro advocated an "arc of freedom and prosperity" to complement Abe's strengthened alliance ties to Bush. Yet, behind the façade of Abe's embrace of the U.S. alliance in the manner of his predecessor Koizumi Junichiro was awareness that his obsession with historical revisionism had the potential not only of arousing tension with South Korea, as occurred in 2007 when the "comfort women" issue flared, but also of focusing on the United States. The problem was not limited to LDP conservatives. When the DPJ was voted into power in September 2009, it promised in pursuit of goals such as an East Asian community to distance Japan from the tight, unequal U.S. embrace. These striking reversals in bilateral relations make no sense from the perspective of realist threat assessments. If some lay the blame on specific triggers – progressive South Koreans objected to Bush's "axis of evil" speech and policy toward North Korea, while the DPJ was generally opposed to the Iraq War and resort to unilateralism – others recognize that these reversals are best understood within a long-term context focused on historical memory. U.S. leadership remains surprisingly dependent on matters of history in a region where China's record of sinocentrism, Japan's record of militarism, and the way the U.S. government handled the final stages of World War II and its aftermath, including in South Korea, continue to arouse controversy.

Northeast Asia has faced a series of challenges to U.S. leadership since the end of World War II: the spread of revolutions after the Chinese communist victory in 1949; the Korean War; the Soviet military buildup and increasingly assertive posture until the mid-1980s; two North Korean nuclear crises after the cold war; and the rise of China marked by growing insistence on its values. All of these confirmed for most Japanese and South Koreans the importance of a close alliance with the United States. Recognition of shared adherence to democratic principles and human rights also reinforced U.S. leadership in recent decades. Yet, neither dependency on U.S. protection against threats to freedom nor respect for U.S. universal values suffices to align attitudes toward a broad range of values. Clashing perspectives on history stand in the way, casting a shadow on bilateral relations.

The first challenge we address in this book, starting in the next section, is how to exercise U.S. leadership on values, in which historical memory plays a large role in the Northeast Asian context. This subject figures repeatedly in the following chapters and needs further clarification than the dichotomy between one side pressing for consistency with U.S. values by forcibly criticizing states that violate them and the other side urging pragmatism by avoiding acrimonious insertion of values and history into diplomacy. The second challenge is raised in the chapters in Part I by Kazuhiko Togo and Gi-Wook Shin on how the Japanese, led by conservatives, and South Koreans, with progressives in the lead, have shown an interest in bringing historical issues to the fore in relations with the United States. In response, I discuss the implications of U.S. responses to each ally. The third challenge is raised in the chapters in Part II by Togo and Cheol Hee Park on the U.S. role in clashing historical memories between Japan and South Korea. Again, I respond with an assessment from the U.S. side on what may be feasible and effective. A final challenge raised in the exchange in Part III between Jin Linbo and Scott Snyder is the nature of the Koguyro history issue and the U.S. role in dealing with it. My response is to reflect more broadly on the significance of the dispute as a sign of intensifying sinocentric history.

Much has been written about the history disputes between Japan and its neighbors, but this book is distinctive in putting the U.S. role at the center of attention and linking the historical disputes in Northeast Asia to a sustained narrative about U.S. leadership. At times of intensifying emotionalism over history, the prime goal may be to calm matters and refocus concern on common interests. At other times, however, it may be possible for U.S. leadership to strive for more, framing historical memories in the broader context of values. When states focus their dissatisfaction on the negative memories they have about U.S. behavior, there may be no alternative but to take a more active role in dealing with history. The prevailing U.S. diplomatic strategy of avoidance is increasingly untenable.

Recent U.S. Leadership, Values, and History

Bush took office in 2001 guided by thinking that Bill Clinton had lacked a moral compass for U.S. foreign policy. He had been too compromising, too reluctant to use the unprecedented assets of American power on behalf of moral objectives. Many supported Bush on the basis of fundamentalist religious beliefs. Others started from a messianic outlook on U.S. leadership to transform the world. Their assessment reflected widespread malaise among conservatives that American society was becoming relativist, losing faith in clear principles in favor of some sort of eclecticism of various cultures, each with some claim to truth, having the right to coexist. It also signaled frustration with the limited levers then being employed to reshape a world at odds with their ideals.

At home, the Clinton approach had allegedly cast doubt on the melting pot of all peoples embracing a common American tradition. Abroad, it

accepted globalization on the basis of diverse values rather than under-
taking an assertive civilizing mission on behalf of American values with
universal validity. Specifically, Clinton was accused of erring in policies
toward North Korea, China, Japan, and the region as a whole because he
was not making correct value choices. In contrast, Bush began by forging
an agenda for a values-based foreign policy in East Asia: placing North
Korea in the "axis of evil," treating China as a "strategic competitor"
rather than coddling it as a "strategic partner"; upgrading alliance ties
with Japan on the basis of not only a shared "realist" worldview but
also attention to the depth of shared values; and pressuring South Korea
to embrace the same agenda within the U.S.-Japan alliance framework.
Bush initiated a values-based regional strategy repudiating Clinton's supposedly reactive, compromising ways.

In time, Bush's regional strategy failed as he fell back on policies that
resembled those of Clinton; yet values kept disrupting regional relations
even after U.S. pragmatism was evident. In the fall of 2005, despite U.S.
acceptance of the Joint Statement in the Six-Party Talks that approved the
principles for pursuing a compromise approach with North Korea, a new
U.S. push to put priority on human rights in North Korea damaged ties
with the North and with South Korea, where Roh was trying to build on
the Joint Statement even after Bush imposed financial sanctions on a bank
in Macao for handling the North's ill-gotten funds and thus severed the
North's ties to the international financial system. A year later, however,
after the North's nuclear test, there was no stopping U.S. pragmatism in
moving through bilateral talks to a plan with the North encapsulated in
the Joint Agreement of February 2007 and the deal to complete phase 2
to secure disabling of the Yongbyon reactor and a declaration of nuclear
assets, even if belatedly in 2008.

Values rose to the forefront again in the spring of 2008 when
China repressed Tibetan demonstrations and reacted to violent actions
with demonization of the Dalai Lama and his supposed threat to state
sovereignty. While many in the West agreed with the Dalai Lama that
China was guilty of "cultural genocide" and crushing any freedom of
religion, Chinese citizens apparently accepted the rationale of their government that core values of the state were endangered. Eager to sustain
progress in working with China on many global issues including the
Six-Party Talks, Bush downplayed the values at stake or any need for
a sharp response such as not attending the opening ceremony of the
Beijing Olympics. Russia's punishing military offensive in Georgia during the Olympic Games put values on trial again, amid uncertainty over

China's stance and on the U.S. ability to rally states behind its insistence that democracy hung in the balance as opposed to claims that Georgia's "colored revolution" and use as a symbol of universal values were just a smokescreen for expanding the North American Treaty Organization (NATO) and the intrusion of U.S. power into the sphere of operation of another civilization centered on different values. The U.S. position on values had softened, but as Bush reasserted his worldview, he found reinforcement from John McCain, the Republican candidate for president, playing the values card against Obama, who became the latest Democrat accused of not standing behind U.S. values.

As the contest intensified over how to shape and interpret the reorganization of Asia, Obama's election drew an international outpouring of hope that the United States would change policies that had aroused unprecedented anti-Americanism. Much of the world looked to Obama for reaffirmation of American ideals. If conservative leaders in Japan and South Korea were nervous that this could mean a softer approach to China or North Korea, leading to some marginalization of these allies, and Chinese leaders were nervous that the role of human rights would be raised in U.S. relations, many people in these countries shared in the optimism about America's renewal. Yet, even an inspiring leader cannot avoid the complexity of value differences linked to history in this region. At the start of Obama's administration, the challenge remained to solidify recently shaken alliances with Japan and South Korea, coordinate with China and Russia too in blocking North Korea's plan to become a nuclear power without improving its human rights record, and establish a regional security framework backed by agreed norms and principles. If it seemed to some that the only path to these goals is to ignore different views on historical transgressions, we argue that even for the U.S. alliances centered on shared interests and values focused on current issues, it is risky to overlook value differences over the past.

Obama was awarded the 2009 Nobel Prize for his series of speeches and policy directives that charted a different course than that of Bush on foreign policy. He revived globalization centered on the importance of climate change; a renewed commitment to the abolition of nuclear weapons and arms talks to reduce their number; reaffirmation of the role of the United Nations Security Council as the central force in dealing with crises; willingness to balance carrots and sticks through multilateral and bilateral talks aimed at changing the behavior of states with threatening nuclear weapons programs or egregious human rights violations; and a respectful tone toward nations and groups most suspicious of

U.S. intentions. In some regions, especially Europe, this non-economic globalization resonated well with local sentiments. Among some groups in Northeast Asia, it was also welcome, but at the state level it had limited impact. Democratic Party hesitation on free trade agreements (FTAs) mattered more in this region, where the U.S.–South Korea FTA remained in doubt without Senate ratification, and strong notions of sovereignty left support soft or fragmented for non-economic globalization. Many in Japan welcomed the new antinuclear tone. Many in China approved of the renewed reliance on the Security Council. South Koreans were inclined to favor a more moderate tone than in most of the Bush years in dealing with North Korea multilaterally. Yet, rhetoric and principles were not high priorities for these countries. Concrete national interests mattered much more.

Obama would have to speak directly to recent national identity concerns in order to make notable progress on values in Northeast Asia. For Japan, led by the DPJ under Hatoyama from September 2009, this meant redefining the balance between the U.S. alliance and Asianism as represented by the East Asian community. Many Japanese were seeking a symbolic breakthrough to signify rebalancing. One possibility was for Obama to visit Hiroshima or Nagasaki, as the first U.S. president to do so and a sign that the country that had dropped the atomic bombs recognized their devastation and gave its support to discussion of this sensitive historical topic in a way that could release Japan from one stifling effect of U.S. dependency. For South Korea under Lee, no equivalent step existed, but U.S. deference in dealing with North Korea gives reassurance that on the history issue that matters most, the South's centrality is recognized. For China, the challenge is greatest. Sinocentrism clashes more consistently with U.S. values, and the Chinese recognize less shared positive history prior to 1971. Despite the fact that there is no equivalent of the U.S.-Japanese war in 1941–5 and the Korean sense of betrayal that U.S. leaders winked at Japan's annexation of their country in return for Japan's tolerance for U.S. imperialism in the Philippines, Obama and future U.S. leaders are likely to find China to be the biggest hurdle on matters of bilateral and regional history.

In the spring of 2010, after the sinking by North Korea of the South Korean naval vessel the *Cheonan*, history was eclipsed by military concerns. As during the cold war, when danger lurks attention shifts from national identity to national survival. In these circumstances, awareness of historical grievances tends to follow images of security threats. To the extent that China is seen as out of step in countering North Korea's threat, South Koreans and Japanese are likely to become more attuned to the legacy of sinocentrism while downplaying the history issues that divide them and shadow their bilateral ties to the United States. The two-decade interlude after the end of the cold war opened a window on lingering historical disputes that were separate from current security concerns. As tensions revived, historical memories shifted. The rise of China would be tested not only for China's responsibility in maintaining an atmosphere of peace and stability, but also for its agility in restraining alarm linked to reconstructed memories of sinocentrism.

The Challenge Ahead

Under Roh, reunification assumed historical consensus without value clashes being taken seriously. Under Abe, revisionism assumed constitutional revision with growing historical assertiveness without a steep price to pay from new value clashes. Under Hu, sinocentrism assumes that value clashes will accompany sharper differences over history, but a rising China can manage them. While Lee and Hatoyama take sharply different approaches to the themes of reunification and revisionism, these issues continue to divide their nations, complicating any consensus on history. In contrast, Hu remains in charge in China and his successor is already being groomed with expected continuity in boosting sinocentrism. After all, this theme is now associated with the legitimacy of the Chinese Communist Party and with the conflict against U.S. hegemony. It pervades coverage of history. The old ideological struggle of communism against capitalism had a strong historical component. While a new struggle over history is not wedded to the tenets of Marx, Lenin, Stalin, and Mao, it covers many of the same issues, especially focusing on imperialism. Narrowing the divide over history between Japan and South Korea and between the United States and each of these allies is likely to be an important step in confronting the sharpening historic divide with China.

In the eyes of many in Northeast Asia, a new age is dawning when the Western-centered histories dominant since the nineteenth century are giving way to a focus on their own region. For the Chinese, this means putting the Chinese Revolution and liberation from Western dominance in the forefront. Koreans may dissent over China's past, while agreeing with the critique of Japan's historic role. Yet, the battles over how to evaluate Japan are familiar and may be better managed to serve community-building goals. In the search for a shared history, the target could shift to a critique of the West, especially the excesses of U.S. foreign policy.

To avoid this outcome, a parallel effort should define the Asia-Pacific community with an emphasis on the positive outcomes of the cold war. For both this community and the emergent East Asian community, historical memory serves to build cohesion and provide legitimacy. Avoiding controversial issues cannot be a long-term strategy in this unfolding competition over memories steeped in victimization, but also capable of generating trust through a shared vision linked to mutual security and prosperity. The United States should enter this process confident that it is, in general, well positioned to face historical scrutiny, even if it too must be prepared for criticism.

As Republicans strove to undermine Obama's moral authority and cast doubt on pragmatic concessions, they ignored the challenge of incorporating history into foreign policy toward Northeast Asia. Simplistic approaches are not suitable for a region where historical memories are vivid and often fail to conform to U.S. expectations. Demonizing all who search for a balanced approach that boosts multilateralism divides allies and allows China to gain an edge in advancing its worldview. In both the North Korean nuclear crisis and the parallel pursuit of an Asia-Pacific and an East Asian community, U.S. flexibility in working with China and countering its sinocentric objectives will require leadership of the sort that Bush explored in his final years and Obama has favored from the outset rather than a reversion to "axis of evil"–type rhetoric.

PART I

HISTORICAL MEMORIES AND
BILATERAL TIES WITH ALLIES

I

Japan's Historical Memory toward the United States

Kazuhiko Togo

I face two difficulties in writing a chapter on Japan's historical memory toward the United States. First, for a Japanese to write a chapter as an analyst summarizing the debate in Japan on the subject objectively is not easy. I have lived my life with the controversy on historical memory, and I cannot dissociate myself entirely from the judgments which I have made in these years. Also, because of my past involvement with this issue, my chapter will be interpreted with a certain value judgment by any reader, Japanese or foreigner, whether I like it or not.[1] Second, to give an adequate analysis covering the political left, right, and center as distinct threads of Japanese thinking on historical memory is a voluminous task that goes beyond the scope of this chapter. Nevertheless, there are two reasons that propelled me to write this paper. First, although the United States has never been a major factor in Japan's historical memory controversy, and there is no reason to make it a major factor at this point, Japan's historical memory toward the United States has always been in the consciousness of the Japanese as an underlying theme of Japanese identity and values since the end of World War II. Proper analysis of Japan's historical memory toward the United States, distinguishing democratic values and national identity, could clarify the state of political thought in Japan in a new way. Second, recent events in international relations suggest that some Asia-related historical memory issues have brought

---

[1] I have difficulty claiming objectivity, because I was born as a grandson of Togo Shigenori, Japan's foreign minister in the Tojo cabinet, which started the Pacific War, and then in the Suzuki cabinet, which ended it. Some of my fundamental recognition of historical events dates back to my childhood memory from my mother's narratives, which constitute important primary sources for me.

the United States into the picture. Koizumi Junichiro's Yasukuni visits and rising tension between Japan and China created real anxiety within the Bush administration.[2] Abe Shinzo's statement on comfort women in March 2007 and the House of Representatives' resolution on this issue in July 2007 brought the United States more overtly into history politics.[3] When the Takeshima/Dokdo issue arose again in Japan-Korea relations in July 2008, the U.S. Board on Geographic Names changed the country to which these islands belong from "Korea" to "Undesignated Territory," apparently in a technocratic manner without seeing the policy significance, but strong protests by South Korea led President George W. Bush to reverse this, showing how sensitive U.S. involvement could become. At the basis of these three issues is the fundamental matter of the U.S. historical view of Japan to 1945. In that context, a deeper understanding of the question "why does the United States matter in Japan's historical memory issue?" may make it possible to deal with concrete international issues in a more constructive way.

The Origin of Japan's Identity Problem

How does historical memory toward the United States affect values and the identity of postwar Japanese? I argue that, first, the existing rift between the political left and political right on historical memory toward the United States is related to the question of identity, and second, that, consequently, diverging views on democratic values are not the major dividing factor between the Japanese left and right. Democratic values could, therefore, be considered an important factor governing the fundamentals of the Japan–United States alliance. Japan's defeat in 1945 gives grounds for this conclusion.

Japan's Defeat in 1945

All problems regarding Japan's historical memory and identity started in the summer of 1945, when Japan lost World War II.[4,5] It is now

---

[2] David Straub, "The United States and Reconciliation in East Asia," in Tsuyoshi Hasegawa and Kazuhiko Togo, eds., *East Asia's Haunted Present: Historical Memory and the Resurgence of Nationalism* (Westport: Praeger Security International, 2008), pp. 213–14.

[3] Ibid., pp. 212–13.

[4] An excellent article concerning Japan's post–World War II identity and the significance of defeat in August 1945 was written by Owada Hisashi, "In Search of a New Identity," in Rien T. Segers, ed., *A New Japan for the Twenty-First Century: An Inside Overview of Current Fundamental Changes and Problems* (London: Routledge, 2008), pp. 234–49.

[5] The author has already written several articles with historical analysis related to this section, including "Japan's Foreign Policy: Achievements and Future Directions," in

hard to understand, even for a Japanese person – not to mention outside observers – the physical and spiritual shock experienced by the Japanese people then. For the Japanese, it was the first time their country felt the sting of defeat. The two wars that remained in the people's memory were the Yuan attack in the thirteenth century, from which Japan was saved by *kamikaze* (a "divine wind"), and Toyotomi Hideyoshi's invasion of Korea, which was largely remembered as an unsuccessful attempt at aggression by a dictator in the sixteenth century. These wars could not be compared to this total defeat, which entailed, for the first time in Japan's history, an occupation by outside forces. Japan lost practically everything it had accumulated from the time of the Meiji Restoration. Not only was it reduced to approximately the size it was soon after the Restoration, but also the whole value system that had been embraced since that time became seriously questioned. As Owada Hisashi wrote, "the defeat signified a total collapse of the national polity of modern Japan, together with all the value systems that had supported this polity, in which people had placed their total faith and devotion since the tide of modernization started in the Meiji period."[6]

The occupation started in these circumstances. The American forces brought in new values: democracy, peace, and economic reconstruction. Combined with preservation of the imperial system, intended to ensure some continuity with prewar Japan, these became Japan's four fundamental postwar values. On the whole, Japan accepted these new values smoothly, without waging strong resistance. Forming the basis of the postwar political system, democracy was accepted by a majority of the people without reservation, and there were several reasons for that. First, within the previously described spiritual vacuum of postwar Japan, there was little in Japan to oppose or prevent the introduction of a new political and value system brought in by the occupying U.S. forces. Second, after

---

Japan Aktuell (February 2008), pp. 38–54. Recently he published, in Japanese, *Rekishi to gaiko: Yasukuni, Ajia, Tokyo saiban* (Tokyo: Kodansha gendai shincho, 2008).

[6] Owada further states:

> ... *the process of modernization was made possible, and even successful from certain angles, by creating the polity of Japan as a modern state in the Western constitutional sense, grafting the ideology of the modern state in the image of nineteenth century Europe onto the socio-political culture of traditional Japan . . . Essentially the whole nation – not just the military but the majority of leaders in government, the business community and the intellectual community – believed in the nationally identified goal of making Japan a 'modern state' in the image of the West through the imperialistic design (which was still fashionable in those days) and supported the general direction in which the country was heading.*

Owada Hisashi, "In Search of a New Identity," pp. 235–7.

the catastrophic defeat, people posed the natural question, "Why have we lost the war?" "[I]t is an undeniable historical fact that the rise of the military in Japan in the 1930's . . . allowed the virtual usurpation of power by the military, thus leading the whole country into the abyss of military adventurism and the fatal defeat in 1945."[7] Negation of totalitarian military power fit in well with democratic values in the postwar years. Third, it would be wrong to conclude that democracy was completely new, suddenly introduced by the American occupation. Democratic values as understood as "people's rights and freedom of individuals" were one factor in the national polity of prewar Japan, and some argued that acceptance of new democratic values was made considerably easier as a result of post-Meiji democratic experience.[8]

The Constitution, which represented new postwar values, was adopted in November 1946 and went into effect in May 1947. Sovereign power residing with the people, respect for fundamental human rights, and the Diet as the highest organ of state power were the key democratic concepts. In addition, Article 9 renounced war as the sovereign right of a nation and as a means of settling international disputes and negated the right of belligerency. The emperor was recognized as the symbol of the state and the unity of the people. Many new political measures were implemented, particularly in the initial years of the occupation, including universal suffrage for women, a labor union law, educational reform, the punishment of war criminals, the dissolution of *zaibatsu* (financial conglomerate), and land reform. In Japan's initial postwar period of reconstruction and reemergence, democratic values and new national identity were basically not in conflict. It looked as if values and identity were operating hand in hand without fundamental contradictions.

A Fundamental Contradiction

This initial marriage between values and identity in general did not last long. Japan had to face a fundamental contradiction, which resulted from the deep spiritual vacuum that had engulfed it in the summer of 1945. In this nihilistic environment, thinking spread that the entire political

---

[7] Ibid., p. 236.

[8] Three turning points toward democracy following the Meiji Restoration should be indicated: the five principles of the Charter Oath in 1868; the Jiyu Minken Undo (freedom and people's rights movement) in the 1880s, which led to the establishment of the Meiji Constitution in 1889 and the first parliamentary elections in 1890; and the aptly called Taisho democracy era, symbolized by the election of the first prime minister, Hara Takashi, in 1918 and the passing of the universal male suffrage law in 1925.

system and all international relations from the Meiji Restoration had to be negated because they had led finally to a militarist, totalitarian Japan. This excessive self-denial naturally began to invite a backlash from conservative and nationalist politicians and opinion leaders:

> In the immediate post-war years, there was a period when the whole coun-try was totally polarized in a societal sense, and especially in the intellectual domain.... [T]he revisionist approach to history prevailed to such an extent that the Marxist-Leninist doctrine of the materialistic reinterpretation of Japan replaced the historiography based on the Kokoku-shikabun (nation-alist school of Japanese imperial history) of the prewar days. In due course, however, as Japan gradually restored her self-confidence and a sense of balance, with the fading of the post-war trauma and especially with a gen-erational change, such total repudiation of the past came to be viewed with a growing degree of suspicion.[9]

Following Japan's independence in 1952, the conservatives in 1955 formed a two-party coalition called the Liberal Democratic Party (LDP). Under the party's almost unitary rule, power shifts and policy changes occurred based on LDP factions. An experienced and highly motivated bureaucracy and an energetic and hard-working business community cre-ated, together with the LDP, the so-called golden triangle of Japan's polit-ical and economic power. The contradiction stated previously became a serious issue in domestic politics, where it took the form of the LDP-led government versus a cold war coalition of the media/opinion lead-ers/public opinion/opposition parties. After the end of the cold war, efforts were made to find common ground, but no national consensus has emerged.

In this struggle over historical memory from Meiji to World War II (the contradiction between total negativism and those who argue that not everything that Japan did before the war was evil), the countries that happened to be at the forefront were China and Korea. Yet, it was well understood that the United States defeated and occupied Japan, forging the fundamental framework for viewing Japan's relations with its past. Military tribunals of war criminals were held immediately following Japan's surrender – including the International Military Tribunal of the Far East, where class A war criminals were judged – and it was the United States that led them. At the core of the historical memory issue lies the issue of how to understand fundamental problems related to the ending of World War II in the context of the role played by the United States. In

---

[9] Ibid., p. 242.

the entire postwar era of gradual restoration of Japan's "self-confidence and a sense of balance," as Owada put it, the question of how to view the United States has remained an underlying, if sometimes unspoken, theme that could not be permanently ignored.

The U.S. Role in Overcoming Japan's Passive Pacifism

Before assessing Japan's efforts to overcome the contradiction between the total deniers of pre–World War II and those who tried to maintain some honor from the Meiji period, I need first to note the role of the United States in overcoming a second contradiction that resulted from the spiritual vacuum of August 1945. It was a rejection of anything related to the military or the use of force despite the troubled circumstances of the cold war that was unfolding in Asia as well as elsewhere. This rejection became so intense that many Japanese began to plea for passive and one-country pacifism.

Opposition parties from the political left, many intellectuals, an important part of the media, and public opinion took this position. The conservative-led government took a more realist approach, but for the entire cold war era, the domestic split between the ultrapacifists and government-led realists constituted what Owada called a "mini-cold war in cocoon,"[10] and it even continued thereafter. In the gradual shift toward greater realism, the U.S. role proved essential. From around 1948, with the onset of the cold war in East Asia, the United States changed its policy from molding Japan into a pacifist country, which would be totally incapacitated militarily, to requiring Japan to become a vanguard of the democratic camp against the rising communist power of the Soviet Union, the People's Republic of China, and North Korea. The government first responded with the Yoshida Doctrine, realistically concentrating Japanese power on economic reconstruction and maintenance of minimal self-defense forces, while letting the United States fill the power vacuum. During the cold war and thereafter, the United States has consistently encouraged Japan to adopt a more responsible and assertive defense policy. Whenever the government took the initiative to make its security policy more responsible and proactive, U.S. support made that easier. The fundamental compatibility of realist government policy and U.S. policy is no doubt one of the reasons that overcoming passive pacifism has been reasonably successful.

[10] Ibid., pp. 237–9.

In the wake of the cold war, it was the United States that scorned Japan's inability to send personnel to the 1990–1 Gulf War and Japan's $13 billion contribution as "check book diplomacy" and "too little too late." Traversing the security turmoil of the North Korean nuclear crisis of 1993–1994 and the Taiwan missile crisis of 1995–6, the Japanese government realized that a more responsible defense policy was essential to ensure its national interest and, hence, the Japan-U.S. alliance. This resulted in the reconfirmation of the alliance in 1996, agreement on new defense guidelines in 1997, and the adoption of a domestic law to underpin these guidelines in 1999.

This realist-responsible policy line was substantially strengthened under Koizumi. Faced with 9/11, he stood with Bush and considered the terrorist activities a threat to Japan, sending the Maritime Self-Defense Force (MSDF) to the Indian Ocean to assist coalition forces in November 2001. The North Korean threat, which exploded from 2002 with the abduction issue[11] and the second nuclear crisis, became the next trigger to strengthen security ties with the United States. Succeeding Koizumi, Abe set the objective to revise Article 9, which was deemed to be at the root of idealistic, passive, and irresponsible pacifism. After Abe's colossal defeat in the Upper House election in July 2007 and unexpected retirement in September, Fukuda Yasuo halted this push, but he was not inactive regarding the Japan-U.S. security relationship and made every effort to keep the MSDF in the Indian Ocean, succeeding in January 2008.[12] Prime Minister Aso Taro, whose main challenge was to combat the worldwide recession starting in the fall of 2008, took a dual decision on March 13, 2009, on the one hand, to send two vessels from the MSDF for patrol activities based on current MSD law, and on the other hand, to submit a new law to the parliament to deal with piracy in a more comprehensive manner.[13] All of these decisions were made with strong encouragement by the U.S. administration, whether Republican or Democrat.

---

[11] At the end of the 1970s and the beginning of the 1980s, perhaps twenty Japanese were abducted by North Korea. Kim Jong-il acknowledged to Koizumi at their September 2002 meeting that there were thirteen abductees and eight had already died. This aroused national anger in Japan. http://www.sukuukai.jp/index.php (accessed May 24, 2008).

[12] The Democratic Party, led by Ozawa, won the majority in the Upper House. It insisted that the decision to send the MSDF to the Indian Ocean to assist the coalition forces in combating terrorist activities in Afghanistan lacked sufficient legal authority based on the UN Charter and therefore the MSDF had to be withdrawn.

[13] *Asahi shimbun (evening)*, March 13, 2009.

Historical Memory Issues Primarily Related to China and Korea

The Japanese Domestic Split in the 1950s–1970s

Because various actors had their own reasons for not accepting Japan's endeavor to restore some honor for the Meiji Restoration–World War II period, everything that happened in relation to this turned out to be much more complicated than what happened in relation to Japan's efforts to move away from passive pacifism. The postwar treaties framework became the foundation for bringing Japan back into the international community. After the San Francisco Peace Treaty, many treaties with Asian countries were concluded separately to settle issues of peace and reparations, but this proved very difficult with South Korea and China. In relation to Korea, despite strong feelings rejecting prewar Japanese totalitarianism, the Japanese negotiators failed to understand that the fundamental perception of postwar Korea became total negation of anything done during the occupied period. Any positive assessment of the annexation became a fatal blow toward the establishment of diplomatic relations. After fourteen arduous years of negotiations, Japan and South Korea finally established diplomatic relations in 1965. With China, the peace treaty was first concluded with the Republic of China (Taiwan) in 1952. It was an inevitable choice under the cold war, and it took another twenty years to establish relations with the People's Republic of China in 1972 under the détente policy led by the United States. Concerning the serious damage that Japan caused in the past, the Joint Communiqué registered that "the Japanese side deeply reproaches itself."

From the 1950s through the 1970s, historical memory also became a significant domestic issue in Japan. From the initial question, "Why have we lost the war?" there gradually emerged the question, "What did we do wrong in relation to other people?" The story of the Nanjing massacre, as revealed at the Tokyo Tribunal, and other atrocities committed in China narrated by returned soldiers began to spread. There emerged a tendency among opposition political leaders, center-to-left opinion leaders, and media-led public opinion to negate Japan's prewar values entirely. Nikkyoso (the Teachers' Union) was powerful enough not to let the public schools use national flags or national anthems for many decades, because these represented pre-1945 militarism and excessive statism. The situation was so extreme that at the Tokyo Olympics in 1964 some children thought that Hinomaru (the national flag) and Kimigayo (the national anthem) were symbols for the Olympics.

This direction toward total negation of pre-1945 Japan was challenged by conservatives. In some cases, they gained wider public support; in other cases, the polemics led to polarization between the right and the left. There was broad support for clemency for war criminals after Japan's independence in 1952. The Ministry of Education and Nikkyoso were deeply divided on the extent to which Japanese wrongdoings should be incorporated into textbooks. Ienaga Saburo, generally considered the champion of postwar Japanese "consciousness," began in 1965 to file lawsuits against state-approved textbooks.[14] The Yasukuni Shrine also became an object of intense debate in the Diet. Conservative ruling forces tried to have a new law on the shrine's nationalization approved, but resistance prevented its passage.

The Resurgence of Historical Memory Conflict with Asia in the 1980s–1990s

The conflict over historical memory issues continued into the 1980s. *The Devil's Gluttony*, a nonfiction novel published in 1982, which disclosed the horror experienced by three thousand Chinese prisoners who fell victim to human experiments with biological weapons, had a profound impact on many people's war memory in Japan. The first textbook controversy exploded in 1982 in South Korea and China, and Nakasone Yasuhiro's official visit to Yasukuni in 1985 became another explosive diplomatic issue involving these two countries. In both cases, the Japanese government showed understanding for the feelings of these neighbors, since Nakasone had already succeeded in improving political relations with each, underpinned by his personal friendship with Hu Yaobang and Chun Doo-hwan.

Seen from the Japanese side, reconciliation with China and South Korea reached its height in the wake of the cold war. The imperial visit to China in 1992 and the "deep sorrow" that the Emperor expressed there, for many Japanese, was the height of reconciliation with China. With regard to South Korea, negotiations that began regarding the comfort women under Miyazawa Kiichi resulted in 1993 in the Cabinet Secretary

---

[14] Ienaga Saburo's lawsuit lasted for thirty-two years, and the final verdict by the Supreme Court was announced in 1997. Ienaga's view that the screening system is censorship was not acknowledged, but his assertion that Japanese wrongdoings during World War II should be described more clearly was approved.

Kono Yohei's statement, which acknowledged Japanese military involvement and apologized to them for their suffering.[15] This apology policy reached its height with Murayama Tomiichi's statement of August 15, 1995:

> During a certain period in the not too distant past, Japan, following a mistaken national policy, advanced along the road to war, only to ensnare the Japanese people in a fateful crisis, through its colonial rule and aggression, caused tremendous damage and suffering to the people of many countries, particularly to those of Asian nations. In the hope that no such mistake be made in the future, I regard, in a spirit of humility, these irrefutable facts of history, and express here once again my feelings of deep remorse and state my heartfelt apology.[16]

The latter half of the 1990s proved, however, to be a complicated period. In 1995, when Murayama expressed his historic words of apology, the Nanjing massacre exhibition was shown in all primary schools in China. In South Korea, the colonial governor general's office, which had been used as a national museum, was demolished. In turn, nationalist opinion leaders gathered together in 1996 to create Tsukurukai (the Japanese Society for History Textbook Reform), which produced a junior high school textbook that portrayed pre–World War II Japan with greater honor. Kono's statement on comfort women came under strong criticism from the right, and Chinese claims that Japan was not learning adequately from history were increasingly met with frustration.

The two prime ministers who led Japan in this period, Hashimoto Ryutaro and Obuchi Keizo, both recognized the necessity of reconciling with Asia. Kim Dae-jung's visit to Japan in October 1998 was considered an historic occasion for reconciliation. Jiang Zemin's visit, which took place a month later, was not that successful because of the negative response by the Japanese side to Jiang's excessive preaching to learn from history, but there were also substantial agreements about future-oriented projects. In 1999, indicative of this upbeat mood, Obuchi led in launching a tripartite breakfast meeting among Japan, China, and South Korea within the spectrum of the ASEAN + 3.

---

[15] Kono's statement was later embodied in the work of the Asian Women's Fund. See http://www.awf.or.jp/ (accessed September 18, 2008).

[16] http://www.mofa.go.jp/announce/press/pm/murayama/9508.html (accessed May 19, 2008).

Koizumi and Thereafter

Unfortunately, the five years of Koizumi's tenure are now remembered as having damaged Japan's relations with China and South Korea, because of the single issue of his yearly visit to the Yasukuni Shrine. With the Takeshima/Dokdo controversy erupting, the spring of 2005 was the lowest point in political relations with both countries in many decades. Abe's succession in September 2006 and his new policy of "not to confirm nor to deny whether he will visit Yasukuni or not" succeeded in moving this issue away from the center of the relationship. Abe's declaration that he was going to "inherit" Murayama's statement of apology and Kono's statement on comfort women also contributed substantially to improved political relations. Fukuda, who succeeded Abe in October 2007, immediately made it clear that he had no intention to visit Yasukuni.

Successive leaders' visits, by Abe in October 2006, Wen Jiabao in April 2007, Fukuda in December 2007, and Hu Jintao in May 2008 brought Japan-China reconciliation over history to its apogee, to the point that this stopped being a major focus with Hu's visit.[17] As for South Korea, Lee Myung-bak's election as president in December 2007 and his initial position of concentrating on future-oriented issues favorably impressed the Japanese, but Japan's handling of Takeshima/Dokdo outraged Koreans again in July 2008. On the surface at least, the two leaders managed to fend off the history issue and keep the basic tone of future-oriented relations through Aso's visit to South Korea in January 2009 and regular meetings at multilateral fora. At any rate, in the instances of attention to historical memory issues, the countries with which Japan had to deal were basically China and South Korea. Except for the Yasukuni Shrine under Koizumi and the comfort women controversy under Abe, the United States was out of the picture in history-linked foreign policy issues. Yet, in the background there was always the underlying U.S. role in Japan's historical memory.

The Origin of the Problem with the United States: The Tokyo Tribunal

The Tokyo Tribunal indicted class A war criminals who were charged with committing crimes against peace, that is, a conspiracy whose "...main object...was to secure the domination and exploitation by the aggressive states of the rest of the world," which "intended to and

---

[17] Aso made his visit to China in May 2009, keeping the positive tone in relations.

did plan, prepare, initiate, or wage aggressive war" from 1928 to 1945.[18] Out of twenty-five who were pronounced guilty, twenty-three were found guilty on this count and seven were put to death. At the time that the tribunal was held, the prevailing public mood was that of general acceptance. John Dower writes, "As the Tokyo tribunal came to a close, the media assessed its meaning in the by now talismanic language of peace and democracy."[19] This situation typically represents the period of convergence of newly introduced values and formation of Japanese identity directly based on those values. Yokota Kisaburo and Kaino Michitaka are generally known to be the leading international law scholars to have supported the verdict of the Tokyo Tribunal.[20] Maruyama Masao wrote in 1949 a critical article on the psychology of the war leaders to have led Japan into a fanatical war, not by premeditated organized conviction, but by a system of irresponsibility and adherence to decisions coming from above. He did not take the logic of the crime against peace at its face value, but was equally critical of all class A war criminals for having conducted a fanatical war.[21]

These affirmative views of the Tokyo Tribunal, however, were gradually supplemented by critical views. Democratic values remained a driving force in society but Japan's identity in relation to its historical recognition took a different path after the immediate postwar years. The defense's positions were reported and had already won some sympathy, including the basic position that whether the war waged between 1928 and 1945 was an aggressive war or not, punishing it as a crime against peace was against the sacrosanct principle of "without a law there can be no crime, without a law there can be no punishment." Even if one concurs that there was a coordinated wish to wage aggressive war against China and

---

[18] Richard Minear, *Victor's Justice: The Tokyo War Crimes Trial* (Princeton, NJ: Princeton University Press, 1971; reprinted by the University of Michigan Press, 2001), pp. 24–5.

[19] John Dower, *Embracing Defeat* (London: W.W. Norton, 1999), p. 509. He summarizes various newspaper assessments to underline that people were not exempt from the crime against peace (*Mainichi*), that they have to make sure that leaders would not make the same mistake (*Nikkei*), and that the newspaper regrets that it could not resist the dictatorial control (*Asahi*).

[20] Yokota argued that "in time of great change, when there is a fundamental change of values there is a period when retroactive application of law is inevitable and desirable." Kaino wrote that "the verdict of the Tokyo Tribunal must be considered as part of a democratic revolution and not as an implementation of existing international law." Ienaga Saburo, *Senso sekinin* (Tokyo: Iwanami shoten, 1985), reprinted in 2002, pp. 394–5.

[21] Maruyama Masao, "Gunkokushihaisha no seishin keitai," in *Gendai seiji no shiso to kodo* (Tokyo: Miraisha, 1964), pp. 88–130.

eventually against the United States among Japanese leaders, is it correct to make these actions criminally punishable and, in addition, to prosecute individuals who happened to be at the commanding post when these actions were taken? The only treaty that might have relevance here was the 1925 Kellogg-Briand Treaty, which pronounced war illegal, although wars of self-defense were excluded, and nowhere was it prescribed that individuals may be punishable on this account. After Japan regained independence, on August 3, 1953, the Lower House adopted by vast majority vote a resolution requesting clemency for all war criminals, and it was so decided for class A war criminals on March 31, 1956, and for class B and C war criminals on May 30, 1958.[22] As to the crimes committed under conventional military law, all seven who received death sentences were found guilty on this account. There was a serious issue whether those who were sentenced at the Tokyo Tribunal were actually responsible for the crimes committed, as was challenged by Judge Radhabinod Pal, but in general, there was greater acceptance of this category of crime among Japanese opinion leaders and intellectuals. Yet, if Japan needed to answer internationally for the atrocities committed during fifteen years of warfare, then what about the atrocities committed by the victors' side? Was it not just victors' justice to punish atrocities committed by the vanquished? The examples that frequently arise are the atomic bombs and carpet bombings committed by the United Sates and brutalities committed by Soviet soldiers after their entry into the war on August 9, 1945. The Tokyo Tribunal also drew criticism from the left, particularly because it left out any judgment on major aspects of Japan's aggression toward Asia, except for symbolic judgments such as the Nanjing massacre, and that it did not pronounce any judgment on the Emperor's role.[23]

Criticism against the Tokyo Tribunal was not limited to Japanese. U.S. defense lawyers such as Blakeny, Logan, Brooks, and Cunnings left a strong impression among many Japanese for their professional dedication

---

[22] Shinto seiji renmei, *Iwayuru Akyuusenpantoha Nanda* (Tokyo: n.a., 1987), p. 22.

[23] Onuma Yasuaki left a vivid account in 1983: "Many Japanese people thought that there was something suspicious (*okashii*) in the Tokyo Tribunal. For sure, Tojo and other military and government leaders plunged people into a hell.... After the war, they needed to be punished. But are the hands of those who punished them clean? How about Hiroshima and Nagasaki? What should one say about Russia which violated the neutrality pact? What about four centuries of Asian colonialization by European powers? What about Vietnam, Hungary, Czechoslovakia, and Afghanistan?" Onuma Yasuaki, "Bunmei no sabaki shosha no sabaki o koete," *Chuo koron*, August, 1983, reprinted in Onuma Yasuaki, *Tokyo saiban kara sengo shiso e* (Tokyo: Toshindo, 1993), p. 23.

in defense of the accused.[24] Judge Pal pronounced all of the accused "not guilty" because the strict implementation of international law removes all legal ground for accusing them. The content of his argument came to be shared by the Japanese only after the occupation ended, and it left a profound impression as well. General Douglas MacArthur's statement to the Committee on Foreign Relations of the U.S. Senate on May 3, 1951, indicating that fundamentally the war waged in the Pacific by Japan was a war to ensure Japan's security, commonly understood as a war of self-defense, gradually came to the knowledge of Japanese opinion leaders: "They feared that if those supplies were cut off, there would be 10 to 12 million people unoccupied in Japan. Their purpose, therefore, in going to war was largely dictated by security."[25] Richard R. Minear's "Victor's Justice: The Tokyo War Crimes Trial,"[26] published in 1971, was an early publication assessing the verdict reached on the crimes against peace.

Debates are proceeding. In 1983, an international conference to gather views primarily from the left was held in Tokyo.[27] In 1996, a compilation of views of eight-five foreign opinion leaders who criticized the Tokyo Tribunal was published.[28] The right argues that the "Self-negating Tokyo Tribunal historical view" (Tokyo Saiban jigyaku shikan) is the primary cause of the Japanese spiritual estrangement after World War II. Yet, many serious scholars and intellectuals, deferring in various degrees to the judgment of the verdict, are conducting serious research to comprehend its multiple meanings. Onuma Yoshiyasu,[29] Awaya Kentaro,[30] Higurashi Yoshinobu,[31] and Totani Yuma[32] are just recent examples. Wikipedia in Japanese described the Tribunal largely from the rightist point of view, but there are many who do not associate themselves with this analysis:

> In this tribunal, none of the actions committed by the allies were subject to judgment and no witness was investigated for perjury. It is quite evident that the principle of "without a law there can be no crime, without a law there can be no punishment" or prohibition of punishment for retroactive crimes was not ensured.... Almost all international law experts have negative

[24] Kiyose Ichiro, *Hiroku Tokyo saiban* (Tokyo: Chukobunko, 1986), p. 133.
[25] http://www.sankei.co.jp/seiron/koukoku/2004/maca/01/MacArthur57.html   (accessed August 24, 2008).
[26] Minear, *Victor's Justice.*
[27] Onuma Yasuaki, *Tokyo saiban kara sengo shiso e*, pp. 17–19.
[28] Sato Kazuo, ed., *Seakaiga sabaku Tokyo saiban* (Tokyo: Jupiter, 1996).
[29] Onuma Yasuaki, *Tokyo saiban kara sengo shiso e.*
[30] Awaya Kentaro, *Tokyo saiban e no michi*, Vols. I and II (Tokyo: Kodansha, 2006).
[31] Higurashi Yoshinobu, *Tokyo saiban* (Tokyo: Kodansha, 2008).
[32] Totani Yuma, *Tokyo saiban* (Tokyo: Misuzu shobo, 2008).

views on this Tribunal, but that does not mean that they consider it invalid. There are a few minority views which affirm the Tokyo Tribunal, arguing that its denial destroys the "pacifism" which Japan built after WWII or that the Tribunal enforced accountability on war leaders and clarified activities of Japanese soldiers that the Japanese people did not know.[33]

The Japanese government and a vast majority of opinion leaders consider the framework of postwar treaties that allowed the defeated Japan to rejoin the international community an unshakable foundation. The San Francisco Peace Treaty of 1951 is one of these key treaties and Article 11, in accordance with which "Japan accepts the judgment of the IMTFE" (International Military Tribunal for the Far East), has critical significance. Yet, when it comes to intellectual debate on the IMTFE, views in Japan are moving from uncritical acknowledgment of the verdict toward its critical evaluation, even if the debate is far from over. There are fundamentalist-rightists who believe that the verdict should be officially abrogated and consider the Wikipedia description too compromising, while others, including myself, think that it does not accurately take into account the multifaceted significance of the IMTFE.[34] This unfolding debate in Japan is worth watching closely.

Was the War against the United States a War of Aggression?

The Tokyo Tribunal and War of Aggression

The main emphasis of the previously discussed debate on the Tokyo Tribunal was its legal aspect, whether the tribunal was justifiable from the point of view of international law or not. But closely related to this was the issue of historical recognition of what was the nature of the war fought in Asia and against the United States. Was there a continuous war of aggression starting from around the period of the Manchurian incident stretching right into the war with China from 1937 and to the Pacific War from 1941, as described by the majority verdict of the Tokyo Tribunal? Or should the wars between 1931–2 and 1945 be analyzed separately by period and geography? The most distinguished scholar in Japan, who argued that the fifteen years of war should be looked upon as a continuous war of aggression, supporting the Tokyo Tribunal majority verdict, was

---

[33] http://ja.wikipedia.org/wiki/%E6%A5%B5%E6%9D%B1%E5%9B%BD%E9%9A% 9B%E8%BB%8D%E4%BA%8B%E8%A3%81%E5%88%A4 (accessed May 17, 2009).

[34] Togo Kazuhiko, "Watashi no naka no Tokyo saiban," in *Rekishi to gaiko* (Tokyo: Kodansha, 2008), pp. 257–300.

Ienaga Saburo. "Japan intended to continue its war against China and, therefore, launched war against the United States, Great Britain, and the Netherlands, which intended to halt Japan's action. The war against the three began as an extension of the war against China. It is not possible to divide the two and consider them as separate wars."[35] He pointed out the fact that even after Japan's establishment of Manchuko, the United States and future Allied countries continued their supply of oil, iron, and other strategic commodities to Japan. He stressed that the cause of war was Japan's aggression in China and not the so-called ABCD (American, British, Chinese, and Dutch) encirclement, which in reality tried to oppose Japan's aggression toward China. Ienaga also introduced in his writing Nakanishi Tsutomu, who argued that "for the United States and Great Britain, there was an aspect of protecting their imperial interest, but from the point of view of Japan, which waged the war, the war as a whole bore the character of imperial aggression. The nature of war was dictated not by the countries with which the war was fought but by the purpose of the war, namely the aggression in the Asia-Pacific region."[36]

Apart from Ienaga's views, others on the left, such as Kamei Katsu-ichiro and Takeuchi Yoshimi, argued that Japan's aggression toward China was undeniable but its war against the United States, Great Britain, and the Netherlands was war among the imperialists. They clearly distinguished between two wars. While on the left views of a continuous war over fifteen years were more influential for some time, as the years passed, those who made a distinction between the two wars gained more influence. It is also noteworthy that this distinction between the war against colonial Asia and the war against the Euro-American imperial powers was shared by some on the right. As in the case of the legality of the Tokyo Tribunal, the debates are far from being concluded.

Okawa Shumei and Shigemitsu Mamoru

For the origin prior to 1945 of the view that the war with China was the result of an unintended and poorly conducted policy but the war with the United States was a consequence of conflicts of interests, we can turn to two class A war criminals, Okawa Shumei and Shigemitsu Mamoru. Okawa was a highly reputed ideologue, so popular and considered to be so dangerous by the Allies that he became the only ideologue who

---

[35] Ienaga Saburo, *Senso sekinin*, p. 135.
[36] This is a quotation of Nakanishi's article written in 1971 in ibid., pp. 134–5.

was indicted as a class A war criminal at the IMTFE. Yet his abnormal behavior at the tribunal resulted in his being confined in a mental hospital, and the prosecution eventually waved the indictment because of insanity. Immediately after Japan's attack, Okawa made twelve radio broadcasts on December 14–25 explaining Japan's motives for entering into war with the United States and Great Britain. The content was published in the form of a leaflet in January 1942 and became a best-seller. It explains first how the United States expanded its influence from the American continent to the Pacific, and why the U.S. open-door policy to China was a form of imperialist expansion. The British part explains the nature of British colonial rule in India, countering that Japan's fundamental policy objective was to create a sphere of Asian civilization, where Japan, China, and India would become the three pillars.

In regard to China, Okawa repeatedly claimed that Japan's genuine intention was to liberate China from the intrusion of Euro-American imperialist powers. Yet, he did not hide the reality that such a liberation was rebuked by Chiang Kai-shek's government, which was supported by the Chinese people. He could not resolve this contradiction other than by expressing his hope that eventually the Chinese people would understand Japan's genuine intention:

> Japan made every effort to fight in order to save its own culture and the Oriental civilization which was endangered in China, but China did not stand with us to protect the Orient, fight against those forces which destroy Asia, and began fighting against us.... The majority of the Chinese people consider Chiang Kai-shek's government their leader, do not comprehend Japan's true intention, and fight back against Japan. My sorrow in this situation is infinite.[37]

Shigemitsu belatedly tried to fill the gap left open by Okawa. As a bright and seasoned diplomat, he became foreign minister in April 1943, after Togo Shigenori resigned from the Tojo cabinet over the issue of the creation of the Great East Asia Ministry,[38] and he kept this position until he was replaced by Togo in April 1945 when the Suzuki cabinet was formed. Shigemitsu was known as a China specialist in the Foreign Ministry and after Pearl Harbor, in early 1942, was chosen as ambassador

[37] Sato Masaru, *Nichibei kaisen no shinjitsu* (Tokyo: Shogakkan, 2006), p. 207.
[38] Tojo insisted that a new ministry had to be formed in charge of relations with the occupied countries. Togo disagreed, leading to his resignation in September 1942. The new Great East Asia Ministry was established in November 1942, and Shigemitsu became foreign minister in April 1943.

to China's Wang Qing-wei government. In accord with his long-time ideals, he saw Japan's only sustainable policy as respecting China's full sovereignty, for which complete withdrawal of Japanese military forces would be necessary upon the termination of the fighting:

> The long awaited new policy to China consisted of transferring political and economic leadership to the Chinese, not intruding in any domestic matters of China, and assisting autonomous reconstruction which China requested, or in other words, to treat China as a completely independent state.... If the new China policy is implemented, there would not be any reason for Chiang Kai-shek to fight against Japan, so compromise between Chiang and Wang Qing-wei would emerge and peace with Chiang Kai-shek may well emerge.[39]

As ambassador to China, Shigemitsu took about a year to formulate this policy, and on December 21, 1942, the Tojo government adopted a new China policy embodying his ideal.[40] He was then picked by Tojo as foreign minister to implement his ideas, and on October 30, 1943, Japan and the Wang Qing-wei government concluded a new treaty in which Japan committed itself to complete withdrawal from China upon termination of the war. Shigemitsu was also known for his efforts to expand his new China policy to the newly occupied areas, particularly in Southeast Asia, arguing that respect for the sovereignty and independence of each nation in Asia should become the major purpose for Japan to have waged the Pacific War. Okazaki Hisahiko argues that once the initial purpose of occupying Southeast Asia was achieved and necessary resources were secured, Shigemitsu's logic that the only justifiable purpose of war was to ensure the liberation of Asia from colonialism gained saliency. At the Greater East Asia Co-prosperity Sphere Conference on November 5, 1943, Shigemitsu's ideal of liberating Asia was proclaimed.[41] While his fundamental intention to realize an independent China seems to have been genuine, this policy declaration came too late to leave a trace in history.[42]

---

[39] Shigemitsu Mamoru, *Showa no doran II* (Tokyo: Chuokoron, 1952/2001), pp. 181, 187.

[40] Okazaki Hisahiko, *Shigemitsu Togo to sono jidai* (Tokyo: PHP, 2001), pp. 336–8.

[41] Ibid., pp. 341–4.

[42] The Japanese military achieved overwhelming victory until the naval battle at Midway in June 1942, but after this catastrophic defeat, where the navy lost four carriers, Japan's possibility for future victory was virtually lost.

Takeuchi Yoshimi and Hayashi Fusao

As Japanese debates on pre-1945 Japan unfolded with full vigor, particularly after the conclusion of the San Francisco Peace Treaty, public opinion and the media in general were led by leftist intellectuals who strongly criticized Japanese totalitarianism and militarism. Among them, Takeuchi Yoshimi was well known for his critique of Japan's policy of aggression toward China and eloquently argued against those who did not make a distinction between the wars against China and the United States. His analysis was based on his notion of modernity and the rift that emerged between Europe and Asia. Seen in his early writing in 1948, his framework of analysis was based on a critical view of Europe and America:

> We can acknowledge that Europe was inherently expansionary, and on the one hand, it bore its changeling, America, and on the other hand, it intruded into Asia. This European expansion was a reflex of the European move toward self-preservation.... This movement of European self-assertion took the form of influx of higher culture into a lower culture, or the assimilation of the lower culture by the higher culture.... Resistance from Asia was a calculated factor in that process and the more resistance Asia showed, the more Asia was destined to become European. Asian resistance was merely one factor toward perfection in world history.[43]

Takeuchi's analysis then shifts to the comparison of Japan and China in facing the European expansion. In the 1960s, against the background of rising economic success, Takeuchi acknowledged straightforwardly that the essence of war with China was Japan's aggression and on that basis argued the necessity of establishing diplomatic relations with China.[44] He denied sharply that Asianism lay at the foundation of the war against China and maintained that the Pacific War was at the height of Japan's de-Asianization:

> I wrote that the Greater East Asia War was a product of conflict between *datsua* (rejecting Asia) and *koa* (elevating Asia), but to put it more precisely, Japan's *datsua* absorbed *koa*; Japan ultimately utilized *koa* only in its outward form without its genuine content. Ambition to rule Asia was overwhelming, and Japan refused to understand Asia in reality. That was the reason why Japan failed.[45]

[43] Takeuchi Yoshimi, "Chugoku no kindai to Nihon no kindai," in *Nihon to Asia* (Tokyo, Chikuma, 1964/93), pp. 12–15.
[44] Takeuchi Yoshimi, "Nihonjin no Asiakan," in *Nihon to Asia*, pp. 94–5, 110.
[45] Ibid., p. 103.

For Takeuchi, the notion of the Greater East Asia Co-prosperity Sphere, which was advanced with sincerity by Shigemitsu, was a form of totally useless Asianism.[46] He made special reference to Hayashi Fusao, who wrote articles in *Chuo koron* in 1963–5 entitled *Daitoa senso koteiron* ("Affirmative View of the Greater East Asia War"), stating that he could not, like Hayashi, take a wholly positive view of that war, and that the aggressive part of that war was simply undeniable.[47] Hayashi's articles were widely read and caught the attention of opinion leaders, intellectuals, and the mass media. In the 1960s, the more intellectuals had time to reflect on their past thanks to the economic rise, the more the opinions of the political right began to be expressed. In that context, Hayashi's articles were taken by many as an unusual outcry, describing the feelings of those who had lived through the Meiji to Taisho periods. He maintained that starting roughly ten years before the arrival of the black ships led by Commodore Perry in 1853, Japan spent one hundred years fighting against advancing imperialist powers. There were periods of occasional peace, but they were nothing but a prelude to the next war. The fundamental objective of these wars was to fight against "western powers which move to the east."[48] Thus, Hayashi's description of his own reaction to December 8, 1941, was filled with exaltation:

> I was in Mukden in Manchuko when I heard the first news on the opening of war against the U.S. and Great Britain.... I do not remember whether I heard it by radio or by special newspaper edition. I was hurrying to reach the Mukden station. It was snowing. Even the snow which hit my cheek was so refreshing. It was as if a heavy burden which weighed down on my shoulders was swept away and some dark and heavy spot in my arterial system suddenly melted away.[49]

Hayashi described the same feelings that many people of his generation who lived through Meiji, Taisho, and Showa shared. Takamura Kotaro, Muro Saisei, Miyoshi Tatsuji, Ito Shizuo, and Oki Tsuneo, top poets and novelists of their generation, shared a feeling of relief and exaltation on December 8, 1941.[50] Yet, when it came to war against China, Hayashi showed the same sort of reservations as Okawa. He contrasted the idealism of many Japanese emigrants in establishing Manchuko as

---

[46] Takeuchi Yoshimi, "Nihon no Asiashugi," in *Nihon to Asia*, p. 294.

[47] Ibid., p. 95.

[48] Hayashi Fusao, *Daitoa senso koteiron* (Tokyo: Natsume shobo, 1964/2001), pp. 12–16.

[49] Ibid., p. 400.

[50] Ibid., pp. 416–21.

a dream land of ethnic harmony among the five peoples (Japanese, Han Chinese, Manchus, Koreans, and Mongols) with the harsh political reality. Hayashi emphatically quoted the last public lecture made in May 1936 by Ishihara Kanji,[51] the de facto founder of Manchuko, who warned that the Japanese failed to respect and could not grasp the heart of other Asian nations, and that it was essential to remedy that critical mistake if Japan wanted to succeed in any East Asian cooperation. Viewing war with the United States as inevitable for his generation, but war with China as the result of a series of mistakes, Hayashi wrote:

> The slogan of five peoples' harmony was just unilateral coercion from the Japanese side.... And above all, it was totally unrealistic to shake hands with the Han Chinese and reach mutual understanding with them, since they have been awakened by nationalism through the revolutionary movements led by Sun Yat-sen. Who does dare to accept, if one is beaten on his head by a club and then asked to shake hands?[52]

From Hashimoto Ryutaro to the Confused Situation in the 2000s

Historical memory discourse in Japan continued through the 1980s, when it became an important diplomatic issue with China and Korea, and in the first half of the 1990s it produced the peak of apology policy, culminating in the Murayama Statement. Its language highlights "colonial rule and aggression" as the mistaken past and relates the "damage and suffering" caused to Asian nations. Though no proper names were given, it has been generally assumed that "colonial rule" refers to Korea and "aggression" to China. Hashimoto Ryutaro was the minister of International Trade and Industry in the Murayama cabinet, and he was specifically asked by the socialist prime minister to support the content of the statement. Eda Kenji, his private secretary at the time and later his secretary for political affairs, recalled that Hashimoto's consent was critical for the cabinet to approve the Murayama Statement.[53] Hashimoto's consent was given on the basis that he was ready to apologize to China and Korea regarding the suffering caused by Japan, but he had a different view on the nature of war against the United States, Great Britain, and the Netherlands, with

---

[51] Ishihara Kanji was a member of the general staff of the Kwantung Army from 1928 to 1932. He was the chief planner of the Manchurian Incident and ran the occupation leading to the establishment of Manchuko. He favored an independent Manchuko to stand against the Soviet threat, and he later strongly opposed Japan's expansion to the rest of China.

[52] Ibid., p. 369.

[53] Author's interview with Eda Kenji, February 21, 2008.

which Japan fought a war among equals. Already in October 1994, he revealed his thinking before a committee of the Lower House of the Diet:

> I still continue to think about when Japan's policy began to change to, what is generally called, aggression against the Chinese continent. It might have been some point during WWI. In relation to Korea, our seniors chose an action which cannot but be called colonialism. But when I restrict my thinking to WWII, where Japan fought a war against the United States, the United Kingdom and the Netherlands, there remains some doubt whether we can call it aggression. At least, I have no intention to state that Japan waged a war of aggression against the Soviet Union, which began their attack on Manchuria.[54]

As historical discourse began to take another turn in the latter half of the 1990s, the view to differentiate Japan's responsibility toward Asia and toward imperialist powers did not draw much attention. On the one hand, China resumed its stern criticism that Japan was not learning enough from history, and in Japan resentment grew against China continuously using this issue to demonize Japan. Opinion leaders from the right became frustrated that the historical memory debate became a tool of Chinese diplomacy to intimidate Japan, to the point that humility toward China regarding the past either became mute or openly negated. This trend continued and saw an upturn in the rift caused by Koizumi's visit to Yasukuni and became the major trend among rightist opinion leaders, including Nishio Kanji, Kobori Keiichiro, Watanabe Shoichi, Ishihara Shintaro, Nakanishi Terumasa, Fujioka Nobukatsu, Nishioka Tsutomu, Kobayashi Yoshinori, Sakurai Yoshiko, Yagi Hidetsugu, and Okazaki Hisahiko. On the other hand, this period coincided with rising uncertainty regarding China's military power and the North Korean nuclear threat and abduction imbroglio. For the majority of the opinion leaders listed, the U.S role in ensuring Japan's security had paramount importance. It was no time to provoke it on an issue, after all, which was related to events that took place sixty years ago. Highlighting the U.S. role in historical memory discourse at this point must have been considered nonstrategic.

Since Koizumi's departure from power, historical memory discourse in relation to the United States has been in flux. No clear emphasis in any direction can be firmly observed, but several trends might be discerned. First, whether the current improved political climate with China and

---

[54] October 24, 1994, statement at the Special Committee on Tax Reform of the Lower House, Iwami Takao, *Jitsuroku Hashimoto Ryutaro* (Tokyo: Asahi sonorama, 1995). p. 286.

South Korea would affect the political discourse of Japanese intellectuals toward greater Asianist thinking or not is not clear. Despite rightist warnings about China's rise and growing insecurity from such issues as imports of poisoned dumplings, public opinion in general seems comfortable with improved relations with China. How this may translate into historical memory discourse is yet to be determined. Second, as serious efforts to maintain and strengthen relations with the United States continue, there is no sign of clear resistance by the media and public opinion, but in this atmosphere of general stability there is a rise of historical memory discourse pointedly critical of the role of the United States. China certainly is not exempted from their critical observations, but the strong language directed at the United States is more noteworthy. Kobayashi Yoshinori attacked Bush's war against Iraq, and the latest phenomenon is General Tamogami Toshio's sudden rise as a Gaullist nationalist on the right. On present-day defense and security policy, Tamogami argues for the creation of an alliance of equal footing, where Japan fulfills greater responsibilities. On historical memory, he argues that Japan was not an aggressor country, but a victim that was dragged into war against China and the United States, and that it was the United States and victor countries that unilaterally insisted that Japan be held responsible after its defeat.[55] This combination of self-reassuring historical memory and Gaullist security policy is gaining some media popularity. As this trend gathers force, a third issue looms related to Japan's historical memory toward the United States. This is the matter of atomic bombs dropped on Hiroshima and Nagasaki in August 1945, which has the potential to arouse a more intense debate in Japan.

The United States and the Atomic Bombing

The Atomic Bombing

Complicating historical memory discourse between Japan and the United States is the issue of the two atomic bombs dropped by the United States in the concluding days of the Pacific War. During the U.S. occupation, this issue was subject to censorship. The general recognition by ordinary Japanese was that Japan's leadership in the summer of 1945 could not agree on an expedited decision to end the war, and only through the two

---

[55] Tamogami published eight books where he appears as author or coauthor in the half-year after his resignation, repeating the same theme. This summary is based on *Mizu kara nomiha kaerimizu* (Tokyo: WAC, 2008), pp. 7–10.

atomic bombs and Soviet intervention was Japan convinced to surrender immediately; so it was inevitable that Japan faced the two bombs. This line of thinking exactly matched the U.S. official position, supported by U.S. veterans and U.S. public opinion. Seen from opinion leaders on the right, Japan's inability to challenge the official U.S. position reflected the postwar reality of becoming its junior ally. Japan was protected under the U.S. nuclear umbrella and was not in a position to question the moral validity of these weapons, even when used prior to Japan's capitulation. Opinion leaders on the left should have found it easy to transform their anger about Hiroshima and Nagasaki into anti-American criticism, given their general sympathy to socialism and their criticism of American imperialism, but their position was subsumed under the rubric of idealistic pacifism and developed into a global antinuclear movement. Following this mood, the Japanese government adopted the three non-nuclear principles and took a leadership position at the United Nations on behalf of the ultimate abolition of nuclear weapons.

Both of these approaches – the political right's unwillingness to question the official U.S. position and the left's drift toward the universal antinuclear movement – failed in the scholarly world or in public curiosity. There was no serious study as to why nuclear bombs were dropped and whether they were really necessary to achieve Japan's surrender. Interestingly, despite the firmly established official version that atomic bombs were necessary to save the lives of American soldiers and the Japanese people, this issue aroused serious research and debate in the United States right from the end of World War II. According to Tsuyoshi Hasegawa, in his edited, well-documented book on the dropping of the atomic bombs and the ending of the Pacific War, there were three schools of thought: the orthodox, the revisionist, and the neo-orthodox.[56]

The orthodox school considers that dropping the bomb was necessary and justified because it swiftly ended the war and saved U.S. soldiers' lives as well as the lives of many Japanese. This view became the official position, pronounced clearly by former secretary of war Henry Stimson in 1947.[57] It was confirmed by Bill Clinton in the heated controversy regarding the Smithsonian exhibit of the Enola Gay in 1995.[58] In the scholarly world, Robert Butow's *Japan's Decision to Surrender* (1954) has been

---

[56] Tsuyoshi Hasegawa, "Introduction," in Tsuyoshi Hasegawa, ed., *The End of the Pacific War: Reappraisals* (Stanford, CA: Stanford University Press, 2007), p. 2.

[57] *Harper's* (February 1947), quoted in *Asahi shimbun*, July 23, 2007.

[58] John Harris, *Washington Post*, April 8, 1995, quoted in Shigehiko Togo, *Views of Japan from the* Washington Post *Newsroom* (Tokyo: Kodansha, 1996), pp. 78–9.

considered by many as a classic of the orthodox school. Hasegawa quoted two books, *Fighting to a Finish: The Politics of War Termination in the United States and Japan, 1945* (1988), by Leon Sigal, and *Downfall: The End of the Imperial Japanese Empire* (1999), by Richard Frank, and one paper, "The Shock of the Atomic Bomb and Japan's Surrender" (1998), by Sadao Asada, as the "only three other serious works on Japan's decision to surrender since Butow's book, until early 2005."[59]

As for the revisionists, the United States Strategic Bombing Survey's "Summary Report (Pacific War)," published in July 1946, concluded that in the face of continued American conventional bombing, Japan would have surrendered "certainly" before December 31, 1945, and "in all probability" before November 1, "even if Russia had not entered the war, and even if no invasion had been planned or contemplated."[60] This view was persistently supported by Gar Alpelovitz in his successive books of 1965, 1985, and 1995.[61]

The neo-orthodox school denies at least one of the two factors that constitute revisionist thinking: (1) Japan would have surrendered anyway; and (2) Truman decided to drop the bombs for some other purpose than just enforcing Japan's surrender. Burton Bernstein, who wrote a series of articles in the 1970s, and Tsuyoshi Hasegawa, who published a highly praised but controversial monograph, *Racing the Enemy,*[62] may be most representative of this school. Both agree that some external factor was necessary for Japan's surrender, and it was the Soviet entry into the war that came to be decisive. Bernstein persistently argues that Truman's intention was to ensure immediate Japanese surrender, whereas Hasegawa argues that Truman's intention was to end the war before Soviet entry so as to ensure a stronger strategic position in the postwar context.

In comparison to American scholarly debate, the outcome of Japanese scholarly research pails. Asada, Hatano Sumio,[63] and a few others have produced serious articles, but the research seems to be just getting under

---

[59] Tsuyoshi Hasegawa, "Introduction," p. 3.

[60] Michael Kort, "The Historiography of Hiroshima: The Rise and Fall of Revisionism," *New England Journal of History*, Vol. 64, No. 1 (Fall 2007), p. 32.

[61] Ibid., pp. 33–5, 39. Alperovitz published in 1965 *Atomic Diplomacy: Hiroshima and Potsdam*; in 1985 its expanded version; and in 1995 *The Decision to Use the Atomic Bomb and the Architecture of an American Myth.*

[62] Tsuyoshi Hasegawa, *Racing the Enemy: Stalin, Truman, and the Surrender of Japan* (Cambridge, MA: Harvard University Press, 2005).

[63] See Sumio Hatano, "The Atomic Bombs and the Soviet Invasion: Which Was More Important in Japan's Decision to Surrender?" in Tsuyoshi Hasegawa, ed., *The End of the Pacific War*, pp. 95–112.

way. Minister of Defense Kyuma Fumio stated on June 30, 2007, that "dropping the atomic bomb was inevitable," which was met by strong public anger, and he was forced to resign on July 3. The anger was primarily directed at Kyuma's lack of sympathy for the suffering of those who are still dying as a result of the bombing, but frustration at the delay in Japan in research on why the bombs were dropped and whether they were really necessary might have been a reason. Thus how to view the U.S. atomic bombing in the context of historical recognition is yet to be fully explored. But in contrast to the issues of the legality of the Tokyo Tribunal and the historical recognition of the nature of the war fought by Japan, where the essential aspect is identity rather than values, the atomic bombing issue seems to be more oriented toward values. Whether the kind of bombs used against Japan can be justified or not can be more easily understood and debated on the common ground of human rights and protection of individuals, just as the concrete issues of atrocities in Nanjing and elsewhere are easier to handle from the perspective of mutual respect for human rights.

In regard to value judgments, it is interesting to see that as early as 1985, Ienaga Saburo, one of the most influential postwar critics of Japanese atrocities, defined U.S. atomic bombings as one of the "trio extreme cases of systematic atrocities committed during WWII," together with Auschwitz and Unit 731.[64] Quite recently, on July 16, 2007, the International Peoples' Tribunal on the Dropping of Atomic Bombs on Hiroshima and Nagasaki pronounced guilty verdicts against the U.S. leadership of 1945. This is a clear indication of the shift on the political left to express openly their critical views against the U.S. government, in requesting an acknowledgment of responsibility, apology, and atonement to the victims.[65] It may not be a coincidence that one of the chief figures in the establishment of this tribunal was Tanaka Yuki, who was pursuing diligently Japan's responsibility for comfort women.[66] Second, with a view of achieving reconciliation more on moral grounds with a more realistic objective, Matsuo Fumio, a former Japanese correspondent of *Kyodo Tsushin*, has been pushing forward in the last few years realization of mutual visits of the American president to Hiroshima and the prime minister of Japan to the USS *Arizona* Museum at Pearl Harbor.[67]

---

[64] Ienaga Saburo, *Senso sekinin*, p. 86.

[65] http://www.k3.dion.ne.jp/~a-bomb/indexen.htm (accessed May 17, 2009).

[66] Tanaka Yuki's writing includes *Hidden Horrors, Japanese War Crimes in World War II* (Boulder, CO: Westview Press, 1997); and *Japan's Comfort Women: Sexual Slavery & Prostitution during World War II and the U.S. Occupation* (London: Routledge, 2002).

[67] Tsuyoshi Hasegawa and Kazuhiko Togo eds., *East Asia's Haunted Present*, p. 11.

Barack Obama began taking new initiatives to abolish nuclear weapons and accepted "moral responsibility to act" as the only country which used nuclear weapons.[68] Matsuo seems to have intensified his efforts.[69]

Reconciliation with U.S. Prisoners of War

Against the backdrop of the U.S. atomic bombing, a difficult issue remained unresolved until quite recently. With a view to achieving reconciliation with former allied prisoners of war (POWs), the Japanese government launched a Peace Friendship Exchange Program in 1995 and began implementing various initiatives, including inviting former POWs to Japan with a view to heal the wounds of those who had suffered at the hands of the Japanese military forces. By 2004, 784 former British POWs were invited to Japan, likewise 425 from the Netherlands and 56 from Australia. The Program then ended its formal activities, but its goals continued to be pursued at the initiative of the Foreign Ministry. U.S. POWs were conspicuously excluded from the Program's initiatives. If that omission was not due to some bureaucratic inertia, the only possible reason that one can think of would be the government reluctance to reach out to former POWs from a country that dropped the two bombs, as a consequence of which Japanese people are continuing to die. But one failure to show remorse does not justify another. This negative link had to be cut. As it turned out, on May 30, 2009, Fujisaki Ichiro, Japanese ambassador to the United States, attended the annual meeting of the American Defenders of Bataan and Corregidor, and extended a formal apology.[70] There still remain several tasks to be fulfilled, but a major bridge of reconciliation has been crossed.

Conclusion

For decades, Japan's historical memory issue has been perceived as an issue between Japan and Asian countries, notably China and Korea, but, in reality, there is a deeply embedded U.S. aspect present as well. It is axiomatic because it was the United States with which Japan fought the

---

[68] "Obama Prague Speech on Nuclear Weapons," April 5, 2009 http://www.huffington post.com/2009/04/05/obama-prague-speech-on-nu_n_183219.html (accessed August 22, 2009).

[69] *Mainichi shinbun*, January 3, 2009; an interview by the author with Matsuo Fumio on February 18, 2009.

[70] *Kyodo Tsushin*, May 31, 2009. See also Lester Tenney, "The End of the Long March," *Japan Times*, April 15, 2009; Togo Kazuhiko, "Iyasareru senso no kizuato," *Mainichi shinbun*, evening, May 18, 2009.

Pacific War, it was the United States that defeated Japan, and it was the United States that occupied Japan for seven years. The results of the U.S. occupation, the reemergence of Japan as a country of democratic values and economic strength, and the creation of a new alliance with the United States all have proceeded extremely well to date. Perhaps the underlying historical issue with the United States should not have emerged, in order that the political situation centered on further consolidation of this alliance based on common values could be further strengthened. Yet, in reality, the historical memory issue characterized in Japan as an identity issue remained unresolved not only toward Asia but also toward the United States, as seen from three perspectives: (1) the Tokyo Tribunal, put in the perspective of international law; (2) the nature of the war waged by Japan against China and against the United States; and (3) the atomic bombs dropped on Hiroshima and Nagasaki, and Japan's possibly related approach to U.S. POWs. No definite direction has emerged on any of these issues. Serious efforts are intensifying, but no consensus has emerged in any area.

At this juncture, it is best to stress that Japan's historical memory toward the United States remains obscured after many decades of neglect. This is not a result of lack of importance, but of specific historical circumstances that left the Japanese divided and hesitant to address some sensitive issues directly. These circumstances have been changing, as seen in increased willingness to debate the issues raised in this chapter. Enhanced debate in political and intellectual circles should improve understanding and trust between Japan and the United States.

2

Values and History in U.S.–South Korean Relations

Gi-Wook Shin

The U.S.–South Korean bilateral relationship has increasingly become more than a matter of military alliance or economic relations, although security and trade are still the two defining issues. As a result, it has become much more complex and challenging to manage. With emphasis on Korean reasoning about values influenced by memories of history, this chapter explores relations in the first decade of the twenty-first century between Washington, in search of a response to a more insecure world, and Seoul, newly attentive to fellow Koreans in the North and to a regional role in dynamic Northeast Asia.

Largely based on state-to-state interactions, U.S.–Republic of Korea (ROK) relations until the 1970s remained robust if not free of tension and conflict. If a rift occurred, it centered on policy matters such as U.S. plans to withdraw troops from the peninsula. South Koreans did not question the rationale for the military alliance, and any anti-American voice was immediately suppressed by the authoritarian regimes that ruled the country. For instance, discussing the killings of civilians by U.S. troops during the Korean War, which would become a hot issue later, was taboo in the highly anticommunist state. U.S. cooperation with authoritarian regimes during the cold war era occurred in sync with its lead on matters of national security.

Things began to change as South Koreans struggled to realize democratization, led by the development of a vibrant civil society, along with the end of the cold war, which undermined the rationale for anticommunism.

I have benefited from insightful comments from Gilbert Rozman, David Straub, and Donald Keyser. Hilary Izatt and Soo-Kyung Kim offered research assistance for the chapter.

Many South Koreans began to rethink the rationale for relations with the United States and North Korea, the two significant others that shape their national identity. As the U.S. role in Korea's unfortunate past came under scrutiny, three issues, in particular, spurred this questioning: alleged U.S. complicity with the dictatorship and the Kwangju massacre; the U.S. role in national division and the mass killings of innocent civilians during the Korean War; and the issue of policies toward North Korea. Closely linked, they all relate to issues of history, values, and national identity.

Led by progressive intellectuals and nongovernmental organizations (NGOs), the reassessment of historical issues contributed to a new perspective that significantly differs from the American one and from what both countries shared in the past. This not only led to strains between the allies but also aroused intense contention between conservatives and progressives within the South, who remain split in their views of the alliance.

The first issue led South Koreans to rethink the U.S. role in Korean affairs, which in turn provoked anti-American movements in the 1980s during the struggle for democracy. Many appreciated the value of the alliance, but resented U.S. economic and political dominance over their nation, linking it to perceived collaboration with the dictators. While denying involvement in the Kwangju massacre, the United States seemed to have learned its lesson when it intervened to support South Korean democracy in the summer of 1987, which ended decades of authoritarian rule. Today South Koreans have successfully addressed issues of "transitional (in)justice" during the democratization process, including the Kwangju issue, and it appears no longer to affect relations; yet, activists who had fought for democracy in the 1980s with anti-American slogans became the policy elite (known as the "386 generation") during the Roh Moo-hyun administration and memories of their democratic struggle shaped policies that took a tough stance toward the United States.

The second issue provoked another wave of anti-American sentiment that culminated in the 2002 presidential campaign. Despite a collaborative investigation of the No-gun Ri incident by the U.S. Army and President Clinton's statement of deep regret, the public mood in the South wreaked with anti-Americanism, helping to elect human rights lawyer Roh Moo-hyun as president. Roh, who ran a campaign critical of the United States, paid keen attention during his tenure in office to issues arising from the unfortunate past, including wartime mass killings. Subsequently, the Roh administration established various state-sponsored organizations to deal with these issues, including the Truth and Reconciliation Commission (TRC), which revealed additional cases of mass killings of Korean civilians by U.S. troops during the Korean War.

Progressive activists continue to raise this issue, demanding another U.S. apology as well as compensation. Although an unexpected event such as the death of the two schoolgirls in 2002 could provoke renewed anti-American sentiments, it is unlikely that this issue will directly impact U.S.-ROK relations in any significant way.

Finally, the Democratic People's Republic of Korea (DPRK) issue has been a point of strain on U.S.-ROK relations in the recent past. The progressive governments of Kim Dae-jung and Roh Moo-hyun had differing views from the Bush administration regarding weapons of mass destruction (WMDs) and human rights, on the one hand, and inter-Korean relations and unification on the other. At a fundamental level, the differences stemmed from the fact that these matters were closely tied to the larger question of national identity for Koreans, while they were a matter of security policy for Americans.[1] Thus, despite sharing values such as democracy and human rights, the different approach toward the North Korean issue created a schism within the alliance. Although policy coordination has improved and the Lee Myung-bak government promotes a DPRK policy that is much more similar to that of the United States, South Korean society is deeply divided about its approach toward North Korea and the politics of identity continues to pose a policy challenge for the United States.

Given South Korean historical perceptions, memories, and value inclinations, we must pay closer attention to the nonmilitary, non-economic aspects of this bilateral relationship grown out of the military alliance. As perceptions matter in international relations, so too do views of history, as they shape those values and perceptions. This chapter concludes with policy suggestions to mitigate and manage potential sources of tension resulting from the increasing role of values in U.S.–South Korean relations.

Security and Trade in U.S.-ROK Relations

Beginning in 1945, when Korea was liberated from four decades of Japanese colonial rule, the United States became involved in Korean affairs in earnest. It established a military government in the South (1945–8) and fought the communists in defense of the southern regime during the Korean War (1950–3). U.S. aid and market access were instrumental to South Korean modernization. In the process, the United States became,

---

[1] For more discussion on the perception gap existing between South Korea and the United States regarding the DPRK, see Gi-Wook Shin, *One Alliance, Two Lenses: U.S.-Korea Relations in a New Era* (Stanford, CA: Stanford University Press, 2010).

arguably, the most important "significant other" shaping identity, along with North Korea and Japan.

Security and trade have been the two main pillars of the bilateral relationship. Formed as a response to a common threat – communist North Korea – at the end of the Korean War, the military alliance developed into a robust relationship in the following half century. Along with the U.S.-Japan alliance, the U.S.-ROK alliance formed the hub-and-spokes of U.S. security arrangements in East Asia, a region with no multilateral security architecture. The United States enjoyed rights to a strategically significant forward deployed location – at the conjuncture of three major powers in the Northeast Asian region, Japan, China and Russia – at a relatively low cost, and was even able to garner South Korean troops in Vietnam in support of the U.S. fight against communism. For decades, the U.S.-ROK alliance represented an exemplary military partnership, not only because it continued successfully to deter the North but also as a result of both governments and their constituents believing that the purpose for the alliance continued to serve their respective interests.

The other pillar has been economic and trade relations. With the U.S. security guarantee and large amounts of economic and military aid, the ROK accomplished impressive economic growth, boasting today the thirteenth largest economy in the world. The United States was South Korea's largest trading partner until recent years and the South rose to become the seventh major trading partner of its ally. Recently the two negotiated a free trade agreement aimed at strengthening economic ties. Yet, South Korean trade with China has grown rapidly over the past two decades to far exceed trade with the United States, altering the calculus of economic dependency.

That security and trade have been the two dominant issues in defining the bilateral relationship is well illustrated by the media coverage of the relationship. In the Korean media, as Table 1 shows, security issues account for almost 60 percent of the coverage of U.S.-ROK relations, while economic and trade issues comprise 15 percent.[2] In the U.S. media, economic and trade issues receive more coverage than security (45.47 versus 33.77 percent). Yet, looking closely, the *Washington Post* pays much more attention to security than economy/trade and the *New York Times* also gives slightly more attention to security (see Table 1).

---

[2] The Korean data are based on 1,724 editorials and columns that appeared in the two Korean newspapers from July 1 1994, to July 31, 2003, and the U.S. data are based on 5,122 articles that were published in the three American papers from July 1, 1994, to January 31, 2004. For more detailed information on the data, see Chapter 2 in Shin, *One Alliance, Two Lenses.*

TABLE 1. *Most Prevalent Issues in South Korean and U.S. Media*

	Chosun (%)	Hankyoreh (%)	Total (%)	
Security	48.62	68.27	59.09	
Economy/Trade	18.43	13.45	15.78	
General Diplomacy	18.82	8.97	13.58	
Others	14.13	9.31	11.55	
Total	100	100	100	
Issues	**Nyt (%)**	**Wp (%)**	**Wsj (%)**	**All (%)**
Economy/Trade	34.34	15.46	70.53	45.47
Security	38.55	46.39	23.16	33.77
General Diplomacy	13.25	13.40	2.11	8.61
Others	13.86	24.75	4.2	12.15
Others	100	100	100	100

Notes: NYT = *New York Times*; WP = *Washington Post*; WSJ = *Wall Street Journal*.
Sources: Gi-Wook Shin, *One Alliance, Two Lenses: U.S.-Korea Relations in a New Era* (Stanford, CA: Stanford University Press, 2010), pp. 85 and 118.

Despite these variations, it is fair to say that citizens from both countries see security and trade/economy as the main pillars of their bilateral relationship.

Although the U.S.-ROK relationship was built upon security and trade, it has become much more complex, including people-to-people ties as diverse groups are increasingly involved. Consequently, the importance of nonsecurity, non-economic issues has increased. Incorporating history and values into the analysis, we can better understand the new relationship that is emerging in an era defined by Korean democratization, the end of the cold war, inter-Korean reconciliation, and the U.S. war against global terrorism. Policy makers in both countries need to pay close attention to these factors in order to manage the alliance successfully in the coming years.

Kwangju: U.S. Complicity with Dictators and Anti-Americanism

South Korea is considered an exemplary nation that has achieved economic modernization and political democracy in a relatively short period of time. Few would dispute the fact that the United States was a key player in both developments. It gave massive economic and military aid, its market access was instrumental to South Korea's export-oriented industrialization, and the military alliance shielded the South from the North's threat. At the same time, the United States supported coopera- tion with a series of authoritarian and military regimes from Syngman Rhee to Park Chung-hee to Chun Doo-hwan. As democratization pro- ceeded, this past record of the U.S. role in the country was brought to the forefront and provoked emotional debates and reactions.

One event that triggered the reevaluation of the U.S. role in the South was its alleged involvement in the Kwangju massacre in May of 1980. Until then, most Koreans held highly favorable attitudes toward the United States. As Gregory Henderson points out, "We [Americans] were more than a friend to Seoul, we were *the* friend; until the late May 1980 Kwangju uprising anti-Americanism was about as common in South Korea as fish in trees."[3] Even most Korean activists considered the United States a friendly power, an ally to the democratization movement. This sentiment, however, was shattered when the American commitment to human rights and democracy was tested in Kwangju. Originating as a student demonstration, the movement escalated into a struggle that mobilized hundreds of thousands of citizens against the seizure of power by General Chun Doo-hwan, who responded with brutal suppression.[4] Many Koreans expected the United States to help to stop the confronta- tion. Yet to their dismay, the U.S. military command was alleged to have released South Korean troops for redeployment in Kwangju who pro- ceeded to kill hundreds of antigovernment protesters.

The United States denied any involvement, claiming that the Special Forces who first entered Kwangju and caused most of the deaths were not under U.S. operational control. However, many Koreans were suspi- cious of the U.S. role in the massacre and an invitation to Chun to pay a state visit to Ronald Reagan's White House in early 1981 was seen to confirm these suspicions.[5] While the United States complained that Korea's government-controlled media painted a distorted picture of its role in the tragedy, many Koreans began believing that the United States was using their country only for its own strategic purposes and that talk about democracy and human rights was no more than placating rhetoric.

Alleged U.S. involvement at Kwangju and support of the autocratic Chun regime shaped the subsequent development of Korea's democratic

---

[3] Gregory Henderson, "Why Koreans Turn against US," *Washington Post*, July 1, 1986.
[4] See Gi-Wook Shin and Kyung Moon Hwang, eds, *Contentious Kwangju: The May 18 Uprising in Korea's Past and Present* (Boulder, CO: Rowman and Littlefield, 2003).
[5] His invitation was part of a deal to keep Chun from executing Kim Dae-jung, but it was not known to the Korean public at the time.

movement. As the leaders reflected on their previous struggles, especially on reasons for the failure to prevent the Kwangju tragedy, they came to realize that they had fought in the absence of a well-articulated strategy and ideology. If past mistakes were to be avoided, they concluded, it would be necessary to specify properly the nature of Korean society and articulate a coherent ideology and strategy based on this analysis. Subsequently, the early to mid-1980s saw a wide range of debates among activists and progressive intellectuals, such as "social formation debates," "debates on Korean capitalism," "debates on modern and contemporary Korea," and "debates on the character of Korean society."[6] They also sought to reexamine their history, especially the U.S. role in the unfortunate events of peninsula division, military occupation, the Korean War, and political dictatorship.

Based on this reexamination of history, Korean intellectuals and activists questioned their previous appeal for American support and began to argue that democratization could not be obtained without liberation from American dominance. As Tim Shorrock points out, the Korean democratic movement began to change from "a Western-oriented movement based largely on middle-class resentment of Park Chung-hee's military dictatorship" to "a nationalist struggle for independence from foreign intervention and eventual unification" in the 1980s.[7]

Some activists even took direct action against American facilities such as the American Information Center and the American Chamber of Commerce. Mun Pusik, leader of the 1982 arson incident at the Pusan American Information Center, explains in his letter to Cardinal Kim, "We chose the method of setting fire to a building in broad daylight because we felt there was no other way left to chastise the U.S. for acting as the mother-in-law for this [Chun] dictatorship."[8] While the arson was initially considered "radical activism," even by student activists, the mid-1980s witnessed a series of attacks on American facilities: from May 23 to May 25, 1985, seventy-three students occupied the U.S. Information Center in Seoul demanding a formal U.S. apology for "its role in the Kwangju massacre"; on August 12, five students unsuccessfully sought to

---

[6] See Gi-Wook Shin, "Marxism, Anti-Americanism, and Democracy in South Korea: An Examination of Nationalist Intellectual Discourse," *Positions: East Asia Cultures Critique*, Vol. 3, No. 2 (1995), pp. 508–34.

[7] Tim Shorrock, "The Struggle for Democracy in South Korea in the 1980s and the Rise of Anti-Americanism," *Third World Quarterly*, Vol. 8, No. 4 (1986), p. 1205.

[8] Bu-Shik Moon (Mun Pusik), "Why Did I Commit Arson?" UCLA Archival Collection on Democracy and Unification, 1982.

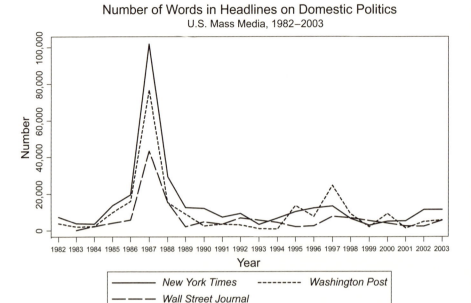

FIGURE 1. U.S. Media Coverage of Korea's Domestic Politics, 1982–2003

invade the U.S. embassy for the same reason; and on November 4, four-teen students occupied the U.S. Chamber of Commerce office in Seoul, protesting reported U.S. pressure to increase agricultural imports into Korea. As Wonmo Dong indicates, "Only a very small fraction of the 1980 student activists shared anti-American sentiments; but by 1985 it was apparent that most student activists subscribed to the view that the U.S. was primarily responsible for the very existence of the military-authoritarian regime."[9] Furthermore, anti-American sentiments gradu-ally spread throughout the country. A June 1990 survey shows that 37.2 percent of the respondents supported anti-American movements and 72.7 percent agreed that "anti-American sentiments in Korea are serious." Support was most evident among those in their twenties (56.5 percent), college students (63.4 percent), the educated (45.3 percent), the new mid-dle class (42.9 percent), workers (45.1 percent), and people in the Chŏlla region (46.3 percent), location of the Kwangju uprising.

The rise of anti-American sentiment during Korea's struggle for democ-racy caught the attention of the U.S. media and government. Figure 1

[9] Wonmo Dong, "University Students in South Korean Politics: Patterns of Radicalization in the 1980s," *Journal of International Affairs*, Vol. 40 (1987), p. 246.

indicates the number of words in articles on Korea's domestic politics in the three major U.S. newspapers.[10] As expected, media coverage peaked in 1987, reflecting massive democratic demonstrations that culminated in the summer of that year, forcing the Chun government to make concessions for political reform. Perhaps learning a lesson from Kwangju, the United States made a critical intervention, sending Assistant Secretary of State Gaston Sigur to deliver a warning to Chun that it would oppose any attempt to impose emergency rule or resort to military intervention.

With democratization in progress, South Koreans sought to redress past wrongs committed during military and authoritarian rule and the atrocities of Kwangju became a central issue in the process of addressing transitional justice: In 1987, public hearings were held in the National Assembly; the Kwangju Compensation Law was enacted in 1990 for victims and their families; the May 18 Special Act passed in 1995, leading to the trials of Chun Doo-hwan and Roh Tae-woo. Once labeled a communist-agitated "incident," the uprising was officially named the May 18 Democratization Movement.

While the U.S. government did not take any position or action in this process of redressing historical injustice, the two top U.S. officials in South Korea at the time of the massacre sought to correct what they regarded as misperceptions nearly two decades later after they had retired. In his book *Massive Entanglement, Marginal Influence*, Ambassador Bill Gleysteen reflects his personal view of the U.S. predicament at the time, lamenting that the U.S. influence on Korean affairs was more limited than widely thought during the times of turmoil in South Korea.[11] Additionally, the commander of U.S. Forces in Korea during the massacre, General John Wickham, similarly contends that the U.S. role had been one of "steadfast commitment" that not only helped to evade an all-out civil war, but also was a crucial long-term factor, contributing to the political economic successes and peaceful power transfers of the 1990s.[12]

By the time that Gleysteen and Wickham had written their memoirs, however, as David Straub indicates, "the South Korean generation that had come of age during that period had long since formed a powerful

---

[10] The figure shows the number of words in the articles on South Korean domestic politics that appeared in the three U.S. papers – the *New York Times*, the *Wall Street Journal*, and the *Washington Post* – during the period.

[11] William H. Gleysteen, Jr., *Massive Entanglement, Marginal Influence: Carter and Korea in Crisis* (Washington, DC: Brookings Institution Press, 1999).

[12] John A. Wickham, Jr., *Korea on the Brink: A Memoir of Political Intrigue and Military Crisis* (Washington, DC: Brassey's, 2000), pp. 124, 190–1.

'collective memory' of events. Even though both books were translated into Korean, very few Koreans may have read them. Basically, South Koreans already knew what they needed to know; the memoirs barely made a dent in Korean thinking about the period."[13] While Kwangju no longer captures Korean attention when they think of the United States, the damage has been done.

Inside Korea, the successful redress of the injustices at Kwangju set a precedent for examining other atrocities that military and authoritarian regimes had committed since 1945. The April 3 massacre on Cheju Island in 1948 and the mass killings of civilians by government troops during the Korean War have both been reinvestigated. Discussing these tragic events had been taboo among Koreans for a long time, because the victims were often portrayed as communists or sympathetic to the North. However, the end of the cold war, along with democratization, loosened the power of anticommunism and opened a new space for public discussion of the unfortunate past. By the 1990s, the state could no longer ignore the histories of those previously marginalized or oppressed. In bringing the issue of transitional justice to the forefront of politics, new scholarship led by progressive social scientists played a crucial role. This new historiography offered an alternative interpretation of modern Korean history by putting ordinary people or *minjung* at the center of historical progress, in contrast to the state-sponsored official history that privileged the elite and the political establishment.

In 2000, the South Korean government established the Presidential Truth Commission on Suspicious Deaths to "promote unity and democracy by uncovering the truth about suspicious deaths which occurred during the democratization movement against past authoritarian regimes." The Commission has received petitions from families of victims to reinvestigate their suspicious deaths during the authoritarian regimes. A year later, the government established the National Human Rights Commission (Kukka ingwon wiwonhoe), with a broad mandate that included the investigation of violations both past and present along with recommendations to improve the condition of human rights. This paved the way for a more thorough investigation of the wrongdoings of the past, including U.S. wartime killings of Korean civilians.

---

[13] David Straub, "Public Diplomacy and the Korean Peninsula," in Donald A. L. Macintyre, Daniel C. Sneider, and Gi-Wook Shin, eds., *First Drafts of Korea: The U.S. Media and Perceptions of The Last Cold War Frontier* (Stanford, CA: Walter H. Shorenstein Asia-Pacific Research Center, 2009), pp. 129–40.

No-gun Ri: Disputes over a U.S. Wartime Massacre

Many Korean civilians, including women and children, were killed during the Korean War. Most of them were sacrificed by Korean troops, both North and South; yet, American military personnel, primarily aviators, are also guilty of killing. Most of the victims by South Korean troops were considered communists, collaborators, or sympathizers with the North, and it was extremely difficult or even dangerous to discuss the tragic events in a society in which anticommunism was the prescriptive national norm under the firm grasp of an authoritarian government. However, democratization and the demise of the cold war system created a more receptive political environment, offering opportunities to revisit the past. In 1997, for instance, taking advantage of the changed political scene, survivors and families of the victims filed a claim with the Government Compensation Committee, demanding recognition and compensation, only to find it rejected in April 1998 on the grounds that a five-year statute of limitations had expired. South Korea was not yet ready to address its troubled history.

Then on September 29, 1999, the Associated Press (AP) reported a case of mass killings in an article "U.S. Massacre of Civilians in Korean War Described: Ex-Soldiers Confirm Villagers' Accounts." Based on interviews with survivors and ex-GIs, the article asserted: "in late July 1950, in the conflict's first desperate weeks, U.S. troops killed a large number of South Korean refugees, many of them women and children, trapped beneath a bridge at a hamlet called Nogun Ri." The article concluded that it could not determine the precise death toll, only offering estimates ranging from one hundred to two hundred (by ex-GIs) to three hundred (by survivors).

The article received the Pulitzer Prize and ignited controversy on both sides of the Pacific.[14] The Korean media, both progressive and

---

[14] *U.S. News and World Report* reported documents that would undermine the credibility of three of a dozen soldiers cited by the AP report. Robert Bateman, a retired U.S. Army officer, wrote a book entitled *No Gun Ri: A Military History of the Korean War Incident* (Mechanicsburg, PA: Stockpile, 2002), in which he also disputed the credibility of some soldiers. Then years later, on May 30, 2006, AP published a newly declassified letter from U.S. Ambassador John J. Muccio to Assistant Secretary of State Dean Rusk, saying that "If refugees do appear from north of US lines they will receive warning shots, and if they then persist in advancing they will be shot." The AP article interpreted the letter as "the strongest indication yet that such a policy [plan to shoot refugees] existed for all U.S. forces in Korea, and the first evidence that that policy was known to the upper ranks of the U.S. government." Charles J. Hanley and Martha Mendoza, "Letter

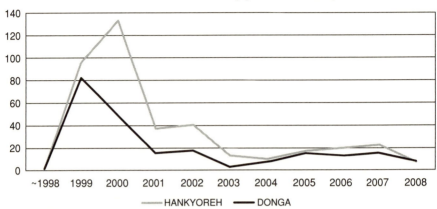

FIGURE 2. Number of Articles on No-gun Ri: Korean Media

conservative, covered the story extensively, as shown in Figure 2. As expected, the progressive *Hankyoreh* published more stories, but even the conservative *Dong-a Ilbo* featured a substantial number of pieces on the topic. South Koreans demanded joint investigations from the U.S. and ROK governments, and the survivors and families of the victims asked for "fact-finding and compensation for the victims."[15] Major U.S. media also followed the AP lead. The *New York Times* reported "the sentiments of many South Koreans, who sharply criticized the United States for long ignoring the claims of massacre survivors and called on their own Government to conduct an independent investigation."[16] *Time* described the No-gun Ri massacre as "the century's second deadliest [bloodbath] committed by U.S. troops, trailing only the 1968 My Lai massacre in Vietnam, where G.I.s killed up to 500 noncombatants."[17] *Newsweek* quoted Edward Daily, one of the veterans who had spoken to the AP, as saying that "a bunch of untrained soldiers were ordered to gun down

on Korean War Massacre Reveals Plan to Shoot Refugees: Historian Discovers U.S. Envoy's Writings Relating to No Gun Ri." On the internal struggle within the AP about publishing the article, see Felicity Barringer, "Reporters and Editors Defend A.P. Story on Korean Massacre," *New York Times*, May 14, 2000.

[15] See editorial by the liberal *Hankyoreh* newspaper on October 13, 1999, "Nogun-ri haksal kongdong chosa haeya" (Need for Joint Investigations of the Nogun-ri Massacre).

[16] Calvin Sims, "South Koreans Call on U.S. to Apologize for Killings," *New York Times*, October 12, 1999.

[17] Mark Thompson, "The Bridge at No Gun Ri," *Time*, October 11, 1999.

Korean civilians," and that "I've made my confession to God and have tried to repent."[18]

Soon after the publication of the AP article, the U.S. and ROK governments launched investigations of the No-gun Ri massacre in close collaboration with each other. After fifteen months, the two governments issued a "Statement of Mutual Understanding between the United States and the Republic of Korea on the No Gun Ri Investigations" on January 11, 2001. The statement recognized that "At some time between July 26th and 29th, 1950, some U.S. soldiers fired toward the refugees... [and] as a result, an unknown number of refugees were killed or injured." However, it left undecided whether U.S. soldiers had received orders to fire or not, due to conflicting testimonies of the veterans interviewed. In terms of the number of casualties, the statement merely mentioned "an unverified number of 248 Korean civilians killed" given by the Korean side, noting "the testimony of U.S. veterans supports lower numbers."[19]

On the same day, right before the release of this statement, the White House issued a statement from President Clinton addressing the No-gun Ri case: "On behalf of the Untied States of America, I deeply regret that Korean civilians lost their lives at No Gun Ri in late July 1950. The intensive, yearlong investigation into this incident has served as a painful reminder of the tragedies of war and the scars they leave behind on people and nations." He added that the United States would construct a memorial to Korean victims to "bring a measure of solace and closure" and establish a commemorative scholarship fund that will serve as "a living tribute to their memory."[20]

It is unusual for a U.S. president to issue an official statement of regret for an incident that had occurred more than half a century earlier in wartime. Although it was not an official apology, as some survivors and families of the victims demanded, and no compensation was given to the victims, Clinton's statement was well received in South Korea. Even the progressive *Hankyoreh* appreciated the inclusion of many Korean

---

[18] Gregory Vistica, "'I've Tried to Repent': An American GI Recalls How a Bunch of Untrained Soldiers Were Ordered to Gun Down Korean Civilians," *Newsweek*, October 11, 1999, p. 58. Daily's testimony was later discredited; documentary evidence proved he was not serving in Korea at the time the incident occurred.

[19] Citation. See also Department of the Army Inspector General, "No Gun Ri Review," January 2001.

[20] Office of the Press Secretary, the White House, "Statement of the President." Also at http://www.pbs.org/newshour/media/media_watch/jan-june01/clinton_1-11 .html (accessed October 1, 2009).

views in the statement as well as Clinton's expression of regret.[21] He and President Kim Dae-jung enjoyed a cordial relationship, making it easier to calm emotions; nonetheless, many survivors and family members refused to accept the scholarship fund, filing lawsuits instead for compensation from the U.S. government.[22]

Moreover, after the AP story, the Korean media reported one highly negative story after another about the United States, especially regarding the U.S. Forces in Korea (USFK). In particular, the progressive media, including *Hankyoreh*, published many editorials and op-eds on U.S. troops in South Korea: Before 1999, the average number was below ten per year but it jumped to forty in 2000.[23] The main topics included controversy over the Status of Forces Agreement (SOFA), the dumping by USFK personnel of formaldehyde in the Han River, an accident at the U.S. Air Force's practice bombing range near Maehyang-ri, Agent Orange exposure of South Korean veterans during the Vietnam War, and a South Korean short track speed skater's loss of a gold medal at the 2002 Winter Olympics in Utah due to an Australian referee's call.[24]

All these stories critical of the United States appeared in the midst of inter-Korean reconciliation, leading many Koreans to rethink the rationale for the military alliance as their sense of the North Korean threat diminished. As the alliance was built on the threat from the North, views of the two were inevitably related. American troops became less valued as a deterrent, and the social and political consequences of U.S. military deployment in South Korea, especially in increasingly urban areas, seemed less tolerable. Then, in the summer of 2002, U.S. soldiers who took a road too narrow for their vehicle tragically crushed to death two middle-school girls walking on the pedestrian shoulder of the road. Because the accident happened while they were on duty, under the terms of the SOFA, both the driver and the commander were tried in a U.S. military court instead of a Korean civilian court. They were found not guilty and immediately transferred out of the country. The Korean public was furious.[25] Protests erupted, demanding justice for the "murders" of the girls, as photos of the

---

[21] "'No Gun Ri' palpy'o naeyong, ŭimi," *Hankyoreh*, January 13, 2001.
[22] Elizabeth Becker, "Army Confirms G.I.'s in Korea Killed Civilians," *New York Times*, January 12, 2001, p. A1.
[23] See Shin, *One Alliance, Two Lenses*, chapter 4.
[24] Straub, "Public Diplomacy and the Korean Peninsula," p. 132.
[25] The incident was reported when it occurred, but did not become a major story until the end of the World Cup tournament then under way. The progressive online news service *OhMyNews* led the reporting.

bodies spread across the Internet inflamed emotions.[26] Bush's statement of "regret" was dismissed as insufficient and insincere since it came late and was read not by him but by the U.S. ambassador. Memory of other tragic events, especially No-gun Ri and Kwangju, became the interpretative framework. As David Straub, head of the political section in the U.S. embassy at the time, explains, "millions of South Koreans interpreted the accident through a prism of attitudes significantly shaped by their understanding of the U.S. role. . . . Their feelings were a product of their history and their culture."[27]

Americans had their own, significantly different, memory of Korea's past, and thus could not understand the extent and furor of protests. Straub recollects:

> . . . for most Americans . . . whose own collective memory tells them only that the U.S. saved the Republic of Korea from a military invasion from the communist North in 1950 and then nurtured the South's near-miraculous economic and political development, the massive protests came out of the blue. What could possibly explain daily protests involving tens and even hundreds of thousands of people over an unintended traffic accident?[28]

The public mood in South Korea influenced the presidential election, as Roh Moo-hyun, a human rights lawyer who represented labor activists and student dissidents, was openly critical of the subservient relationship of his country to the United States and of Korean politicians for their traditional pilgrimage to the United States for "a political blessing." Condemning Bush's hard-line policy toward the North, Roh hit a popular chord with his strong stance. Even his conservative opponent, Lee Hoi-chang, was forced by the public mood to criticize the American government for its handling of the death of the two girls. Once again, Americans could not fully understand the public mood. As Doug Struck, *Washington Post* correspondent at the time, reflects:

> . . . most U.S. news stories . . . focused on the military accident as the cause of the anti-American demonstrations as though it was a discrete event. We wrote the North Korean story as though it was isolated from the other issues. In fact, these issues were all intertwined, and all reverberated on the others . . . we did not weave a broad enough portrait for the events of the

---

[26] Doug Struck, "Democracy, Anti-Americanism, and Korean Nationalism," in Macintyre, Sneider, and Shin, eds., *First Drafts of Korea*, pp. 61–8.
[27] Straub, "Public Diplomacy and the Korean Peninsula," p. 130.
[28] Ibid., p. 130.

time. . . . The reporting wasn't wrong. It just did not encompass enough of the emotional mix of the time.[29]

Riding this public mood, Roh was elected Korea's new president.

Once in office, Roh paid keen attention to redressing the nation's unfortunate past. In December 2005, he established the Truth and Reconciliation Commission (Chinsil hwahae wiwonhoe). Modeled after the South African group, the Commission was set up for a nationwide investigation to uncover the history of atrocities by each Korea, including "past incidents, such as the anti-Japanese independence movement and the history of Koreans residing abroad during the Japanese occupation, mass victimization of civilians before and during the Korean War, human rights violations and politically fabricated trials from August 15, 1945 to the end of authoritarian rule." Its establishment, however, provoked controversy within South Korea as conservatives were suspicious of the underlying political motivation.[30]

With fifteen commissioners, three subcommittees, and one reconciliation committee, the TRC aimed to finish its investigation by April 2010.[31] Its leaders were historians and social scientists who had led the effort to challenge the elite-centered conventional view of Korean history in favor of a view that puts the marginalized and oppressed people at the center of their inquiry. The Subcommittee on the Investigation of Mass Civilian Sacrifice headed by Kim Tong-choon, a noted sociologist, had as its main task to investigate "cases during the Korean War period," which comprised almost three-quarters of the TRC's petition cases. Unlike mass killings of civilians by the North Korean Army, those by South Korean or U.S. troops were not well-known during the cold war era.[32] According to Kim, "without addressing the deep trauma suffered by some members of Korean society, we cannot go forward to the bright future, and in order to approach the peaceful unification of the country, we have to verify the truth in such tragic events of our history."[33]

[29] Ibid., pp. 62–3, 68.
[30] See, for instance, Pak Dusik, "Yŏ mŏrit sogen 'kwakŏ' ibron 'mirae,'" *Chosun Ilbo*, August 1, 2004.
[31] Truth and Reconciliation Commission, Republic of Korea, "The Just Settlement of the Past Wrongs Promises an Integrated Society and a Bright Future," February 2008.
[32] There were reports in the United States at the time of such killings, including in the *New York Times*, but the ROK government and the U.S. public basically ignored them and focused on what the "bad guys" were doing.
[33] Subcommittee of Investigation on Mass Civilian Sacrifice, "The Just Settlement of the Past Wrongs Promises an Integrated Society and a Bright Future," March 2008. TRC, p. 7.

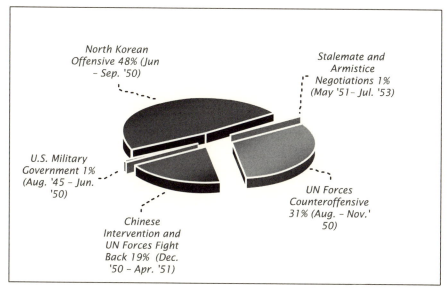

North Korean
Offensive 48% (Jun
– Sep. '50)

Stalemate and
Armistice
Negotiations 1%
(May '51– Jul. '53)

U.S. Military
Government 1%
(Aug. '45 – Jun.
'50)

UN Forces
Counteroffensive
31% (Aug. – Nov.'
50)

Chinese
Intervention and
UN Forces Fight
Back 19% (Dec.
'50 – Apr. '51)

FIGURE 3. Petitions by Period

Team 5 under the subcommittee was in charge of investigating "civilian killings by American bombings, strafing and shootings during [the] Korean War period." It considered 509 petitions, most referring to events at the early stage of the war, that is, during the North Korean offensive and UN forces' counteroffensive in the latter part of 1950 (see Figure 3).

In early August 2008, there were reports on the main findings by the TRC on the three cases concerning the mass killings of Korean civilians on the part of U.S. military personnel. According to declassified U.S. military documents that the TRC reviewed, on September 10, 1950, five days before the Inchon landing, forty-three American warplanes swarmed over Wolmi Island, dropping ninety-three napalm canisters to "burn out" its eastern slope in an attempt to clear the way for American troops. The TRC report suggests that "it was quite possible that the U.S. Forces were aware that numerous civilians were living in Wolmi-do, but no actions were taken to reduce the casualties such as warning or avoiding civilians. On the contrary, U.S. forces napalmed numerous small buildings, strafing children, women, and old people in the open from early morning. The weather was clear and one of the firing altitudes was only 100 feet." The report said that at least ten of the victims were verified by the TRC, but "many more residents were believed to have been killed." It concluded "the devastation of Wolmi-do cannot be justified under the principle of discrimination nor the principle of proportionality."[34]

The other two cases that the TRC investigated occurred as communist forces barreled down the peninsula. As the allies fell back, they were attacked by guerrillas that could not be easily distinguished from refugees. On January 19, 1951, the U.S. Air Force conducted three bombing raids, dropping napalm in the Sansong-dong area, which killed at least fifty-one residents, the TRC report said. Using declassified U.S. documents, the report ruled that the bombing was "not necessary" because North Korean soldiers were not present in the area, so that only "innocent civilians," including women and children, were killed. The attack on Tanyang followed on the next day when American planes dropped napalm near the entrance of a cave where refugees had sought shelter. According to the TRC, at least 167 villagers, more than half of them women, were burned to death or asphyxiated.[35] The TRC has urged the ROK government to seek U.S. compensation for victims, but the government has not disclosed how it plans to follow up.

The TRC also charged that the United States did not stop mass executions by its ally. In the early days of the war, the South Korean government is believed to have killed a large number of leftists and supposed sympathizers, usually without charge or trial. For instance, as war broke out, South Korean authorities rounded up members of the three hundred thousand–strong National Guidance Alliance, a "reeducation" body to which they had assigned leftist sympathizers and whose membership quotas were filled by illiterate peasants lured by promises of jobs and other benefits. Extrapolating from initial evidence and interviews with family survivors, the TRC reported that most alliance members had been killed in the wave of executions. It also asserted "they [Americans] were at the crime scene, and took pictures and wrote reports," but "did not stop the executions."[36]

Right before its dissolution, the Commission recommended that the Korean government enact a special law to compensate those wartime victims and establish a state-sponsored foundation to commemorate the

---

[34] Ibid., p. 19.
[35] Choe Sang-Hun, "South Korea Says U.S. Killed Hundreds of Civilians," *New York Times*, August 3, 2008. See also Charles Hanley and Jae-Soon Chang, "Korean Commission Finds Indiscriminate Killings of Civilians by US Military," *AP Impact*, August 4, 2008.
[36] Charles Hanley and Jae-Soon Chang, "US Wavered over S. Korean Executions," *AP Impact*, July 6, 2008.

unfortunate past. However, the conservative Lee government has not accepted such proposals from the Commission. Instead, it closed the Commission when its term expired in April 2010. In addition, President Lee, unlike his predecessor, is not likely to make this a major issue with the United States, which so far has largely remained silent on the Commission's work. Given that Clinton already issued a statement of regret in 2001, it is unlikely that there will be another in the near future.[37]

DPRK: Clashes of Identity and Interests

In the recent past, the U.S.-ROK alliance has shown visible strains attributed to divergent perceptions of the North Korean threat.[38] No alliance can survive unless it is anchored on a congruence of strategic interests (such as a common threat) and a willingness to share risk. While the end of the cold war loosened alliances in general, the U.S.–South Korean alliance remained robust through most of the 1990s, when both nations still shared a similar view of the threat, as illustrated by their common approach to the first North Korean nuclear stand-off. Yet, various developments of the late 1990s and early 2000s, such as the South's prolonged engagement policy and the U.S. war against terrorism, have eroded the congruence of interests between the two nations. The two parties no longer shared the same perception of the North Korea problem.[39] In contrast to the U.S. global approach to the nuclear issue, South Korea has paid most attention to peninsula stability. The idea of a nuclear North Korea has raised U.S. fears that the North would sell fissile material or transfer nuclear technology to terrorist groups. On the other hand, many (especially progressives) in the South believe that the threat has been exaggerated and fear U.S. military action against the North would most likely lead to a full-blown military confrontation on the peninsula.

---

[37] The fact that the United States conducted one study on such an issue, ironically, has probably made it *less* likely it will do another. Relevant is the fact that the U.S. military continues to be charged with mass killings of innocent civilians even today in places such as Iraq and Afghanistan. Of course, the U.S. archives are open to everyone and the ROK government and scholars can and will continue to do research in them.

[38] See Eric Larson, Norman D. Levin, Seonhae Baik, and Bogdan Savych, *Ambivalent Allies? A Study of South Korean Attitudes toward the U.S.* (San Diego, CA: RAND Corporation, 2004); Derek Mitchell, ed., *Strategy and Sentiment: South Korean Views of the United States and the U.S.-ROK Alliance* (Washington, D.C.: Center for Strategic and International Studies, 2004).

[39] This theme is more systematically addressed in my book, *One Alliance, Two Lenses.*

In particular, the progressive governments of Kim Dae-jung and Roh Moo-hyun, concerned with the costs of regime collapse in the North, sought to keep the failed regime in Pyongyang alive to engineer an eventual "soft landing." In contrast, the Bush administration initially advocated "regime change" in the North and Bush himself was known to "loathe" Kim Jong-il.[40] While Seoul tried to engage Pyongyang to thaw relations, Washington sought to isolate and press it into submission until the North's nuclear testing led to a change in U.S. strategy. Moreover, this difference was not simply a matter of policy discord between the allies. Its roots were deeper. While U.S. officials approached the DPRK as a matter of security policy, North Korea and inter-Korean relations have been central to the evolution of South Korean *national identity*. Led by progressives, South Koreans have sought to redefine their national identity in the newly evolving regional and global order of the post–cold war era.

A turning point in South Korea's politics of national identity vis-à-vis the North and the United States occurred with the implementation of Kim Dae-jung's "sunshine policy." The election of this long-time opposition leader to the presidency not only signaled a maturing democracy in the South but also marked a new policy orientation toward the North. Kim forcefully promoted his vision for bringing reconciliation, peace, and eventual reunification to the Korean peninsula. Two key assumptions underpinned the policy: First, the two Koreas should not continue their cold war animosity and confrontation; and second, the northern regime is reasonable enough to accept changes to improve the quality of life for its people and appreciate its common ethnicity with the South. Kim's policy set business and political relations on separate tracks and advocated economic aid to the North to foster and support DPRK efforts at reform.

The sunshine policy led to a series of diplomatic achievements as well as concrete projects, including South Korean tourism to Mount Kumgang in the North. Most notably, the June 2000 Pyongyang summit between Kim Dae-jung and Kim Jong-il marked the first meeting between the top leaders of the two Koreas since the peninsula's 1945 partition. Unprecedented high-level military talks between North and South Korean delegations followed. These achievements led to a change in the tenor of the

---

[40] Secretary of State Condoleezza Rice also called the North Korean regime an "outpost of tyranny" at her Senate confirmation hearing in January 2005.

relationship, and the North came to be viewed less as a threat and more as a "compatriot."[41]

This shifting view of the North triggered a corresponding change in views of the U.S.-ROK alliance. The North's economic decline led many to perceive their neighbor as weak while new contact decreased the sense of threat South Koreans felt – long-held notions of the North as a strong, threatening "other" were shattered. Therefore, the need for a U.S. security guarantee was no longer as sharply felt.[42] Under these new circumstances, American forces appeared to some as an unnecessary inconvenience, or even worse as an infringement on sovereignty, a source of interference in Korean politics, and a symbol of national stigma. Some even came to portray the United States and the alliance as obstacles to improved inter-Korean relations and eventual unification.

The Roh administration went further in seeking to reorient Korean identity away from the nation's close ties with the United States. While continuing his predecessor's policy of engagement with the North, Roh also pressed for a more region-centered foreign policy. Proclaiming an "era of Northeast Asia" (*tongpuka sidae*), he asserted that the ROK must actively participate by becoming a hub in the region, going so far as to make the case that it could serve as a "balancer" in Northeast Asia. This initiative was widely interpreted as a veiled strategy to weaken the U.S.-ROK alliance and move closer to China, and it proved controversial both within and outside South Korea.[43]

This regionalist outlook reflected Korea's new politics of identity. As Gilbert Rozman points out, "national identity is the foundation of state power and foreign policy. To accept regionalism means to redefine one's

---

[41] For example, see Do-Yeong Kim, "After the South and North Korea Summit: Malleability of Explicit and Implicit National Attitudes of South Koreans," *Peace and Conflict: Journal of Peace Psychology*, Vol. 9, No. 2 (June 2003), pp. 159–70.

[42] See, for example, Kurt Achin, "South Korea–US Alliance in Difficult Transition," Voice of America, May 2, 2005; Balbina Y. Hwang, "Minding the Gap: Improving U.S.-ROK Relations," Heritage Backgrounder # 1814, Heritage Foundation, December 21, 2004; Robert Marquand, "How S. Korea's View of the North Flipped," *Christian Science Monitor*, January 22, 2003.

[43] David C. Kang, "Rising Powers, Offshore Balancers, and Why the US-Korea Alliance Is Undergoing Strain," *International Journal of Korean Unification Studies*, Vol. 14, No. 2 (2005), pp. 115–40; Scott Snyder, "The China-Japan Rivalry: Korea's Pivotal Position?" in Gi-Wook Shin and Daniel Sneider, eds., *Cross-Currents: Regionalism and Nationalism in Northeast Asia* (Stanford, CA: Walter H. Shorenstein Asia-Pacific Research Center, 2007), pp. 241–58.

country's identity."[44] South Koreans, led by progressives, have been actively seeking to (re)define their position vis-à-vis the United States and China, in addition to the DPRK. Former activists who had fought for democracy in the streets with anti-American slogans in the 1980s became influential in the Roh government and this progressive orientation reflected their memory of and experience in their activism. Yet, not all Koreans' views have shifted in this way. Progressive ideas of the kind of relations South Korea should have with the North and the United States provoked strong dissent from conservatives in the South. Though not necessarily opposed per se to engagement with the North, they remained skeptical that the North would change and demanded greater reciprocity in inter-Korean relations.[45] In their view, its nuclear activities were a clear violation of bilateral North-South agreements and the northern threat has not diminished. Pursuit of rapprochement under these conditions seemed disconcerting at best. South Korean conservatives have come to underline the importance of the U.S.-ROK alliance. The bitter contention between progressives and conservatives has been described as the "South–South conflict" or "a house divided."[46]

Spurred by intense debate over how to approach North Korea and the alliance, the politics of identity reemerged in the South in earnest. As J. J. Suh asserts, South Korea has been "caught between two conflicting identities: the alliance identity that sees the United States as a friendly provider and the nationalist identity that pits Korean identity against the United States."[47] The former is an established viewpoint that conservatives have maintained, while the latter is a new framework promoted by progressives as well as a reaction against the past. The nationalist identity of progressive administrations clashed with the Bush administration's tough line on the DPRK, engendering tension in relations. Policy incongruity was

---

[44] Gilbert Rozman, *Northeast Asia's Stunted Regionalism: Bilateral Distrust in the Shadow of Globalization* (Cambridge: Cambridge University Press, 2004), p. 364.

[45] Conservatives were enraged when they found that the Kim Dae-jung government had paid cash to Pyongyang to facilitate the breakthrough with the North, and the under-the-table payoffs became a big issue in debates over engagement.

[46] Byung-Hoon Suh, "Kim Dae Jung's Engagement Policy and the South-South Conflict in South Korea: Implications for U.S. Policy," *Asian Update* (Summer 2001), at http://www.asiasociety.org/publications/update_southkorea.html (accessed October 1, 2009); Hahm Chaibong, "The Two South Koreas: A House Divided," *Washington Quarterly*, Vol. 28, No. 3 (Summer 2005), pp. 57–72.

[47] J. J. Suh, Peter J. Katzenstein, and Allen Carlson, *Rethinking Security in East Asia* (Stanford: Stanford University Press, 2004), p. 169.

only part of the larger "identity" story that explains strains in U.S.-ROK relations.

In the United States, Clinton's North Korea policy came under heavy fire from conservative critics. In 1999, for instance, a House Republican advisory group on North Korea issued a report that questioned the merits of engagement and claimed that "the comprehensive threat posed by North Korea to our national security has increased since 1994 . . . [as there are] a number of serious weaknesses concerning current U.S. policy toward North Korea."[48] Another 1999 report by Asia specialists and more moderate Republicans (who would assume key positions under Bush) called Clinton's approach "politically unsustainable" and urged a more comprehensive approach that conceptualized the Agreed Framework[49] as the *beginning* of formulating a coherent, disciplined North Korea policy rather than as any kind of resolution.[50] President Bush pursued an ABC (anything but Clinton) approach toward the DPRK. When Kim Dae-jung visited the White House in March 2001, Bush lent rhetorical support to Kim's sunshine policy but unequivocally expressed his lack of trust of North Korea and asserted that there must be a better verification mechanism for nuclear compliance. Although Bush had not yet formulated a specific North Korean policy, it became quite clear that it would come into conflict with Kim's position.[51]

The terrorist attacks of September 11 further transformed U.S. strategic thinking. The greatest threat came to be perceived as the nexus of "rogue states" with WMD capabilities and terrorist intent to strike the U.S. homeland or its interests abroad. Thus, when the second North Korean nuclear crisis broke out in October 2002, it was immediately couched

---

[48] North Korea Advisory Group, "Report to the Speaker U.S. House of Representatives," November 1999. http://www.fas.org/nuke/guide/dprk/nkag-report.htm (accessed October 1, 2009).

[49] The Agreed Framework was a 1994 agreement between the United States and North Korea for gradual denuclearization and normalization of relations between the two countries. The agreement broke down with North Korea's withdrawal from the Nuclear Non-Proliferation Treaty (NPT) in early 2003.

[50] Richard L. Armitage, "A Comprehensive Approach to North Korea," Institute for National Strategic Studies, Strategic Forum, No. 159, National Defense University, March 1999, at http://www.globalsecurity.org/wmd/library/news/dprk/1999/forum159.html (accessed October 1, 2009).

[51] Sebastian Harnisch, "U.S.–North Korean Relations under the Bush Administration: From 'Slow Go' to 'No Go,'" *Asian Survey*, Vol. 42, No. 6 (November/December 2002), pp. 856–82; Andrew Moens, *The Foreign Policy of George W. Bush: Values, Strategy and Loyalty* (Ashgate, 2004). pp. 109–11.

in terms of nonproliferation. Though the administration would eventually engage in multilateral diplomacy, for months Washington pursued a policy of isolation by refusing to talk to North Korea until it abandoned its nuclear weapons programs. At the same time, South Korea vowed to continue inter-Korean engagement, despite the nuclear crisis. The two governments were out of sync – while Washington viewed the North as part of an "axis of evil" and sought a policy to contain this threat, Seoul had no intention of suspending or even toughening its engagement policy. As Victor Cha points out, "at the heart of this gap are parallel paradigm shifts in foreign policy that have taken place in Washington and Seoul" in the post-September 11, post-sunshine era, respectively.[52] The DPRK was a clear case in which the allies' interests, as defined by these foreign policy paradigm shifts, came into direct conflict.[53]

With the change of power in both countries, there are optimistic expectations on both sides of the Pacific that the four-year period of the Lee and Obama administrations represents an opportunity to strengthen the U.S.-ROK relationship. This seems especially true, considering that the last five years featured the overlap of President Roh and his progressive advisers with President Bush and the neoconservatives, which was possibly the least workable combination of leadership for the alliance. Indeed, in the first meeting of presidents Bush and Lee Myung-bak, at Camp David in April 2008, the leaders stressed the allies' common values and shared challenges in the twenty-first century, calling for a broad-based "strategic alliance" that on the basis of "freedom, democracy, human rights and the principle of market economy . . . will contribute to global peace and security."[54] President Obama has similarly stressed the importance of consulting with key U.S. allies in pursuing a foreign policy agenda, and so far the two administrations have worked very closely in dealing with the North Korean nuclear issue.

Nonetheless, the United States should be wary of raising expectations for a dramatic change in South Korea as a result of this power shift to a conservative government. As shown in this chapter, the Korean

---

[52] Victor D. Cha, "Korea: A Peninsula in Crisis and Flux," *Strategic Asia* (2004–05), p. 151.

[53] The Bush administration shifted from a confrontational to a more diplomatic approach after the midterm elections and hawks such as Donald Rumsfeld and John Bolton left.

[54] White House press release, "President Bush Participates in Joint Press Availability with President Lee Myung-Bak of the Republic of Korea," Camp David, April 19, 2008, at http://www.whitehouse.gov/news/releases/2008/04/20080419–1.html (accessed January 8, 2009).

political landscape has evolved significantly since democratization, with the development of a vibrant and institutionalized left and civil society. These groups and their ideas (particularly about the North and the United States) persist, and identity politics could reemerge quite quickly in line with events such as the 2002 USFK accident. Indeed, the controversy over the agreement to begin re-importation of U.S. beef to Korea represented the first such case under the new Lee administration. The president has viewed the spread of public anxiety over U.S. beef as politically motivated,[55] and *Chosun Ilbo* has compared the outpouring of emotion and the holding of candlelight vigils to the sweeping anti-American reaction to the 2002 schoolgirl incident.[56]

There exists a good possibility that the establishment of a conservative administration in South Korea may galvanize the progressive opposition in challenging the government's policy agenda, including – and perhaps foremost – its approach to the North. Although the voice of South Korean progressives was weakened by defeat in recent elections, this constituency still remains a significant force in South Korean society, and the United States should not underestimate it or its ideas. In a sense, progressive forces were coopted by the governments of Kim Dae-jung and Roh Moo-hyun, as they reluctantly agreed on policies such as sending troops to Iraq. In the face of a conservative administration, however, the progressives could become more aggressive in advancing their agenda. This may mean intensification of identity politics in South Korea, and the United States could easily be caught between a conservative presidential administration and progressive activists.

Conclusion

Most discussions about strengthening U.S.-ROK relations focus on military alliance and economic cooperation. In recent years, the two allies have worked together on various issues, including relocation of the USFK headquarters from Yongsan to Pyongtaek, transfer of wartime operational control from the United States to the ROK, and free trade agreements. South Korea dispatched its troops to Iraq and Afghanistan in support of the U.S. war against terrorism, and policy coordination toward the DPRK has improved. These developments are all matters crucial to

---

[55] "President Lee Links Public Anxiety on U.S. Beef to Political Motivations," *Hankyoreh*, May 13, 2008.
[56] "U.S. Beef Imports Fuel Online Scaremongering," *Chosun Ilbo*, May 5, 2008.

the alliance and give hope for a brighter future. However, we should recognize that the bilateral relationship has become much more complex and multidimensional, transcending the initial state-to-state interactions and engaging civil society. Korean democratization, the end of the cold war, and inter-Korean reconciliation have brought issues of history, values, and identity to the forefront, and they hold the latent power to affect the bilateral relationship.

The Kwangju massacre and alleged U.S. involvement first provoked reexamination of the U.S. role in Korean history, leading to massive anti-American demonstrations during the democratic struggle of the 1980s. Denying any involvement in the massacre, the United States intervened to support Korean democracy in the summer of 1987. Kwangju became a key issue later when addressing historical (in)justice, as the South Korean government responded with a number of measures, including compensation for the victims. If the issue no longer is a focus for critics of the alliance, it has left an important legacy in South Korean politics and in relations with the United States. Kwangju became the model for addressing historical injustice and reconciliation, as seen in the handling of the mass killings of Korean civilians by American troops. The activists who fought for democracy with anti-American slogans became the policy elite of the progressive governments, and the scholars who led the reexamination of the U.S. role in Korean history have played a key role in state-sponsored institutions that address historical issues such as the Truth and Reconciliation Commission. Thus, the memory of Kwangju and experience with anti-Americanism in the democratic movement led to the development of a progressive perspective and identity that gained important currency under Kim Dae-jung and Roh Moo-hyun. Although conservatives returned to power in 2008, the voice of progressives remains salient in Korean society.

Revelations of the No-gun Ri massacre fueled another wave of anti-Americanism in South Korea from the late 1990s, and motivated the Clinton administration to recognize the occurrence of this tragic event by his unprecedented statement of "regret." Recently the TRC has found more cases of mass killings during the Korean War, urging the ROK government to demand an apology and compensation from the United States. While it is unlikely that there will be any repeat of the emotional reaction to No-gun Ri, U.S. leaders must not underestimate Korean perceptions and the power of collective memory. Another unexpected "identity-evoking event" echoing the backlash after the 2002 death of two schoolgirls could ignite a new wave of anti-American sentiments, damaging the bilateral relationship. Although it would be a hard sell for officials in the U.S. government, collaboration in "fact-finding" about the unfortunate past may increase mutual trust. As the "Statement of Mutual Understanding" for the No-gun Ri case pointed out, fact-finding and reconciliation of the unfortunate past can strengthen the ROK-U.S. alliance by "provid[ing] closure for the past and bring[ing] hope for the future."

As emotions over Kwangju and No-gun Ri fade, the DPRK still remains a challenging issue. Although policy coordination has improved and the Lee government promotes a policy toward the North that is much closer to that of the United States, South Korean society is deeply divided about its approach toward the North Korea and the politics of identity pose a challenge for the United States. The divided political landscape is not likely to change in the near future and this dynamic may hinder the overall capability of the South Korean government to think and act strategically. In fact, as clearly displayed during Lee's first visit to Washington, D.C., in the spring of 2008, his ostensibly pragmatic policy is firmly grounded in the alliance identity, provoking strong reaction from progressive forces that remain critical of the alliance. There is a potential danger that the United States might be caught between a conservative government and progressive activists.

All said, history, values, memory, and identity are significant elements that can influence the "soft power" of an alliance built on "hard power," and policy makers of both nations should not overlook their importance. In the past, these issues have occupied only a marginal place in the policy-making process or tended to be relegated to the area of public diplomacy. However, as a former senior U.S. official reflects from his own experiences working in Korea and Japan, "pubic diplomacy cannot be effective unless the foreign policy it supports is farsighted and reasonable."[57] Accordingly, these "unconventional" aspects of the U.S.-ROK alliance should not be seen as secondary but need to be taken as central to formulating policies regarding the bilateral relationship.

[57] Straub, "Public Diplomacy and the Korean Peninsula," p. 9.

3

U.S. Leadership, History, and Relations with Allies

Gilbert Rozman

U.S. leadership of alliances with Japan and South Korea long avoided history and, by its very nature, stifled candid discussion of differences in historical memories. As part of the Yoshida Doctrine, Japan's leaders deferred to U.S. international leadership while postponing raising sensitive historical issues. Even more reliant on U.S. support, South Korean leaders used their dictatorial power to suppress discussion of the most sensitive historical issues linked to the United States. Given that conservatives in each state feared that progressives would seize any sign of anti-Americanism to attack the legitimacy of the government, censorship served domestic political objectives. Yet, it also allowed accusations and rumors to spread without being adequately answered. During the 1990s and 2000s, conservatives in these states have shown that they have historical grievances too, while progressives have found new opportunities to have their voices heard. Seeking answers to far-reaching national identity questions, both Japanese and South Koreans were prior to the military crisis of 2010 newly poised to raise history issues with the United States in a more insistent manner.

While Japan and South Korea are close allies clearly committed to democratic values, unlike most U.S. allies in other parts of the world they are troubled by memories centered on past American foreign policy that have been artificially and only temporarily suppressed over many decades. This little-recognized reality could become a stumbling block in attempts to sustain U.S. leadership in Asia, especially since these countries are tempted by notions of Asianism or reunification. As China rises as a challenger critical of values embraced by each of these states and Asian reorganization quickens, changing views of regionalism and globalization may test national identities. The previous chapters by Togo and Shin alert us to the force of these critical historical memories, while pointing to the need for anticipatory discussions in the United States on how to respond. To do so requires refocusing alliances on a shared vision as well as on joint strategic demands. In any such vision challenges of today must be linked to future goals and also past successes.

Already there have been wake-up calls warning that the inclination of Americans to assume that universal values supportive of human rights and democracy spill over into a shared outlook on far-reaching historical events in the twentieth century cannot be fully justified. In 2003, Roh Moo-hyun became president sharing a worldview that reflected the progressive side of the South Korean political spectrum, soon straining relations with the United States. In 2009, Hatoyama Yukio assumed the position of prime minister at the head of a center-left coalition in Japan, leading to unprecedented concerns in the United States about the reliability of a longstanding ally. Moreover, while it had appeared that the leadership of Japan's preceding right-center coalition was keen on strengthening the alliance on the basis of a shared worldview, an examination of the leanings of many on the right show that their revisionist views of history center on grievances with the United States. The possibility exists of a left-right convergence aimed at reassessing historical understandings related to the United States. While a similar shift in South Korea appears less likely as long as the right is preoccupied by North Korean threats, new circumstances could induce a spike in nationalism that brings the political extremes in that ally closer in criticisms of the United States too. Whether it is one or two ends of the political spectrum that become agitated over history, Americans should be prepared to face this challenge.

Hatoyama's challenge to U.S. leadership resembled Roh's.[1] Both leaders came to office determined to reduce their country's dependence on its ally and to pursue a policy of upgrading relations in Asia. They sought changes in the alliance more respectful of the sovereignty of their state, a shift in diplomacy to North Korea that had left their state at the mercy of perceived U.S. unilateralism, and fulfillment of a longstanding quest to put their state in the middle between a more solicitous United States and a resurgent Asia. Only in May 2010, after he had unsettled relations with the United States over moving a military base in Okinawa and in

---

[1] "What Hatoyama Has in Common with Roh Moo-hyun," http://english.chosun.com/site/data/html_dir/2009/11/09/2009110900905.html (accessed November 9, 2009).

the midst of the North Korean military crisis, did Hatoyama backtrack, restoring priority to the alliance. In the background in both cases were intense national identity aspirations rooted in history. Succeeding him, Kan Naoto reaffirmed the base agreement while joining Lee and Obama in solidarity against the North Korean sinking of the *Cheonan*. A triangular approach was gaining momentum.

The United States fits squarely into the picture of shifting national identities that can arouse growing regional distrust. In the 1980s through the 2000s, when disputes over history and territorial issues lingering from the past grew more heated in Northeast Asia, Americans generally took comfort in thinking that these were the problems of other nations. During the cold war and the uncertain transition that followed it, such reasoning prevailed. Yet, the potential for U.S. historical actions to be targeted has been rising. We see in the Togo and Shin chapters balanced academic analyses of these critical views, which are often expressed with stronger emotions by Japanese and Koreans who are frustrated by long years when it was widely recognized that the time was not ripe to bring such memories to the fore. In an era of new temptations when shared regional identities may compete with images tied to alliance relations, negative historical memories may have greater relevance.

One impetus to increased focus on historical memory were anniversary events marked in 2010. Already in 2009, interest was building in the region. In Tokyo, Obama was asked whether he would visit Hiroshima or Nagasaki and whether he thought the U.S. atomic bombings were justified. Avoiding the latter question and leaving vague when a visit to either city would be possible, he sidestepped these historical minefields. Yet, expectations that he would mark the fiftieth anniversary of the security treaty when he visited Japan in 2010 left little doubt that history would keep drawing more attention. The history issue also loomed in his next visit to South Korea. When the G-20 meetings are held in Seoul in 2010, he was expected to mark the sixtieth anniversary of the Korean War. After tensions with North Korea kept rising, especially after it was identified as torpedoing a South Korean ship, history slipped into the shadows. Once again, security took priority.

This chapter treats historical memory in the context of the evolution of U.S. value concerns toward Northeast Asia since the end of World War II. It assesses the impact of war memories from the perspective of liberal values. Then it considers the role of values in forging the foundation of an Asia-Pacific community, while taking into account shifts in Japanese foreign policy after the onset of Democratic Party of Japan (DPJ) leadership in 2009 and the struggle still consuming conservatives and progressives in South Korea. To start, it reviews how liberal values have fared in Japan and South Korea since the time of the U.S. occupation of both.

The Acceptance of Liberal Values in Japan and South Korea

The United States has long been seen as spreading its values to Japan and South Korea, but that does not mean its allies received a strong, consistent dose of liberal values. More concerned about countering the feared domino effect of communist expansionism than nourishing the sprouts of democracy that had been planted, U.S. policy makers gave their approval to Japan's "reverse course" that brought back to positions of power many who had guided the war effort and to Rhee Syngman's autocratic methods that used the North Korean threat as justification. In the cold war, anticommunist appeals centered more on what the United States opposed than on the overall meaning of its "free world" stance. Later, under George W. Bush, unilateral policies such as early interest in inducing regime change in North Korea as well as the lingering spillover from the war in Iraq clouded a positive picture of U.S. values again. Although U.S. media/movies had considerable success in spreading consumer values, these did not smooth the way for similarities in political culture. Often compromising its principles in order to achieve a higher-priority goal, the United States did not present a clear, steady message about its values. Even if it had, its two allies were not inclined to heed such a message, given their own troubled national identities overwhelmed by the trauma of events in 1945, defeat and partition, and the reinforcement of their abnormal situation in the Tokyo Tribunal and the Korean War. Neither ally has adequately debated the significance of these epochal events. As visits to the Yasukuni Shrine transfixed many, these powerful concerns remained in the background. Japan remains in an historical limbo,[2] and without reunification South Korea does too.

These allies encouraged distorted views of national identity for their own foreign policy objectives. No wonder that the cold war era later came to be seen as an abnormal period, not as a source of pride in what one's nation could accomplish. The United States long abetted demonization

---

[2] Togo Kazuhiko, *Reikishi to gaiko: Yasukuni, Ajia, Tokyo saiban* (Tokyo: Kodansha gendai shincho, 2008), p. 20.

of the Soviet Union and neglect of reconciliation with China. Japanese claims to victimization at the hands of the Soviets served U.S. interests even if they operated in unrecognized ways also to limit trust in their ally, as in the late 1980s divergence of opinion on how to respond to Mikhail Gorbachev. Tight censorship and alarmism under South Korea's dictators interfered with well-rounded reflection. However convenient it may be to capitalize on value distortions by one's ally, when shared liberal values may later be sought, the lack of balance may come back to haunt your own country. Decades later under new circumstances the legacy remains of expedient value choices. The Liberal Democratic Party (LDP) was reluctant to become more centrist – its right wing was obsessed with eventual realization of revisionist dreams – while the leftist opposition refused to move toward the center in light of its own secure base in the Diet and local governments. On both sides, ideological assumptions steered politicians away from centrist values associated with U.S. leadership.

We can identify at least three factors that help to explain the indifference or even suspicion of liberal values. First, state-centered values predominated – even on the left. Although Republicans long wore the mantle of antistate or laissez-faire thinking on domestic affairs, their international image is that of a backer of strong states that make convenient partners on realist issues. Second, economic protectionism has been a high priority. Democrats were associated with opposition to economic protectionism, long a vital part of statism for the left as much as the right, while Ronald Reagan, George H. W. Bush, and George W. Bush were too preoccupied with other objectives to show much concern. The periods 1993–4 in Japan and 1998–2000 in South Korea, when conservatives lost their grip on power and Bill Clinton might have moved toward a value consensus with them, were marked by the two most intensive campaigns to open these economies. Third, no value-driven cross-national network has existed in East Asia to cultivate trust in liberal institutions, as occurred in the West in the arts, the academic world, and elsewhere over many centuries. Ties with the United States produced some new networks of this sort, but centralized state practices overshadowed them. Not only did grass-roots organizations not fill this void, but the Democrats have not developed a corps of foreign policy advisers with strong ties to political elites in Japan and South Korea. However much of this springs from Japanese lack of interest in liberal thinking, it perpetuates reliance on Republicans.

In Japan and South Korea, the debate over values involved three political forces: the ruling elite; the progressive opposition; and, in the post–cold war years, an increasingly vocal right wing. The ruling group that wholeheartedly embraced the U.S. alliance at the same time proved to be much less committed to liberal values than most Americans had expected. The LDP from the outset became deeply beholden to forces that rejected some essential values, while paying lip service to other liberal values and accepting democracy with the expectation that the party could keep a monopoly on power. Even more inconsistent with U.S. expectations, Rhee Syngman put South Korea on a track of arbitrary executive power that continued with military dictators. Excessive centralization, discouragement of civil society, and weakness of centrist forces in policy debates left value transmission in jeopardy. In both U.S. allies, progressives offered an alternative view of values, steeped in Marxism or pacifist idealism, which garnered the bulk of attention in opposition to the ruling elite. This narrowed the scope for liberal values to spread, even as on the political right a more traditional approach to national values as unique retained its hold, seeping into the discourse of the ruling elite. While from the late 1990s the right wing held sway in Japan and the progressives set the agenda in South Korea, in both cases liberal values were not gaining ground. U.S triumphalism and unilateralism did not set the right agenda.

Liberalism in foreign affairs rests on hopes of bridging differences with states considered to be threats or potential threats. Conservatives in Japan and South Korea feared overtures to China, the Soviet Union, or North Korea that were normally attributed to Democrats. Although it happened that the most shocking overtures were made by Richard Nixon in 1971–2, Reagan in 1986–8, and Bush in 2007–8, the idea persisted that the Democrats are the party apt to sell out their country – Carter with North Korea, and Clinton with North Korea and China. Liberal ideas for reconciling differences in East Asia also did not gain traction because mutual perceptions in the region saw other states as unreceptive. China might be approached on realist or economic complementarity grounds, but its communist regime was a doubtful respondent to liberal values. In the eyes of its neighbors, Japan's obsession with historical revisionism left it beyond reach for shared values too. Given their own predilections, neither China nor Japan was prepared to test South Korea on liberal values. Ties within the region restrain interest in liberal values as does the pervasive impact of historical predispositions on perceptions of U.S. politics.

In Japan and South Korea, as in China, little interest was shown in the Democratic Party candidates who ran for high office in the United States and their liberal values. The pro-Bush bias in Japan as in China was accompanied by a pro-Bush bias among South Korean conservatives, while progressives were prone to dismiss the Democrats even if they showed no sympathy for Bush. One explanation is the narrow realism of some conservatives that expect stronger alliance ties from a Republican president. Yet, other explanations reflect more directly on the values underlining foreign policy views. For conservatives in Japan and South Korea, there is hesitation about liberalism with its idealistic appeals that could challenge their own narrow nationalism. Many on the left, meanwhile, are driven by a different sort of nationalism – in Japan linkage to pacifism or regionalism as a means to boost Japan's unique international role, and in South Korea romanticism about the reunification process. These progressives lack the idealism of global citizenship and institution building widely seen in the West. The result is a weak middle range for liberalism between conservatism and progressivism. The agenda is driven instead by unrealized goals of nation-building linked to international status.

South Korean and Japanese media split in their approach to the U.S. presidential election in 2008. The Japanese political elite hardly disguised their preference for John McCain, who had Japan's favorite first-term Bush officials as advisers and who promised an assertive response to North Korea, Russia, and others. While Lee might have leaned to a fellow conservative McCain, the early tribulations of his administration had made him cautious amid media enthusiasm for engagement diplomacy. In neither state did those leaning to Obama focus on the values his candidacy represented, in contrast to American intellectuals attracted to liberal values and angered over Bush's extreme disregard of them at home and abroad as well as McCain's low-road campaign that threatened more of the same. Unlike European ardor for a revival of liberal values, the Asian allies took a narrower approach, demonstrating again the difficulty of achieving value consensus in a context where historical memories continue to cast a dark shadow on the region. After Japan's prime ministers stopped visiting the Yasukuni Shrine in 2006 and Lee took office downplaying historical resentments, a kind of moratorium ensued, but this did not lead, as Kazuhiko Togo had urged, to a national debate narrowing differences.[3] The history gap persists.

In contrast to Japanese revisionists and South Korean progressives steeped in discourse about historical unfairness and victimization, Hatoyama and Lee have toned down such rhetoric. This makes it easier to pursue both regionalism and globalization. In the United States,

---

[3] Kazuhiko Togo, "A Moratorium on Yasukuni," *Far Eastern Economic Review* (June 2006), pp. 5–15.

Barack Obama championed liberal values in his rhetoric and met with these visiting allied leaders. He traveled to Asia in November 2009, aiming to refocus discussions about alliances, regionalism, and the rise of China in a broad perspective. If much of the attention in Tokyo centered on relocating a U.S. base on Okinawa and in Seoul on finalizing a free trade agreement, there were at least four big themes capable of testing the extent of agreement on liberal values. Although Sino-U.S. talks garnered the most attention among observers alert to the difficulty of narrowing differences on these themes, U.S. bilateral discussions with allies provided another meaningful test. First, in preventing the proliferation of nuclear weapons through Iran, North Korea, and Pakistan (linked to the war in Afghanistan), Obama sought allies with international responsibility. Japan prepared to assist in the rebuilding of Afghanistan with $5 billion and South Korea planned to send about 350 soldiers to train the army there, but in the wake of U.S. plans to add 30,000 troops bringing the total near 100,000, they were not doing a lot. Japan's support, after retreating from a refueling mission in the Indian Ocean, was more suspect.

Second, in facing the world financial crisis and the need to restructure the global economic system, both Japan and South Korea were continuing to move away from their protectionist history of export-led growth. Notably, South Korea, in anticipation of being the host to the G-20 meetings in late 2010, was taking a leadership role. With many Democratic Party backers more inclined to preserve jobs than to open markets, Obama was not in a good position to expound liberal values to Hatoyama or Lee. Yet, certain features of both allies, notably their agricultural protectionism, reinforced their longstanding images as reluctant to open their economies wide.

Third, with the Copenhagen climate change meeting looming, Obama lacked a mandate from the U.S. Congress to give substance to his own rhetoric in favor of strong combative measures. Both Japan, symbolized by its association with the previous Kyoto Agreement, and South Korea, assertive about its "green revolution," had no reason to defer to the United States as a champion of this vital test of responsible behavior.

Finally, with regard to a collective response to China's rise in Asia in pursuit of a regional framework dismissive of universal values, Obama found the situation reversed from a few years earlier. Instead of South Korea being hesitant to join the United States in a broad Asia-Pacific community, Japan was now less enthusiastic. Even so, they both awaited greater clarity on the U.S. vision while searching for ways to make it compatible with a still vague vision of an East Asian community, which each had endorsed. In the spring of 2010, firm U.S. support for Lee in the military showdown with North Korea provided the necessary clarity at a time when security trumped history, as Hatoyama and then Kan Naoto gave priority to addressing this crisis.

Value Concerns in U.S. Policies toward East Asia since 1945

As wars are prone to do, the war against Japan sharpened U.S. thinking about how its values operate in the struggle for Northeast Asia. In the first one hundred years of U.S. history, the paramount value in this region as elsewhere was self-determination, continuing the struggle against old-world colonizers such as Great Britain by supporting the rights of nations to gain freedom and exercise sovereignty. Increasingly, the United States also aligned with Great Britain as a champion of free and unrestricted trade. Differences over other matters receded as agreements advanced over economic freedom. Forcibly opening Japan, the United States claimed to have no imperialist designs, only the imperative to bring it into the world of international commerce in a manner that would require the usual legal protections. At the start of the twentieth century, in spite of its own imperialist thrust into the Philippines, the United States insisted on an "open-door" policy, keeping China a sovereign state where other states would all enjoy freedom of trade. Naturally, dissatisfaction arose when Japan insisted on making demands that threatened Chinese sovereignty at the end of World War I, again in its invasion of Manchuria, and then in its full-scale invasion of the country in 1937. In 1945, the United States emerged victorious in World War II, proud that it had stood against naked, imperialist aggression and had no territorial aspirations as it started occupations in Japan and South Korea intended to make those states democratic and free market participants at the core of a new regional order. Defining the war against Japan's militarists and Germany's Nazis in starkly dichotomized terms, Americans were ready for a world in which their quest for freedom would oppose any totalitarianism.

Occupying Japan and South Korea in 1945, the United States began its most ambitious experiment in value transmission. The goal was not only to establish bulwarks in the global struggle against communism and exemplars of democracy and free market economies, but also to nurture societies that embrace liberal values. Recognizing that the "free world" extends from its center in the United States along two principal fronts – the trans-Atlantic front deeply rooted in humanistic values, and the East

Asian front with a tiny toehold as China joined the communist bloc and North Korea became its aggressive champion – U.S. leaders faced their biggest challenge in converting the Japanese and South Korean nations to a worldview that would make them dependable not only as allies but also as advocates of liberal values. For at least half a century, Americans felt growing pride in the success of this endeavor, giving them confidence in the durability of this region's triangular civilizational core of mutual understanding and treating it as a model for value transmission to other nations. Yet, the true test for whether the U.S. alliances in Northeast Asia are buttressed by shared values could come only after three conditions were met: the disappearance of a common, dangerous enemy; the success of the allies in economic prosperity and diversification, reducing dependence on the United States; and the emergence of new challenges in the reorganization of the region that would arouse uncertainty about common national interests. These circumstances would put to a test the degree to which liberal values outweigh distinct, nationalist values in each country.

Japanese who consider the war with the United States and World War II to be a struggle among imperialists attack the very essence of U.S. thinking about the war and their history. If this issue rises to the surface, the national identities of the two countries will be opposed on a matter of fundamental importance. Even if Americans tend to ignore their lingering imperialist holdings and their alliance with states with vast colonies, they are convinced that the age of imperialism was rapidly fading away and that Japan's goal was to colonize, not to liberate, while the United States supported China's sovereignty as part of its overall struggle against fascism and militarist authoritarianism. Consistent with these values, U.S. occupations and foreign policy championed postwar democracy.

The cold war, especially in its early days in opposition to Josef Stalin/Stalinism, served to reinforce an orientation toward values that left little room for compromise. The other side in Northeast Asia combined three communist states: the Soviet Union, China, and North Korea. The United States stood with Japan, which by the 1950s had become romanticized as pacifist, democratic, and even an attractively exotic nation. The Korean War demonized North Korea as barbaric brainwashers; by the Great Leap Forward, the image of China had become that of rabid fanatics without limits; and Leonid Brezhnev's Soviet Union, despite Nikita Khrushchev's de-Stalinization speech and peaceful coexistence overtures, could not escape the image of a military juggernaut bent on world domination.

The main challenge for the United States became how to temper its just commitment to freedom and the free market in ways that would avoid nuclear war and the expansion of Soviet power in places where values did not give the United States an unmistakable advantage. Although South Korea did not embrace democracy for most of the four decades after World War II, the fact that it faced great danger from the North left many justifying its extenuating circumstances.

Consistent with this dichotomy of the two Koreas, the United States depicted its agreement to the partition of the peninsula as the only way to permit the population in the South to escape from totalitarianism. Unable to prevent the Soviet Union from occupying the North, U.S. leaders did what they could in assisting the South to promote economic, social, and political freedoms. Accordingly, the Korean War was fought not only to make clear to the Soviet Union that it could not get away with spreading communism by force, but also to protect the freedoms of the South Korean people and make clear to the Japanese and others the U.S. commitment. Those in South Korea who blame the United States for the partition, support for dictatorship, and failure to promote reconciliation with the North can find little solace in the values Americans associate with their historic role. Even if specific decisions over half a century may be debated, there is little room in U.S. thinking for challenging the values that are perceived as driving support for this valued ally.

At times, U.S. preoccupation with threats skewed its consideration of values. In 1942 through 1945, Japan's conduct of the war left the impression of fanaticism that would not lead to rational calculations at a time of war. Americans doubted that Japan would surrender even as its defeat became increasingly likely; U.S. images of a sneak attack without a declaration of war, abusive handling of prisoners, suicidal obedience, and defense of the homeland to the last person altered the calculus of what U.S. war actions were appropriate. Japanese criticism of U.S. behavior ignores the provocations from Japan's own war conduct. In 1950 through 1953, the United States was drawn into war again, facing an enemy whose fanaticism knew few bounds. U.S. values again were skewed in the war against North Korea. Three decades later, the Soviet invasion of Afghanistan and belligerent foreign policy raised fear in some circles, notably officials at the start of the Reagan administration, that a tougher U.S. stance in the cold war required an adjustment in values. Similarly, in 2001 through 2005, the Bush administration responded to the 9/11 attacks on the United States by insisting on a reordering of U.S. values. Whatever one's opinion may be of early Reagan and early

Bush value shifts, they represent anomalies in U.S. foreign policy since the 1940s. For Japanese and Koreans to generalize from the extreme moments in U.S. policy, to ignore the background factors, and to raise historical issues as if they can bring redress without a damaging process of give and take on both sides is a troubling sign of national identities that lack sufficient roots in liberal values. One does not have to justify U.S. actions to conclude that Japanese conservatives, focused on revisionism, and Korean progressives, prone to denial regarding North Korea, lack a balanced basis on which to raise history issues. Whether the United States faced Japanese or South Korean obstinacy about opening their economies or Soviet/Russian, Chinese, or North Korean obstinacy about opening their political systems, there has been continuous reluctance by strong states to agree to the widespread penetration of Western organizations and some of their values.

Sovereignty values serve not only secure borders, when military intrusions are feared, but protection for existing jobs and economic interests. They conflict with the values advocated by the United States, which may support self-determination for areas in which minority groups reside, be eager to break down barriers to economic and financial flows with potentially worrisome short-term consequences for vested interests, and seem intent on the spread of information and culture that could change the way people think. All of the countries in Northeast Asia have taken measures to impede the inflow of culture imbued with the values the United States is keen on spreading. The struggle against sovereignty values in allies as well as adversaries kept reappearing in U.S. thinking during the cold war.

Victory in the cold war stimulated financial globalists under Bill Clinton and even more assertive power-projection globalists under George W. Bush to press confidently for the extension of U.S. values. In the former case, there was no overarching value agenda, but optimism prevailed that a world with fewer barriers would realize faster economic growth and greater openness of communications along with greater trust. Many of the main targets were countries with which the United States had close ties, such as Japan in the early Clinton years and South Korea in the Asian financial crisis. Yet, the values that colored U.S. views of economic relations with these allies narrowly focused on realizing freer markets without wider implications for bilateral relations. Other targets were states, notably Russia, where U.S. leaders expected pressure to open their doors to advance the transition to democracy and a market economy. In the latter case, neoconservatives were driven by a combination of strong convictions on the need to transform domestic values and confidence that the United States now had the power to press areas around the world to embrace values, claimed to be universal, espoused by one country and according to a timetable largely determined by that country. The "axis of evil" speech and unilateral war in Iraq with pressure on allies to lend their support reflected Bush's value-laden agenda.

Doubtful about the prospects of bridging value differences in Northeast Asia, U.S. officials after the cold war gave little thought to multilateralism in the region. As George W. Bush took office, given his proclivity toward unilateralism and export of American values without regard to local receptivity, prospects dimmed. Yet, in August 2003, with narrow objectives in mind, Bush did agree to Six-Party Talks. In September 2005, after a shift of course in these talks, he also accepted a Joint Statement, treated as a roadmap for a broader regional agenda. And in February 2007, he approved the Joint Framework as an action plan that involved five working groups, including one assigned to establish a multilateral Northeast Asian Peace and Security Mechanism. In preparation for that working group and in an effort to sustain all-around progress in the Six-Party Talks, the question of how to incorporate values along with security drew attention. Parallels were made with the Helsinki process of the 1970s, which introduced values into planning to bridge differences between the two blocs in Europe. Yet, strategizing was handicapped by sharp differences in worldview inside the administration as well as by departmental narrowness. If some in the State Department under John Negroponte and Chris Hill took this seriously, others showed scant interest and remnants of the neoconservative wing could not overcome their disdain that another empty talk forum could emerge. Echoing this split were differences over the future of the Six-Party Talks, not only about the future of North Korea but also about the benefits of continuing a process that had boosted Sino-U.S. strategic cooperation, pressured Japan to overcome troubled bilateral ties in pursuit of a much-needed regional orientation, and laid a foundation for U.S.–South Korean joint efforts as well as more responsible Russian behavior toward long-term goals. If the North should collapse or choose to defy all the other states, the U.S. challenge is to strengthen cooperation with the others, requiring not only a means to address security concerns, but also a vehicle for reaching agreement on basic values – backed by norms and principles.

Neoconservatives had a catastrophic effect on the image of U.S. values around the world. Their triumphalism was seen as arrogant, unilateral, insensitive, and often hypocritical as well as contrary to the pragmatic legacy of U.S. diplomacy. Messianic fervor replaced idealistic appeals. Yet, awareness of divisions with the United States and a reservoir of approval for overall U.S. principles and its past policies eased the way for a new president to embrace values in foreign relations without becoming tainted by their legacy. By avoiding the impression that the goal is to make the world in the U.S. image and resorting much more to multilateralism, U.S. leadership may be renewed. As the first African American president and a leader with no association with controversial policies such as the decision to start the Iraq War, Obama succeeded through his election victory to arouse widespread hope that the neoconservative approach and triumphalism are gone.

Any new effort to reach agreement on regional security with a values component will undoubtedly raise comparisons to the approach taken in Europe in the final decades of the cold war. Views in the United States and China differ on the Helsinki accords and the process that led to the collapse of world communism and the Soviet Union. If Obama should press for a document similar to the Helsinki accords as a statement of values that can shape the future of Asia, the Chinese are likely to worry that these values and the NGOs or others who would invoke them could become a force for limiting sovereign authority and setting in motion a repeat of the threats that undermined the Soviet system. It is hard to imagine that Washington would stand much chance of persuading Beijing unless a new understanding is first achieved with Tokyo and Seoul. The road to values consensus on a regional level starts with agreement on a trilateral level among U.S. allies.

In the cold war era, at least prior to Nakasone Yasuhiro's upgrading of alliance cooperation with Ronald Reagan, the Japanese were thought to downgrade the role of values, even as late as the 1990s distancing themselves from American "fundamentalism" in defense of Asia's distinctive ways (i.e., Asian values). Under Roh Moo-hyun, South Koreans were reluctant to bring up values with North Korea, insisting that building trust comes first. In 2008, there were signs that the situation was starting to change. In contrast to December 2005, when Roh and his staff shunned Jay Lefkowitz, the U.S. special representative for North Korean human rights, Lee Myung-bak arrived in New York on his first visit abroad as president placing values above interests in strengthening the alliance. Also, despite the tensions in the United States over Abe Shinzo's moves to reconsider Japan's past apology over "comfort women" followed by the critical resolution of the House of Representatives, both sides recognized a renewed alliance as desirable.

War Memories and Liberal Values

Wars have an unusually strong grip on nations' emotions with the power to shape thinking about values on current as well as past matters. In the case of Northeast Asia, the meaning of five wars is subject to ongoing controversy, while echoes of three earlier wars stay alive through their connection to these events. The list of five includes the Japanese invasion of China/ Pacific War, the Korean War, the Vietnam War, the cold war/ Sino-Soviet split, and the war against terror. The earlier three wars in a span of one decade are the Sino–Japanese War of 1894–5; the Russo–Japanese War; and, in between the two, the Spanish–American War, in which the United States acquired the colony of the Philippines. Superficially, these wars appear to be either in the distant past or a matter of only minor controversy, but on closer examination they have become embroiled in disputes over national identity that amplify their impact on the way public opinion perceives values. A consensus on liberal values is difficult when the public is tugged toward narrow thinking.

The most serious affront to liberal values is the way Japanese increasingly see the war they fought in China, the occupation they imposed on Korea, and the nature of the Second World War fought primarily against the United States. Liberal reasoning holds that Japan fought a barbaric war of aggression to conquer China; tightened its unjust domination of Korea to commit cultural genocide; as an ally of Hitler's Germany, attacked the United States in a war to impose racist totalitarianism and eradicate the humanistic and free traditions of the West; and was necessarily punished in the brutal ending to the war and in the Tokyo Tribunal for its own record of atrocities and blind obedience that left little hope for a negotiated surrender. In contrast, Japan's refusal to apologize in a substantial, sincere manner to its victims in Asia, to take actions that show repentance, and, most importantly, to recognize what was at stake in the war are a worrisome sign of a values gap. Increasingly from the mid-1990s, the message from Japan's political leaders about the war (even after 1993 through 1995, a political interlude that briefly brought to the forefront some leaders with a different mindset) was a renewed, weak statement of regret about adverse reactions and new, defiant tone of justification about Japan's real intentions. Instead of invading Asian countries, Japan allegedly occupied them for their own benefit, standing up to Western colonial powers in Asia. Instead of reflecting the weight of their families' suffering, Chinese are supposedly insincere in playing the "history card" for a geopolitical advantage. And, instead of justifiably recalling their humiliation, Koreans are seen as ungrateful for the foundation to modernization provided by Japan. Five of the past six Japanese prime ministers – Hashimoto Ryutaro, Obuchi Keizo, Mori Yoshiro, Koizumi Junichiro, and Aso Taro – have displayed this reasoning or shown no inclination to oppose it. With rising potential for a clash over history with the United States and no sign of optimism about greater U.S support for liberal values, Japan is not headed in the direction of values reconciliation in the region.

A poll on the fiftieth anniversary of the Pearl Harbor attack revealed concerns that were widespread even before the Japanese people had been aroused by nationalism from the mid-1990s. Eighty-three percent of the Japanese labeled the atomic bombing of Hiroshima and Nagasaki morally wrong, with 73 percent calling for an apology, compared to 55 percent who conceded that Japan should apologize for Pearl Harbor. Given frequent discussion in the Japanese media of issues of wartime apologies, an extension to U.S.-Japan relations looms. For every two Japanese who acknowledged that Japan had been the aggressor in the war, one justified it by claiming that Japan was surrounded by hostile powers and had no choice.[4] As long as Americans largely believe that Japan was a fanatical nation ready to commit suicide and fight until the death rather than surrender no matter the odds and the Japanese largely think that the United States could have ended the war with assurances of what came to pass rather than atomic bombs and did not do so with suspicious motives, the two nations remain far from reconciliation over history, even if it is little discussed.

The Korean War is also reemerging as a problem, dividing South Korea from the United States and complicating the fragile reintegration of North Korea into the region. If Americans have long assumed their country's sacrifice in defending South Korea from a tyrannical regime with the world's worst, prolonged human rights record would establish the war as a monument to close relations based on shared values, they can be shocked by the extent to which South Koreans blame them for the unavoidable 1945 division of the peninsula and aspects of the war. An image has spread not of liberal values driving U.S. support for the endangered South Korean people, but of callous U.S. support for brutal warfare and the lingering military dictatorship that made a mockery of democratic values. In the sympathy of progressive South Koreans toward North Korea and the

---

4 Steven R. Weisman, "Japanese Think They Owe Apology and Are Owed One on War, Poll Shows," *New York Times*, December 8, 1991, p. L26.

repeated appeal of anti-Americanism over symbolic issues, we see a nation struggling with the legacy of war and division in ways that marginalize liberal values. These issues are playing out against the background of the North Korean nuclear crisis and potential reunification.

The third war that arguably affects prospects of a liberal consensus is the Vietnam War. In this case, the problem is the erosion of U.S. recognition that the war was fought under false pretenses since it did not produce a domino effect for communist expansion and rather led to a reunited nation with an independent foreign policy. Those who denied the earlier antiwar thinking were instrumental in insisting that the United States had to free itself of the post-Vietnam War way of thinking consistent with liberal values and then repeating the error of starting a war under false pretenses and interpreting it in ways that continued to distort those values. Under these circumstances, U.S. leadership in the spread of liberal values has been weakened, repeating the error in the Vietnam War when the U.S. demanded support from its allies South Korea and Japan against the judgment of much of the public that sympathized with Vietnamese nationalism and even of officials who cynically used this support for nationalist and regime-strengthening goals. As long as Americans lose perspective on their own misuse of values, they not only are in danger of repeating their error but also failing to recognize the overall picture of postwar history.

The fourth war is different from the others because it was prolonged without real fighting; yet memories of how it ended in the period 1986–92 may be as significant for reaching consensus on liberal values as any of the hot wars. Again, the problem centers in the United States, where glorification of Ronald Reagan's treatment of the "evil empire" distorts for many comprehension of Mikhail Gorbachev's "new thinking." The way the U.S. misjudged Russian national identity, the Sino-Soviet reconciliation, the survival and leverage of North Korea, and the lessons to be drawn from the demise of the communist bloc and the collapse of the Soviet Union is critical to understanding values debates. The setback to liberal values and eventual boost to neoconservatism with its simplistic or even fundamentalist divide of "good versus evil" have not done a service to effective policies in Northeast Asia. In this region, three countries sharing the legacy of communism reason very differently about how the cold war ended. Inclinations on the part of some officials to apply their misguided notions of Reagan's legacy to deal with China, Russia, or North Korea and win the support of Japan and South Korea were bound to undermine liberal values.

Finally, the war against terror and its extension in many directions – Middle East policy, Southwest Asian policy, Southeast Asian policy, North Korean policy – failed to bring convergence on values despite international sympathy for the United States in 2001. While criticisms of U.S. motives often demonstrate troubling values in other states, the root of the problem lies in the failure of the Bush administration to win global support for the arguments and values that it presented in support of this cause. In the absence of acceptable U.S. leadership in setting a values agenda for the world, the door was open for cynical responses to values and nationalist interpretations of them. In Northeast Asia, despite the common threat of North Korean nuclear weapons and the joint prosperity from unprecedented economic integration, there was a kind of values anarchy after 2001. Anti-Americanism, alienation by Japan, North Korean manipulation, China's success in deflecting attention from its values deficit, Russia's free hand to revive Soviet-era values, and South Korean flailing in the search for a regional strategy all reflect this vacuum in establishing among key states a values consensus that could set a clear agenda for dealing with the most serious differences that must be addressed.

Japan prioritized dealing with China and South Korea, as necessary over history, while it determined that it would avoid differences over history with the United States. Because the U.S. notion of values placed little importance on thinking about history, this posed little difficulty except insofar as it complicated triangular relations with South Korea, where values centered on history were of major significance. This did not seem to have serious consequences against the backdrop of anticommunism that in the first half of the 1980s seemed to boost prospects for triangularity. As the cold war ended, many wrongly assumed that Japan and South Korea would move beyond the history issue. Instead of the end of history, for these states we witnessed a revival of history. Former barriers to turning in this direction had fallen; deep-seated forces for doing so found a more fertile environment, including vivid symbols for mobilizing public opinion; and values advocated by the United States or others failed to draw countries closer together.

U.S. analysts of Japan have been slow to recognize the sharp discrepancy present in interpretations of the history of East Asia. It is not just Japan's hesitancy to apologize for the war with China that divides the two countries, but the overall narrative about Asia versus the West in which Japan's assertive challenges are justified. For instance, when asked in 2008 to list the ten biggest events in the history of East Asia over the past 150 years, Ogura Kazuo, former ambassador to South Korea, Vietnam, and France, opined that the main narrative was the struggle of Asians to throw off Western imperialism. The Meiji Restoration was a model for the rest of Asia. The triple intervention after the Sino–Japanese War as well as "yellow peril" discrimination drove the Japanese people to back imperialism as in the treaty with Great Britain as the only way to survive in international society. The list naturally includes the Russo–Japanese War. The Chinese Revolution of 1911 and Russian Revolution are important, leading to the spread of the communist threat without which fascism would not have arisen. He adds to the list the atomic bombings of Japan, for which the United States has not apologized, while the Japanese have not yet sorted out the contradictions and moral meaning of being a U.S. ally. Finally, the list includes the anti–Vietnam War movement, which rallied the world against wars of aggression.

Many have underestimated Japan's shift toward nationalism. They have confused rising revisionism with realism, as if the latter alone mattered. If revisionism was noted, they often narrowly focused on one or another symbol, such as the publicized Yasukuni Shrine visits of Koizumi, failing to notice that even when Abe was silent about the Shrine he pressed a more nationalist agenda: making the ideological case, securing Diet approval for a national referendum to realize constitutional reform, and centralizing state requirements for patriotic education. Mechanisms, such as textbook commissions, were in place to sustain the nationalist thrust, as seen even under Fukuda Yasuo, when South Koreans were shocked to discover the new coverage of Dokdo/Takeshima in Japan's textbooks.

Conservatives in Japan and, to a lesser extent, South Korea questioned U.S. values after Bush's foreign policy changed course, especially in 2007. The Japanese showed disappointment that their preferred policies had failed to gain international support – the abductions position with North Korea, the demand for four islands from Russia, and the firm resistance to China's pressure such as on the Taiwan issue.[5] On all of these matters and others, the United States had shifted away from earlier positions, leaving many in Japan resentful and their country essentially a bystander on matters of vital interest to it. In such critiques, we often find exaggerations of why and how far the U.S. position had shifted and hints that Japan should switch to a more independent stance with an unstated assumption that Japan not only could better defend moral principles to which the

---

[5] *Sankei shimbun*, February 20, 2008, p. 13.

United States was only paying lip service, but also it could pursue its own revisionist goals. By failing to stress the values gap with Japan's conservatives, U.S. officials had not prepared for a split over realist goals driven by those with revisionist objectives. They also failed to anticipate the rise of a left-center party to power, capitalizing on rising anxieties.

In South Korea, foreign policy changes have had the greatest impact on national identity. While China and Japan have anchored their images of the outside world since the 1980s on rather consistent perceptions of the United States, South Koreans shifted toward North Korea in 2000 and the United States in 2001–3 in ways that defied earlier expectations. Unlike the well-established great power identities in the other two, South Korea is more conscious of its limited power and vulnerability. It is also more openly divided over social issues. Religious consciousness matters more. Localism has proven more divisive in national politics. Generational divisions are especially pronounced on political matters. On many dimensions, identity issues provoke intense reactions in South Korea. Toward the United States this is manifested in the debate over dependence on a lasting alliance versus autonomy, albeit only in stages. Toward North Korea it appears in the divide over unconditional economic assistance versus staged reciprocity, postponing reunification. Under Roh, these divides were pronounced, even inside the government.

In 2009, a duel of rival lists of historical transgressions transfixed South Koreans. On the one side was the *Biographical Directory of Pro-Japanese Collaborators* issued in late 2009 in three volumes with 4,389 names, including former president Park Chung-hee. It instantly became a thorn in the side of conservatives, whose status and wealth appeared sullied as a result of assisting imperialist pillage of their nation's sovereignty. Some even angrily charged that publication of the list weakened the legitimacy of the South Korean government in the struggle with North Korea, countering supporters who asserted, "This encyclopedia project is significant in that it allows us to examine the twisted structure of our modern society in which pro-Japanese figures have entered the social mainstream."[6] In retaliation, conservatives prepared their own biographical dictionary of pro–North Korean activists, intent on exposing activities over the years deemed antagonistic to the constitutional order of South Korea.[7] While

---

[6] "Yim Hun-yeong Speaks on Encyclopedia of Pro-Japanese Figures' Publication," english hani@hani.co.kr (accessed November 27, 2009).

[7] "Rightwingers to Name and Shame 'Pro-N.Koreans,'" englishnews@chosun.com (accessed November 27, 2009).

these two targets were in the forefront, the contrasting images of historical ties to the United States also mattered to both sides.

In the fall of 2009, South Korea was wooed by Washington to strengthen alliance ties and by Beijing to join in a regional community, while Tokyo seemed to be aligning with Beijing. Chinese vice president Xi Jinping called for "realization of both the Korea-China free trade agreement and an East Asian community in the not so distant future," as Ozawa Ichiro, secretary-general of the DPJ, appealed for enhanced solidarity among the three Northeast Asian states. Some saw this as a chance to enhance South Korea's status as a mediator between its neighbors.[8] Yet, plans were proceeding to draw up new defense guidelines with the United States, strengthening the alliance. Growing rapport between Lee and Obama amid alarm about North Korean intentions justified this decision. In contrast to the Roh era, when Tokyo was closer to Washington, Tokyo was distancing itself from its ally. This abruptly ended in 2010, however, as shared security concerns spread.

Conclusion

The values conflicts with traditional allies in NATO fit a long-established pattern. The United States was confident that after World War II it had overcome tendencies toward narrow nationalism, while increasingly embracing universal values. At times, the United States faulted one or another ally for shirking international responsibilities, taking the easy road as a free rider while leaving the heavy lifting to American forces. In turn, some allies turned universal values against U.S. policies, warning of excessive patriotism and reliance on military force. Differences could become serious, as in the U.S. decision to go to war in Iraq in 2003 or even in U.S. frustration with the small number of allied troops in Afghanistan in 2007–8. Yet, the parameters for these divisions are pretty clear, and problems are blamed on current leadership or public opinion, not on historical forces or deep-seated value differences. We continue to assume that the West is largely united in its fundamental values, drawn from a shared civilization and solidified through a largely common worldview during the cold war. The path is open for leaders to narrow the gap.

The situation is different with Japan and South Korea, but the United States has not found a ready explanation. Value differences of each with

[8] "East Asian Union: Is Korea Really Ready Itself for Regional, Global Changes?" *Korea Times*, December 16, 2009.

the United States, between the two of them, and of each with other Asian states cannot escape U.S. attention, even if the response may not do justice to the problem. Sometimes U.S. leaders insist that the issue at stake demands only a realist outlook, assuming that the U.S. role as the driving force ensures that value differences do not get in the way. The Soviet threat, the North Korean threat, and even the rise of China as a military power are deemed sufficient to justify the conclusion that the ally is bound to be realist, rendering value differences of little consequence. A second U.S. response is compartmentalization, consigning value differences to the category of Asian-Asian problems separate from cross-Pacific values that bind. Yet a third response is to recognize that the differences matter for U.S. relations but to relegate them to a minor, declining role, as shared values are primary and time is on the side of convergence. All such responses lead to underestimating value divergence.

Japan and South Korea are the two most important U.S. allies who do not share Western traditions, and they are expected to support the long-term reinforcement of U.S. interests in the vital region of East Asia. If we look at the alliances with these states not in the usual manner of military burden sharing but through the lens of shared values in the face of changing challenges, we find intensifying incomprehension of the differences that exist and the way values issues operate in a regional context. Assumptions drawn from relations with allies elsewhere little prepare Washington for the challenges in East Asia.

An overview of U.S. relations with both Japan and South Korea since the 1990s reveals that overlapping, substantial disagreements over values are recurrent. In the first half of the 1990s, a lingering concern was protectionism, symbolized by the impossibility of selling U.S. or other foreign automobiles in either country as each built up its own manufacturers with the aim of competing successfully with United States firms in the global market and in various niches within the U.S. market. Each nation also had a strong tendency to contrast its harmonious, community, state-directed values with U.S. discordant individual values, objecting to U.S. efforts to impose some notions of human rights or sympathizing with advocates of Asian values. A closer look also reveals that each state was anxious to gain its voice toward the United States, long stifled under one-sided dependence, and to achieve some breakthrough with one or another state that would confirm its emergence as a partner worthy of equality. In the background, signs of serious historical grievances with the United States could be detected, which would have to be aired at some date even if most believed that the time was not ripe. Finally, both

Japanese and South Koreans were prone to romanticism about approaching Asian regionalism that could free them to pursue values distinct from those embodied in relations with the United States. After the cold war, value differences burst into the open with increasing intensity.

Recently, Japan and South Korea have brought value differences with the United States to the surface in similar ways. The public has quickly been mobilized to explode over seemingly minor incidents, including accidents or unexceptional crimes. They have taken offense at U.S. values–driven regional policies, such as South Korean reactions to regime change policies toward North Korea or Japanese reactions to democracy-building support for Russia after the collapse of the Soviet Union. After the United States was attacked in 2001 and began a long-term war on terrorism focused on Islamic fundamentalist militants, Japan and South Korea sympathized and did what was militarily necessary given the state of their alliances, but did not become deeply engaged in reflecting on the values at stake. The two states are driven by their own separate values priorities. There are overlapping values that buttress the two alliances, but they should not obscure the instrumental nature of much cooperation and the urgency of strengthening the foundation of shared values.

A frequent argument is that under the U.S. umbrella, the Japanese forgot their own international responsibility. For many on the right, the remedy is more patriotism and a stronger defense of sovereignty. The essence of responsibility is to shrug off apathy and support one's national territory and use of pressure on behalf of Japan's interests. Others on the left are still enamored with the idea of becoming a bridge to Asia, lessening the U.S. role. Neither side pays much attention to compromising on narrow national goals in order to work more closely with the international community to solve serious crises.

It was long assumed that historical reconciliation depended largely on Japan, as it proceeded sequentially: first assuaging South Korea as it apologized for the annexation of 1910 as well as policies that led to Japanization; then calming emotions with China by a full rendering of wartime atrocities; and finally finding common ground with the United States that would put Pearl Harbor, the atomic bombs, and the Tokyo Tribunal in context. This sequence is not being followed, as all three challenges are becoming intertwined in a renewed search across Northeast Asia for a sufficiently shared narrative ranging to today in order to pursue community building in a newly competitive environment.

PART II

HISTORICAL MEMORIES, JAPANESE–SOUTH KOREAN RELATIONS, AND U.S. VALUES

4

Japan–South Korea Relations and the Role of the United States on History

Kazuhiko Togo

"I consider that there were clearly things which Japan overdid during the colonial period. I think that the Japanese people should know about them, remember them, and then maintain a feeling of remorse." This was the author's position, which he actively communicated to interlocutors with whom he had the opportunity to talk during his four-month stay in South Korea from September to December 2007. But based on his research and conversations, the historical memory issue is far more complicated than this simple position suggests. Fundamentally, from the point of view of geopolitics and liberal values, Japan and South Korea have so many factors in common, and hence have structural reasons for cooperation, but historical memory drives them far apart. This reality is even negatively influencing cooperation on security (based on common geopolitical interests), values (democracy), and economic integration. This chapter first analyzes the intricate relations among geopolitics, values, and historical identity in Japan–South Korea relations; then it assesses how the rift on historical memory is perceived from the U.S. point of view. Finally, in search of a new strategy, the chapter highlights three distinct approaches open to a U.S. administration: the traditional approach of keeping its distance; the oft-considered but rarely tried approach of taking a judge-mediator position; and an unprecedented integrated approach treating the United States as an integral part of Northeast Asia's history. It concludes by evaluating how Barack Obama is positioning his administration in the face of changes under way in Japan and the Korean peninsula.

In reviewing contemporary Japanese–South Korean relations, this chapter stands on the fundamental principle that a nation cannot accept occupation by another power. Furthermore, the annexation of Korea was done by the Japanese, people of the same Asian race whom Koreans had long considered inferior in the sinocentric order and whom they once regarded as helpers in the quest for reform and independence. The annexation was characterized not only by its initial ruthlessness but also by the extent of full "Japanization" that occurred in the years leading to World War II. Total negation of the colonial period that branded everything that Japan had done in those years as impermissible became obligatory through the entire post–World War II period in Korea. As Japan and South Korea were increasingly sharing many factors in common from the point of view of geopolitics and liberal values, such as human rights, democracy, and market-based free trade, historical memory drove them far apart and touched fundamental issues of honor, pride, and identity in each nation.[1] Even two decades after the end of the cold war and a decade after Prime Minister Obuchi Keizo and President Kim Dae-jung reached a ground-breaking agreement to set history aside and upgrade ties, bilateral relations on the eve of Lee Myung-bak's presidency in 2008 were again struggling to emerge from another sharp downturn where history and territory served as divisive symbols. After eight years of George W. Bush's presidency, Barack Obama took office with a vigorous policy of "reaching out" through dialogue and diplomacy, setting a more positive tone. Attention to a new U.S. role in support of more earnest Japanese–South Korean efforts may help to bypass historical memories, but a more enduring impact may be achieved by striving for a wide-ranging approach that has potential to face the emotions over these troubling issues and calm them.

Japan–South Korea–U.S. Relations: Geopolitics, Values, and Historical Identity

Geopolitics and Power

In terms of geopolitics, South Korea and Japan are two allies of the United States in Northeast Asia dating from the cold war period, and despite some difficulties in respective alliance management, they remain

---

[1] In the broadest sense of the word, both "liberal values" and "historical memory, honor, and identity" may be categorized within the same terminology of "values." But in this chapter, "values" are used in regard to what are generally understood as "liberal values" in conjunction with the liberal theory of international relations. Historical memory and "identity and honor"–related matters are handled separately in conjunction with the constructivist theory of international relations.

so. For Japan, U.S.-Japan relations, based on the Security Treaty concluded in 1960, are the cornerstone of its foreign policy. It was so during the cold war, and it remains so as public support grows in light of the North Korean threat and the rise of China. The alliance is acquiring a global character, particularly after Japan's "defeat" in the Gulf War in 1991 for failure to offer more than financial support, joining the coalition of forces after 9/11 in 2001, and sending the Self-Defense Forces (SDF) to Iraq for humanitarian and reconstruction purposes in 2003. But management of this alliance has faced many difficulties, including anti-Americanism from the left during the cold war and resistance of local residents against American bases, notably in Okinawa. The government has adopted a series of policy measures in order to make the alliance credible, such as a substantial increase in host-nation support from 1978; the conclusion of new defense guidelines in 1978 and 1997; a reallocation effort (still unimplemented) since 1996 for Futenma airport in Okinawa; and transformation, as agreed in 2006, of the U.S. Army command and control at Camp Zama. None of these issues had an easy or quick resolution, and with a change in Japanese leadership after the August 30, 2009, elections, uncertainty has grown after two years of sparring over whether the Maritime SDF (MSDF) would be allowed to continue its supportive activities in the Indian Ocean.

For South Korea, the Korean War and the U.S.-Korea Mutual Defense Treaty of 1953 concluded after the armistice that ended that war determined the fundamental nature of its security position during the cold war. The cold war ended in parallel with the strengthening of the South Korean economy as symbolized by the Seoul Olympics in 1988 and the process of democratization shown by four successive democratically elected civilian presidents from 1993 onward. But as is clearly described in Gi-Wook Shin's chapter, several factors emerged as wedges impairing U.S.–South Korean security ties. U.S. economic and political dominance and perceived complicity with dictatorial regimes, symbolized in the Kwangju massacre in 1980, were the first blow. A wave of anti-Americanism by students and leftist opinion leaders determined the preelection mood in 2002, symbolized by the protests against the death of two students who accidentally perished under American tanks, and inflicted another blow. The two presidencies of Kim Dae-jung and Roh Moo-hyun shifted the emphasis of foreign policy toward eventual reunification with North Korea, dealing ties a third blow. These factors led to some reconsideration of the status of American bases in South Korea. With Washington eager to transfer troops to Iraq and achieve force realignment, an agreement was reached in 2004 to reduce the number of soldiers at South Korean bases by 12,500, to reallocate other troops from the area between Seoul and the armistice line to the south, and to shift as of April 2012 wartime operational control over South Korean troops to the South Korean government. These changes were in line with Roh's goal of letting South Korea become a "balancer" in the Korean peninsula, rather than just adhering to the position of U.S. ally. When elected as president, Lee declared his intention to mend the troubled state of relations and stated that his "aim was to ensure the improvement of relations damaged during the past ten years."[2] In Lee's visit to the United States in April 2008 and Bush's visit to Seoul in August 2008, both sides confirmed the consolidation of their strategic partnership; improved communications and greater trust followed.

As the two critical ends of the spokes stretching from a common hub, Japan and South Korea forged direct security cooperation through enhanced exchanges and dialogue after the end of the cold war. From 1994, top defense ministers of the two countries began regular visits to the other country and defense exchanges also began at the director-generals' level.[3] Notwithstanding this progress, the Six-Party Talks from 2003 proved to be a hard-core security issue fraught with clashes of interest among Japan, South Korea, and the United States. Roh Moo-hyun took the most conciliatory position of relying on "carrots" to entice North Korea to dismantle its nuclear weapons, as seen in the July 2005 proposal to supply 2 million kilowatts of electricity if the North abandoned its nuclear weapons.[4] Japan was known to be the toughest in advocating the use of "sticks," largely due to its insistence on the return of abductees. Japan's nonparticipation from February 2007 in the supply of heavy fuel oil to North Korea if it proceeded in disabling the facilities at Yongbyon symbolized its approach.[5] The initial position of the United States in the Six-Party Talks to require comprehensive, verifiable, irreversible denuclearization (CVID) suited Japan's rigid position, but the more flexible U.S. approach from February 2007 to provide "carrots" in line with the North's step-by-step concessions caused tension with Japan even as South Korea welcomed it. Under Fukuda and Lee Myung-bak, the Japanese and South Korean positions drew closer, because Fukuda was less fixated on the abductions and Lee took a tougher stance, asserting, "During my

[2] Interview with Funabashi Yoichi, *Asahi shimbun*, February 2, 2008, p. 5.
[3] Ministry of Defense, *Boei hakusho*, 2007, p. 303.
[4] *Asahi shimbun*, July 13, 2005.
[5] http://www.mofa.go.jp/mofaj/area/n_korea/6kaigo/6kaigo5_3g.html (accessed January 9, 2008).

tenure in office I will let North Korea abandon its nuclear weapons and realize its de-nuclearization."[6] In the Lee-Bush talks in 2008, the two sides emphasized the importance of North Korea meeting its obligations as prescribed by the roadmap agreement from February 2007.

The Obama administration launched its North Korea policy by pushing forward the Joint Agreement made at the Six-Party Talks.[7] Hillary Clinton's first trip to East Asia and her willingness to reach out to the North through dialogue was answered, however, by North Korean brinkmanship in launching missiles on April 4–8 and then testing a nuclear weapon on May 25. While Japan and South Korea fully supported the UN Security Council sanctions resolution that followed, they would be tested anew only after North Korea softened its stance, beginning with a visit by Bill Clinton to free two journalists. With Obama insisting that he would undertake bilateral talks only after Kim Jung-il returned to the Six-Party Talks and would press for a commitment for verifiable denuclearization, triangular consensus prevailed in the following months.

Liberal Values

South Korea and Japan have something fundamentally in common: Despite their specific circumstances, these two countries are considered to be among the most successful examples of democratic development after World War II. In the case of Japan, democracy did not exactly start from its defeat in 1945. From the Meiji Restoration in 1868 onward, in the process of modernization, a democratic tradition was developing as witnessed by the movement for freedom and people's rights in the 1870–80s as well as the Taisho democracy in the 1920s. But after the totalitarian and militaristic rule of the 1930s, which resulted in total defeat in 1945, a new wave of democratization led by the U.S. occupying forces was the main political trend in postwar Japan. Japan's democracy is often qualified as collectivism, lacking individualism at the center of democratic thinking; yet, in terms of minimum protection of human rights and proper functioning of the electoral system, there is little doubt that Japan has become one of the leading democratic nations in the world.

---

[6] Interview with Yoichi Funabashi, *Asahi shimbun*, February 2, 2008, p. 5.

[7] On February 12, 2009, Deputy Secretary of State Jim Steinberg stated that Secretary of State Hillary Clinton's visit to East Asia would be a good opportunity to enhance Six-Party Talks based on close cooperation with Japan, South Korea, and China. *Sankei shimbun*, February 13, 2009.

Korea went through its initial process of modernization under Japanese colonization. It was an extremely complex process where identification as part of Japan proceeded together with deeply engrained indignation against the occupiers. After the end of World War II, South Korea had to bear such tragic developments as the division at the thirty-eighth parallel and the North Korean attack followed by the raging Korean War in 1950–3. Rhee Syngman's authoritarian rule was followed by military dictatorship for another three decades. Only thereafter was South Korea transformed into an electoral democracy. Riots in parliament, corruption, the undefined role of prosecution, and other traits of a democracy at its embryonic stage were present, but South Korean democracy is clearly a resounding success.

From the economic point of view, after its "economic miracle" of the 1960s and continuing rise for another two decades, Japan still stands as the second largest economy despite its lost decade of the 1990s. Japan is facing new problems of an aging population and a low growth rate economy, as it seeks new ways to overcome these issues. South Korea, in the 1980s, became one of the most powerful newly industrialized economies (NIES), one of the "four dragons" together with Taiwan, Hong Kong, and Singapore, a flying goose immediately trailing Japan, the leading goose in the Asian formation through the 1980s. Signifying its success, it joined the Organization for Economic Cooperation and Development (OECD) in 1996 as the second country from Asia.

Japan tried to take the lead in forging regionalism as early as the 1970s through the Pacific Economic Cooperation Council (PECC), after the end of the cold war through Asia-Pacific Economic Cooperation (APEC) and the Association of Southeast Asian Nations (ASEAN) Regional Forum (ARF), and after the Asian financial crisis of 1997–8 through ASEAN + 3 and later the East Asian Summit (EAS). Kim Dae-jung took a conspicuous initiative in furthering East Asian regionalism by the East Asian Vision Group in 2001 and the East Asian Study Group in 2002. While Roh directed more attention to regional cooperation within the narrower scope of Northeast Asia, the fact remains that both countries have good reason to seek the support of the other in order to advance their respective visions of regionalism. Given the importance of U.S. ties to each, the United States is likely to play an active role in developing a shared vision.

Historical Memory and Identity: Past

On the historical memory issue, the situation is fundamentally different. The thirty-five years of Japan's annexation of Korea left a deep scar on the psychology and perceptions of the Korean people, but it also has left unsettled and polarized historical memories in Japan. First, there was the fundamental issue of resistance that no nation can accept occupation and loss of independence to another power. Second, Korean indignation was particularly profound because the annexation was done by Japan, by a fellow Asian nation, whom they had long considered a junior partner under the Confucian sinocentric world order, but whom some Korean reformers saw as the model for Korean reform, and consequently expected to help in Korean modernization, reform, and independence. Their expectations were betrayed by the occupation and loss of independence. Third, there was improper behavior by the Japanese, ranging from ruthless oppression, particularly at the beginning of the annexation, and a sense of superiority, treating the Koreans as secondary citizens. Fourth, although there was a period of flexible cultural policy particularly after the March 1 movement in 1919, when some "Koreanness" was allowed to develop, toward the end of the 1930s a total wave of "Japanization" overwhelmed Korea under Japan's determination to wage war in China and in the Pacific. Korean pride was crushed. Fifth, many Koreans had to live for thirty-five years under annexation, their identity in peril, and engage in the process of creating a modernized and industrialized Korea, making it an integrated part of Japan. This culminated in the Pacific War, when Koreans fought together with the Japanese as a part of the Japanese Empire.[8] Sixth, postwar Korea firmly set its historical memory on total negation of Japanese colonial rule, exploding with deep indignation against anything Japan had done under its annexation:

> The historical tragedy between Japan and Korea lies in the fact that "cooperation" between Japan and Korea advanced to the extent of engendering Japanization. When Japan's occupation suddenly ended, Korea consequently needed to negate everything in the past, label everything that Japan did as evil, and implement a thorough historical education depicting the colonial history as perpetual resistance against Japanese occupation. Anti-Japanese feeling was emphasized and strengthened substantially after Korean emancipation from Japan.[9]

This analysis coincides well with the author's dialogue with elderly South Koreans who experienced colonization,[10] narratives of those who know

---

[8] Kuroda Katsuhiro describes how Korea was becoming an integral part of the Japanese Empire in waging war against the United States in *Kankokujin no rekishikan* (Tokyo: Bungei shunju, 1999), pp. 50–1. The movie *Hotaru*, made in 2001, describes the fate of a Korean officer in the Japanese Imperial Army who died as a kamikaze pilot.

[9] Ibid., pp. 52–3.

[10] This is an impression that the author had in meeting three senior Koreans from the prewar generation (December 10, 2007).

that generation,[11] the author's impression of places in South Korea that emphasize Japanese wrongdoings,[12] and narratives of young South Koreans who recently went through the educational system.[13]

In contrast to almost uniform negation of the colonial past in Korea, Japanese understanding of the colonial period has been a long and diversified learning process. Immediately after the war, Japanese reaction toward the colonial period was perhaps best represented by the statement of Kubota Kanichiro in October 1953 during the Japan-Korea normalization talks that "not everything that Japan did during the colonial period was wrong." This statement invited extreme anger on the Korean side, and the talks were suspended for four and a half years.[14] But there has been a gradual realization that to state that "not everything that Japan did during the colonial period was wrong," specifically by the Japanese themselves, is unacceptably insensitive, and that Japan should basically stay humble and concede that there were at least certain aspects that it clearly overdid during the annexation. Many Japanese began to realize that it was the disrespect of Korean pride and culture that proved to be fatal.[15]

The first official "regret and remorse" was expressed orally in 1965 at the final stage of the normalization negotiations by Foreign Minister Shina.[16] In the 1980s, when the historical memory issues were highlighted in the international discourse between Japan on the one hand and China and South Korea on the other, the introduction of the "neighbor clause"

---

[11] "The senior generation which lived through the colonial period sometimes recalls the colonial period with a certain sense of nostalgia and an acknowledgment that during the colonial period, there was also respectable life," said an elderly South Korean professor about Japanese politics (November 1 and December 6, 2007).

[12] Among others, the Sodemunton prison museum and the Cheonan independence museum can be cited.

[13] "Whenever modern history under Japanese occupation was taught, the teacher usually became angry against Japan, and he did not hide his anger. So students also became angry against Japan," said a South Korean graduate student (October 27, 2007).

[14] Ikei Masaru, *Nihon gaikoshi gaisetsu* (Tokyo: Keio University, 1992), pp. 277–9.

[15] Okazaki Hisahiko wrote a book in 1977, *Tonari no kuni de kangaeta koto*, strongly criticizing the ignorance and sense of superiority on the Japanese side, urging his fellow citizens to learn more about the richness of Korean history and culture, and noting the sense of indignation that would naturally have emerged by way of being subjugated to foreigners, who once were considered inferior. (The same book was recently published under the new title of *Naze Nihonjin wa Kankokujin ga kirai nanoka* [Tokyo: wac. ink., 2006], pp. 101–5, 300–6.

[16] Kazuhiko Togo, *Japan's Foreign Policy 1945–2003, The Quest for a Proactive Policy* (Leiden: Brill, 2005), p. 159.

after the textbook controversy of 1982[17] and Prime Minister Nakasone's decision to suspend Yasukuni visits after his officially promulgated visit in 1985 are remembered as examples of Japan's will to respect the feelings of Asian neighbors. The end of the cold war and the interruption in LDP rule in the first half of the 1990s brought about a particularly conspicuous wave of apology statements and efforts to reconcile with South Korea. Numerous direct apology statements were made by Emperor Akihito in 1990, Prime Minister Kaifu Toshiki in 1990, Cabinet Secretary Kono Yohei in 1993 toward comfort women, and Prime Minister Murayama Tomiichi in 1995 expressing decisive remorse and apology for colonial rule and aggression. Despite President Kim Young-sam's initial goodwill to improve relations, the explosion of anti-Japanese emotions in this rising democracy failed to appreciate these démarches. But what was done then paved the way to the remorse and apology statement made by Prime Minister Obuchi in the reconciliation talks with President Kim Dae-jung in 1998.[18]

By this time, the mainstream government thinking could be summarized as follows: (1) recognition that there were excesses in Japan's Korean annexation, readiness to apologize for them, and the necessity to transcend these memories in the younger generation; (2) realization that the Koreans have reasons for deeply ingrained indignation against Japanese colonial rule and, against this psychological background, raising any positive aspect of the annexation period, especially in any political context by the Japanese side, is utterly insensitive and unacceptable by the Korean side; (3) positivist search for historical truth, which many Japanese are longing for, is a long-term objective, which may be sought only outside the political arena in a scholarly environment. But these expressions of contrition and the reconciliation talk in 1998 did not prevent the historical memory issue from again occupying center stage in Japan–South Korea relations. Koizumi's repeated visits to Yasukuni from 2001 to 2006, adoption of Fusosha's textbook in 2001 and 2005, Shimane Prefecture's establishment of Takeshima Day in March 2005, the comfort women issue that was revived under Abe in relation to a U.S. congressional resolution from March to July 2007, one after the other, stirred Korean emotions and thus had a negative impact on relations.

---

[17] This clause indicates that in screening the textbooks, the feeling of neighbors should be taken into account.

[18] Jane Yamazaki's analysis of Japan's apologies, particularly directed toward Korea, is a well-documented comprehensive study: *Japanese Apologies for World War I: A Rhetorical Study* (London: Routledge, 2006), pp. 33–56, 100–11.

On the South Korean side, official narratives to assert that "everything that Japan did before the war was wrong" do not seem to lose their strength, except in relatively rare private talks,[19] and some exceptional public statements, such as those by Professor Park Yuha.[20] On the Japanese side, many academic analyses of Korean history still emphasize the harmful nature of Japan's exploitation during the colonial period,[21] but incessant tension with Korea over historical memory may be making some Japanese increasingly weary of following the path of apology further. Kuroda Katsuhiro's recently published book describes this mood vividly.[22]

The split over historical memory affects bilateral relations on security and the economy. Japan's recent security-defense policy, particularly under Koizumi and Abe, can be characterized as attempts to become a "normal country." The revision of the constitution, notably of Article 9, may be considered the most symbolic policy in this direction, and Abe highlighted this as one of his primary political objectives. South Korean reporting on constitutional revision is always accompanied by a note of caution against Japan's drift to the right,[23] underlined in the author's

---

[19] "Korea should also learn from history. There is still an excessive tendency among Koreans that it is simply allowed to argue that Japan has 'an unlimited responsibility' for everything that went wrong in Korea," said a South Korean professor on international law (December 18, 2007).

[20] Park Yuha wrote two books in Korean, both later translated into Japanese, trying to see history objectively and acknowledging that some responsibility should be borne by the Korean side for the formation of modern Korean history (*Hannichi nashonarizumu o koete* [Tokyo: Kawade, 2005]), and to seek a mutually acceptable solution on Yasukuni, textbooks, Dokdo, and comfort women (*Wakai no tame ni* [Tokyo: Heibonsha, 2006]).

[21] In a relatively rare general history of Korea published in Japan, the colonial part takes a very critical tone against Japan's exploitation of Korea. Kasuya Keinichi, "Shokuminchi shihaika no Chosen," in Takeda Sachio, ed., *Chosenshi* (Tokyo: Yamakawa shuppan, 2000), pp. 272–324.

[22] Kuroda's recent book highlights more acutely the Korean tendency to attribute all causes of evil to Japan, and to caution Japan on getting too involved with Asia. Katsuhiro Kuroda, *Nihon banare dekinai Kankoku* (Tokyo: Bungei shunju, 2006), pp. 215–17.

[23] A summary of a *Chosun Daily* article on January 7, 2007, was entitled "Japan's Bent to the Right Is Proceeding Quietly without Any Sound," a headline emphasizing the danger of the Japanese rightist movement. http://www.chosunonline.com/article/2007010700019 (accessed January 8, 2008).

Reporting on the passage of a National Voting Law by the House of Counselors on May 15, 2007, was also written with a cautious tone that the revision may not necessarily be supported by the people. http://www.chosunonline.com/article/2007051500007 (accessed January 8, 2008).

http://www.chosunonline.com/article/2007051500010 (accessed January 8, 2008).

conversations with some South Korean intellectuals.[24] Korean misgivings about Japan are underpinned by historical suspicion that a Japan with a resuscitated military might harm Korea again. Japan's greater desire to play a military role almost automatically arouses Korean memories of Japanese colonization, where undisputed military power overwhelmed Korea.

In the face of these Korean suspicions, a senior Japanese diplomat did not hide his frustration:

> Japan is not happy about the present-day Korean government criticizing vehemently Japan's efforts to strengthen its defense position, for instance through the purchase of F-24s. It does not make sense to consider U.S. troops on the Korean peninsula as a "cap" against Japan. Japan and South Korea should have become allies with the U.S. confronting a common threat, and losing sight of this because of the historical legacy can harm the security interests of all parties.[25]

History-based perceptions about Japan are affecting the outcome of economic cooperation as well. South Korea and Japan had prepared with great effort the conclusion of a free trade agreement (FTA), which reached a stalemate until 2009. The two sides were engaged in a thorough joint study and began negotiations in December 2003, and in the course of summit talks Koizumi and Roh expressed a common desire to conclude the FTA before the end of 2005. But after the sixth round of negotiations in November 2004, the South Korean side stopped showing any willingness to hold the next round of talks. The major reason for this stalemate was reportedly that the South Korean side insisted on substantial concessions on agriculture by Japan before the next round of talks,[26] but the political climate became exacerbated in March 2005 because of the plan for the establishment of Takeshima Day on March 16 by Shimane Prefecture. Newspapers reported that the Takeshima/ Dokdo issue was casting a shadow on the FTA negotiations.[27] In fact, at the following summit meetings in June and November, political issues, notably history-related issues, received a much higher priority, and the two leaders were simply

---

[24] "The Japanese' recent move toward the revision of the Constitution is a reflection of Japan's increasing militarization, and we are very concerned," said a junior South Korean scholar after the symposium on territorial disputes in Northeast Asia (December 22, 2007).

[25] A senior Japanese diplomat in Tokyo, October 17, 2007.

[26] *Asahi shimbun*, February 13, 2005.

[27] *Asahi shimbun*, March 21, 2005.

not in a position to talk about an FTA.[28] An informed source on the
Japanese side maintains that the real reason the South Korean side lost
interest was the deteriorating political climate, particularly in relation to
Dokdo.[29] Even if this assertion cannot be proven, there seems to be little
doubt that because of the political barrier that emerged as the result of
this issue, the two leaders simply lost the opportunity to overcome the
agricultural issue. History is haunting economic relations between the
two countries.

Historical Memory and Identity: Present and Future

Lee Myung-bak's election to the presidency in December 2007 was taken
as a positive development in Japan–South Korea relations. It was so in
all spheres, including on historical memory issues. Lee signaled that he
had no intention of politicizing historical memory issues and wanted to
forge future-oriented relations.[30] Among scholars in support of this, Jin
Chang-soo argued that "there is no system to control the (issue of) past
history" and that "there is a need to establish a system to discuss past
history, to enlarge the Korea-Japan Common History Committee and
to establish a system of long-term resolution based on joint work by
the government and private sector experts. On the territorial issue both
governments should make a declaration not to politicize this issue."[31]

In the initial months after Lee Myung–bak became president, however,
the Japanese side did not take any initiative to ameliorate conditions
related to historical memory. On the contrary, in July 2008, contrary
to Park Cheol-hee's advice "to avoid stepping on the mines scattered in
the field of historical memory,"[32] the Japanese government issued a new
"explanatory paper" on the guidelines for junior high school textbooks.
This called for more detailed teaching about Takeshima in junior high
schools, and it fueled anger on the South Korean side. For a while, dialogue at the leaders' level was frozen again. But the global recession in

---

[28] *Asahi shimbun*, June 20 and November 19, 2005.
[29] A Japanese diplomat in Seoul, November 16, 2007.
[30] "As Japan is the No. 2 economic power in the world, it should be possible for her to
maintain a mature diplomacy with Asia. I will leave to the judgment of the Japanese
(resolution of) the history issue, and I will embark toward the future.... On the history
issue, experts should be engaged in the discussion with an open heart. We should leave
it [the history issue] to the experts, just like the Germans and French created a common
textbook through discussions, and the two countries should embark toward the future."
Interview by Yoichi Funabashi, *Asahi shimbun*, February 2, 2008, p. 5.
[31] Jin Chang-soo, presentation at a seminar held at Keio University, January 18, 2008.
[32] Park Cheol-hee, presentation at a seminar held at Keio University, January 18, 2008.

which the countries were thrown from the fall of 2008 probably became a catalyst for Aso Taro and Lee to resume their dialogue. Aso visited Seoul in January 2009 and the two sides agreed to enhance cooperation on the global economy, Afghanistan, North Korea, and such bilateral issues as the conclusion of an FTA and youth exchanges.[33] During the three democratically elected civilian presidencies of Kim Young-sam, Kim Dae-Jung, and Roh Moo-hyun, the initial position on history was always positive in signaling future-oriented relations without recourse to history. On each occasion, however, during the latter part of the administration, relations turned bitter over the historical memory issue. At the end of 2009, the two sides continued to avoid any rift over Takeshima/ Dokdo; yet as I have argued, the historical memory issue is deeply rooted, and there are no grounds to expect that the issue can be resolved in the near future. Mutual efforts are needed based on shared understanding that there are issues that require a long-term solution.

There are four concrete issues that might ignite emotions on both sides if mishandled: Yasukuni, comfort women, textbooks, and Takeshima/ Dokdo. The prerequisite for managing history issues so that they do not explode again in the forefront of Japan–South Korea relations, in my view, lies in the following guidelines.

Yasukuni

President Lee's statement that Japan should come up with a solution on its own applies best to this issue. There is a deep contradiction on this inside Japan. Until this internal issue is resolved, Japan will not be in a position to resolve it with outside countries. I have outlined my own proposal to introduce a moratorium on the prime minister's visit to Yasukuni. During the moratorium period, fundamental reform of Yasukuni should be implemented.[34] After Koizumi's visits to Yasukuni from 2001 to 2006, the Japanese media seem to have lost interest, and we do not see much debate on this issue. If there is not sufficient energy on the Japanese side to introduce substantial reform in this period of a lull, at least, the current prime minister's position of suspending visits should be continued until the time a new prime minister will be able to launch a reform to make Yasukuni acceptable to the majority of Japanese and the world.

---

[33] http://www.mofa.go.jp/mofaj/kaidan/s_aso/korea_09/gaiyo.html (accessed February 15, 2009).

[34] Kazuhiko Togo, "A Moratorium on Yasukuni Visits," *Far Eastern Economic Review* (June 2006), pp. 5–15.

Comfort Women

This issue was intensely debated between Japan and South Korea in the 1990s. Japanese efforts based on the Kono statement of 1993 and activities of the Asian Women's Fund from 1995 to 2007 were not appreciated by the South Korean government and the majority of South Koreans. Weekly demonstrations by former comfort women in front of the Japanese embassy in Seoul are continuing to this day, but this issue ceased to be a major point of contention in recent government-to-government talks. The three contentious issues under Roh Moo-hyun were Yasukuni, textbooks, and Dokdo. That situation changed abruptly after the press reports on Abe's denial of coercion against comfort women on March 1, 2007. Since then, this issue has caught particular attention outside Asia, as a series of 2007 parliamentary resolutions were adopted in the United States (July 30), the Netherlands (November 8), Canada (November 28),[35] and the European Union (December 13),[36] condemning past Japanese activities and requiring further apologies. The implications of U.S. involvement in the comfort women issue are analyzed later in this chapter, but as for Japan's own handling of this issue, I have expressed my view that after the April 27 Supreme Court verdict rejecting Chinese comfort women cases based on postwar treaties in which all governments and private claims were renounced, the Japanese side may have an historic opportunity to take further action, solely on the basis of humanitarian considerations.[37] This view is not drawing wide support in Japan, but, at least, the government should continue to stand behind the Kono statement and endorse the activities of the Asian Women's Fund.[38]

Textbooks

The situation concerning textbook publications is more complicated. The textbook that appeared to be most controversial in the 2001 and 2005 screening was the one edited by "Tsukurukai" and published by Fusosha. In 2006, Yagi Hidetsugu and his followers, backed by Fusosha, withdrew from "Tsukurukai" on the grounds of differing historical views and decided to publish a textbook edited by "Kaizennokai." Fujioka Nobukatsu and Nishio Kanji, who remained at "Tsukurukai," found another publisher, Jiyusha, and in April 2008 declared that they will

---

[35] *Yomiuri shimbun*, December 8, 2007.
[36] *Sankei shimbun*, December 14, 2007.
[37] Togo Kazuhiko, "Sengo hosho hanketsu, wakai e no shintenki ga otozureta," *Asahi shimbun*, May 17, 2007.
[38] http://www.awf.or.jp (accessed February 8, 2008).

prepare a textbook for adoption in 2009. Thus in April 2009 Jiyusha-"Tsukurukai" and Fusosha-"Kaizennokai" each formulated its textbook and both were approved by Monkasho screening. Jiyusha argued that Fusosha textbook's content was 80 percent the same as its own, and is gaining greater publicity through commercial marketing.[39] But on August 25, a Tokyo district court rejected Jiyusha's lawsuit to suspend the Fusosha textbook.[40] The 2009 textbook screening apparently did not cause an uproar in Japan–South Korea relations. I earlier argued that previous Japanese textbooks, including the one published by Fusosha, were not "whitewashing" history and even the Fusosha textbook saw improvement from the 2001 to the 2005 versions in making its wording more harmonious with the thinking of other countries.[41] To continue this trend, it is important that the Japanese government maintain the "neighbor clause." Further efforts should be made both in government-level committees and in private historians' groups on joint study and textbook preparation to deepen mutual understanding and, where possible, to enlarge common recognition about history. Lee Myung-bak's exemplary remarks on the European textbook experience precisely touch this point. In this situation, probably the most controversial issue is how textbooks handle the territorial issue.

Takeshima/Dokdo

This issue is probably the most explosive among all history-related issues and runs the risk of snowballing out of hand, if mishandled. The inflamed situation in 2005 after Shimane Prefecture's declaration of Takeshima Day is fresh in our memory. The "explanatory paper" for junior high textbooks issued in July 2008 nearly crushed hopes for improved relations early in Lee Myung-bak's tenure. In Korea, the Dokdo issue is seen as an integral and important part of the Japanese annexation. Any Japanese activities in claiming Dokdo immediately evoke a reaction as if Japan is reviving its colonial claim over the whole of Korea. For the overwhelming majority of Japanese, the Takeshima issue is either an issue of historical justice or a practical issue related to fishing rights, and in my view, the Japanese government has never put the Takeshima issue at the center of Japan–South Korea relations. Yet, no common approaches were found

---

[39] http://www.tsukurukai.com/ (accessed August 27, 2009).
[40] *Asahi shimbun*, November 15, 2008; *Sankei shimbun*, http://headlines.yahoo.co.jp/hl?a= 20090826-00000046-san-soci (accessed August 27, 2009).
[41] *Asahi shimbun*, April 6, 2005.

for dealing with this issue. Political determination at the highest level not to make the territorial issue the catalyst of chauvinistic emotions and endeavors by experts outside the government toward greater mutual understanding might help to depoliticize this issue.

U.S. Initiatives to Strengthen Japan-ROK-U.S. Relations

From the U.S. point of view, there is good reason to be concerned about the split over historical memory between two critical spokes of the U.S.-centered hub in Northeast Asia. Given the importance of Japan and South Korea for U.S. interests, the United States should be concerned about their troubles and act to reduce tensions between them. There is at least one example of successful U.S. intervention in their past relations. In August 1998, North Korea launched a Taepodong missile over Japanese airspace, and the many politicians took this as a serious security risk. Tokyo unilaterally suspended its negotiations with the DPRK in Beijing and announced that it would suspend all food aid for the North and financial support for the Korean Peninsula Energy Development Organization (KEDO). The unilateral character of this response revealed the shallow state of coordination in the Japan–U.S.–South Korea triangle. Strong U.S. and South Korean pressure compelled Japan to return to the KEDO process in November, as an alarmed Clinton appointed former secretary of defense William Perry as the senior coordinator for Korean policy. Upon his recommendation, the Trilateral Coordination and Oversight Group (TCOG) at the undersecretary level was created in April 1999 to improve coordination substantially among the three countries. Based on this coordination, Perry announced in October a new proposal for the United States to lift certain economic sanctions in exchange for a North Korean moratorium on missile testing. In December, a parliamentary delegation headed by Murayama visited Pyongyang to lay the groundwork for the resumption of governmental talks.[42] In June 2000, Kim Dae-jung made his historic visit to Pyongyang. Thus, the TCOG successfully kept alive Japanese–South Korean cooperation when it appeared in danger of failing.

The ongoing North Korean nuclear crisis and the respective positions of the three states in the Six-Party Talks are fraught with potential for a collision of interests. In the first half-year of the Obama administration,

---

[42] Michael J. Green, *Japan's Reluctant Realism: Foreign Policy Challenges in an Era of Uncertain Power* (New York: Palgrave, 2001), pp. 124–30.

when appeals for dialogue were not met with a favorable North Korean response, Lee Myung-bak's firm position against the North and Japan's fixation on the abduction issue created a natural harmony in their positions. Yet, from August 2009, when Pyongyang stepped back from brinkmanship, the possibility existed that South Korea would prioritize an appeal for Japan to first make a proper apology and compensation for past abductions of Koreans forced into labor and comfort women. If that point became a focal point of discussion between Japan and South Korea, nationalist politicians and opinion leaders in Japan who have different views on the degree of coercion involved in forced labor and comfort women might explode. Historical memory, so far not a central issue in handling North Korea, may become contentious. The United States may then have reason to consolidate Japan-ROK-U.S. relations in the manner it used in establishing the TCOG. Given the seriousness of the Japan-ROK divide on historical memory in general, the United States has a legitimate interest in expecting that the two countries overcome it and forge a credible alliance foundation as part of a network of countries with which it is fully able to share its values.

Traditional Approach: Stay Away from an Impossible Task

It was the wisdom of the U.S. government, basically supported by both the Japanese and South Korean governments, that, while it has a legitimate interest in expecting closer relations between them, it is best to stay away from concrete historical controversies. The process of normalization talks between Japan and South Korea underlines this conclusion. After the signing of the San Francisco Peace Treaty in September 1951, the U.S. government had expected early establishment of Japan-ROK diplomatic relations: The General Headquarters (GHQ) expected that Japan-ROK relations would be normalized before the peace treaty took effect in April 1952; after the failure of the initial talks, Washington played an active role in getting the two sides to resume negotiations, and in January 1953 General Mark Clark, the commander of the Korean UN forces, invited Rhee Syngman to Japan so that he might meet Yoshida Shigeru.[43] Negotiations were resumed, but negotiations stayed at a stalemate until they gained momentum under Park Chung-hee. Yanagiya Kensuke, a key Ministry of Foreign Affairs (MOFA) official who worked on the negotiations at this final stage until 1965, recalled his experience, saying that "it was clear that the U.S. had an interest in normalizing relations between the

---

[43] Ikei Masaru, *Nihon gaikoshi gaisetsu*, pp. 276–7.

two non-communist countries in Northeast Asia. But to the extent that I know, it has never intervened on concrete issues. Both Japan and Korea were reluctant to have the U.S. intervene on concrete matters as well. We feared that it may complicate the negotiations which were complicated enough."[44]

More than forty years have passed since diplomatic relations were established between Japan and South Korea, but the historical memory issue has become even more complex and difficult. Deeply entrenched indignation entirely negating Japan's colonial rule predominates in Korea, making it important "to avoid any provocation"[45] on the historical memory issue. "Any American involvement which gives an impression of siding with Japan on historical memory is detrimental for the Korean side in keeping sound relations both with Japan and the U.S."[46]

This sentiment can be easily replicated in Japan: "Any American involvement which gives an impression of siding with Korea on historical memory is detrimental for the Japanese side in keeping sound relations with the U.S." This naturally applies to nationalist politicians and opinion leaders who are angered by the incessant nurture of emotional hatred against Japan in education and social discourse in South Korea. Yet, even those who think that Japan should remain humble about history and recognize that Koreans have legitimate reason to be angry about the ruthless policy of "Japanization" mostly feel that over the past four decades there was general recognition about the excesses of Japanese colonial rule, and apologies have already been made many times with genuine feeling. They regret that their message of apology is not penetrating well, recognize that the issue is sensitive, and realize that there are things that need to be done on both sides. But at this juncture, intervention by an outsider who may not understand the sensitivity of this issue may simply evoke a negative reaction:

> The split between Japan and Korea on history and the Korean animosity against the Japanese are so deep. The Japanese side would appreciate it if the Americans show understanding of how Japan tried to understand and accept Korean feelings. But American sympathy toward Japan is out of the question for the Korean side. I do not see any way where the U.S. can play a useful role.[47]

---

[44] Yanagiya Kensuke, former vice minister of foreign affairs (October 18, 2007).
[45] A South Korean professor on politics and international relations (October 30, 2007).
[46] A senior South Korean academician (December 19, 2007).
[47] A senior Japanese diplomat, who had just retired (October 19, 2007).

Creative Approach: Taking a Judge-Mediator Position

In the last decade or so, there have been at least two occasions when the U.S. side showed signs of breaking away from the established practice of non-intervention. The first occasion did not see much success, but the second occasion was not without some results, which merit careful analysis. The 2000 January/February edition of *Foreign Affairs* carried an article written by Robert Zoellick, "A Republican Foreign Policy," in which he gives his thoughts on the U.S. policy with allies, enemies and in-betweens:

> Japan should evolve gradually assuming more responsibility for East Asian security, in concert with America and its allies. Only the United States can help Japan's neighbors accept this historic adjustment, which is the key to transforming Japan's domestic opinion. As a start, Japan, the United States, Korea, and Australia should form closer defense ties.[48]

This article suggests a proactive role on the part of the U.S. government to convince Japan's Asian neighbors, implying primarily China but not excluding South Korea, that postwar Japan has become a trustworthy partner of the United States and, by implication, Asian neighbors should overcome their differences with Japan. He does not mention history issues specifically, but these clearly are one of the main causes of distrust. In Bush's eight years, there was no sign that the line advocated by Zoellick in 2000 bore concrete fruit, but positive evaluation of his article by such nationalist opinion leaders as Sakurai Yoshiko may alert not only Chinese and South Korean policy makers but also American policy makers to the potential in this approach.[49]

As undersecretary of state, Zoellick proposed a joint study of history among Japanese, Chinese, and American scholars on September 21, 2005,[50] reiterating this idea on January 23, 2006, in Tokyo on the eve of his visit to China.[51] But this proposal was not accepted by the Chinese government, which emphasized the "specificity of Northeast Asian history" and the usefulness of joint study among Japan, South Korea, and China.[52] It could be well assumed that Zoellick's positive emphasis

---

[48] "A Republican Foreign Policy," *Foreign Affairs*, Vol. 79, No. 1 (2000), pp. 74–5.
[49] Sakurai Yoshiko, "Naze genbakuha tokasareta noka," *Seiron Extra*, No. 4 (2006), p. 197.
[50] *Kyodo tsushin*, September 22, 2005.
[51] *Kyodo tsushin*, January 23, 2006.
[52] *Kyodo tsushin*, January 24, 2006.

on postwar Japan did not help China enter into a tripartite Sino-Japan-U.S. scholarly exchange on history. Modest U.S. efforts to play a role in enhancing reconciliation were not accepted.

Another issue that needs attention is the way the U.S. Congress dealt with the comfort women issue in 2007. It adopted a resolution on July 30 asking Japan to make an "unequivocal apology" for the comfort women issue. As stated in the previous section, the comfort women issue has been a hot-button issue between Japan and South Korea from the beginning of the 1990s. But when it, while far from being resolved, began to cede its place at the forefront of governmental talks, there emerged a serious effort in the U.S. Congress to rebuke Japan, as a resolution requiring an unequivocal apology was presented four times in the House from 2001, though without success.[53] On March 1, 2007, Prime Minister Abe's press statement, which was reported as a total denial of responsibility for the comfort women system, aroused a negative image in Congress, and a *Washington Post* advertisement on June 14 by nationalist parliamentarians and opinion leaders claiming that the comfort women system was no more than military brothels and not a rape center fueled further anger, contributing to adoption of a resolution.[54]

The Japanese government was opposed to the resolution on the grounds that, based on the Kono statement of 1993, Japan has acknowledged wrongdoing, apologized both publicly and in person to individual comfort women, and compensated the comfort women. On the other hand, South Korean correspondents in Washington reported this development with fascination, particularly on the active role that Korean Americans played in having this resolution adopted by the House.[55] Former comfort women and their supporting organizations made public requests for a formal apology and compensation on the part of the Japanese government.[56] Both the Japanese and U.S. governments took a low profile after the adoption of this resolution, as resolutions were adopted successively in the Netherlands, Canada, and the European Union. On November 26, 2007, Congressman Mike Honda, who led in the passage

---

[53] *Asahi shimbun*, July 31, 2007.

[54] See Kazuhiko Togo, "Comfort Women: Deep Polarization in Japan on Facts and Morality," in Tsuyoshi Hasegawa and Kazuhiko Togo, eds., *Historical Memories and the Resurgence of Nationalism in East Asia* (Westport, CT: Praeger, 2008), pp. 142–62.

[55] *Sankei shimbun*, August 18, 2007.

[56] *Kyodo tsushin*, December 14, 2007.

of this resolution, stated in Seoul that "the resolution is expressing the expectation on the part of the U.S. Congress of what Japanese leaders and people would do."[57]

The comfort women controversy was raised in 2007 more in the United States and Europe than in Korea and Asia. The U.S. government and Japan experts played no small role in advising the Japanese government how to respond to this issue. It was done in a friendly manner, but clearly it was done based on a judge-mediator position. The U.S. side knew what had happened in the 1990s in Japan, had value judgments based on their contemporary notion of human trafficking, and advised Japan not to enter into public rebuttal of possible congressional resolutions, to maintain the Kono statement and to express, one way or another, sympathy toward those who had suffered.[58] These messages were transmitted publicly or privately. It was a successful operation, helping to quench the fire. Mike Green privately advised Foreign Minister Aso, after Abe's March 1 press statement, "not to make a rebuttal against the U.S. media; confirm that your heart aches but do not go further; stick to the Kono statement."[59] It helped to calm what could have deteriorated into a spiraling dispute. In August 2007, Undersecretary of State John Negroponte, while criticizing the prewar system of human trafficking, publicly acknowledged that "the Japanese government has already taken a series of measures, including an apology, and Prime Minister Abe also confirmed this position in October 2006."[60]

This issue is lingering. The United States Congress has taken a clear position and decided to act as a judge on this issue. There exists a powerful group in the LDP and the DPJ membership who consider that the congressional judgment on comfort women is based on grossly distorted facts. The Japanese government argues differently and stated that basically an apology and compensation have already been made.[61] For different reasons, both are not in agreement with the U.S. Congress. In such

---

[57] *Kyodo tsushin*, November 26, 2007.
[58] Interview with Michael Green, *Asahi shimbun*, March 10, 2007.
[59] *Yomiuri shimbun*, April 6, 2007.
[60] *Asahi shimbun*, August 4, 2007.
[61] The author argued in the Japanese media that there has to be an adequate way to continue the activities of the Asian Women's Fund, but, after transmitting the prime minister's apology and paying compensation, the organization terminated its activities in March 2007. "Sengo hosho hanketsu, wakai e no tenki ga otozureta," *Asahi shimbun*, May 17, 2007.

a situation, the United States acted as a friendly judge-mediator, success-fully. There were risks. The South Korean government and media do not appreciate the Kono statement and the Asian Women Fund's activities. Acknowledging a certain value to the Kono statement runs the risk of antagonizing the Korean side, but if the U.S. side is careful not to incite the emotions of either side, there is a possibility of continuing this path.

Historically Integrated Approach: From Outside Judge-Mediator to Inside Participant

The judge-mediator approach, as seen in the preceding example, may produce a successful result if very carefully handled. Another way to deal with the history issue is to take a historically integrated approach. The possibility of taking such an approach was first suggested to me by Dr. Jai-Hoon Yang, a Korean national born in Japan who later became a U.S. citizen.[62] This option consists of considering the U.S. role inside the historical events that took place as an endogenous factor in East Asian history. It could result in a much deeper basis for mutual understanding between with both South Korea and Japan. The historical perspective that emerges from this approach may be different from the traditional historical legacy understood by U.S. mainstream thinking, but, as an insider, it may be able to express its advice more effectively.

A clear example of the historically integrated approach is seen in how one might view the situation in which Korea was annexed to Japan. There is no doubt that the responsibility for the Korean annexation, which mate-rialized from the Protocol of February 1904 to the Annexation Treaty of October 1910[63] and the colonial rule thereafter, lies with Japan and no other state. But at the same time, it is also historically known that Japan's action of annexing Korea was implemented under the approval of the global powers, not only by Russia based on the Portsmouth Treaty of September 1905, but also by Great Britain, the leading hegemonic global power, and the United States, the rising power of the American continent and the Pacific Ocean. Great Britain's approval was given by

---

[62] About a decade ago, Dr. Yang created a network of opinion leaders of the U.S., ROK, and Japan under the name of G3 (Group of Three), seeking to achieve ultimate reconciliation between Japan and South Korea through U.S. participation.

[63] The five agreements are the Japan-Korea Protocol, February 23, 1904; the First Japan-Korea Agreement, August 22, 1904; the Second Japan-Korea Agreement (Protectorate Treaty), November 17, 1905; the Third Japan-Korea Agreement, July 22, 1907; and the Annexation Treaty, August 22, 1910.

the second alliance signed on August 12, 1905. "Korean independence and territorial integrity," which was written into the preamble of the first Anglo-Japanese alliance of 1902, was discarded, and the new treaty was extended to cover India.[64] As for the U.S. position, in the exchange of letters between Prime Minister Katsura Taro and Secretary of War William Taft concluded on July 29, 1905, Japan agreed that the Philippines are best governed by such a powerful and Japan-friendly country as the United States, and the United States acknowledged Japan's protectorate right over Korea.[65]

In March 2005, Dr. Yang told the author about the role of the Katsura-Taft agreement in the context of an historically integrated approach, stating:

> In order that Japan and Korea achieve ultimate reconciliation, as a Korean American citizen who was born in Japan, I have always thought that the United States could and should play a more decisive role. For that it may be useful that the U.S. maintain historical memory of what happened at the time of the colonization of Korea, notably the fact that by concluding the Taft-Katsura agreement, the U.S. acknowledged Japan's free hand in Korea while securing U.S. colonization of the Philippines.[66] Official recognition of Taft-Katsura by the U.S. at the highest diplomatic level and acknowledgment of U.S. acquiescence in the process of Korean annexation may give to the Koreans greater assurance that the U.S. is not, in this historical discourse, abandoning Korea.[67] At the same time, it would give to the Japanese side a new sense of esteem toward the U.S. that the U.S. is acknowledging its role in the process, and this new U.S. position should give further impetus for Japan to think and act more seriously on its own responsibility in the past.[68]

[64] Che Mun-hyon, *Nichiro senso no sekaishi* (Tokyo: Fujiwara shoten, 2004), p. 244.

[65] As for the general analysis of that situation, see Kazuhiko Togo, "The Contemporary Implications of the Russo–Japanese War" in *Russo–Japanese War* (Hanover, NH: Dartmouth University, 2008).

[66] Detailed analysis on the conclusion of the Katsura-Taft can be seen in Nagata Akifumi, *Theodore Roosevelt to Kankoku* (Tokyo: Miraisha, 1992), pp. 97–144. Che Mun-hyon also argued that the Katsura-Taft agreement, the second Anglo-Japanese alliance, and the Portsmouth Treaty should be looked at together as the basis of the Korean annexation five years later. Che Mun-hyon, *Nichiro senso no sekaishi*, pp. 237–45.

[67] According to Yang, "How such official recognition might assuage the deeply embedded Korean anxiety over U.S. abandonment may be seen in the recent Korean translation of Professor Nagata's book cited in footnote 63. His initial title, *Theodore Roosevelt and Korea*, in Japanese was translated into Korean as *America Abandons Korea*." Interview with J. H. Yang, Princeton, March 23, 2005.

[68] Yang, March 23, 2005.

However, in my talks with South Korean intellectuals, I have heard very little support for this historically integrated approach linked to the Taft-Katsura agreement:

- "I do not agree to enter into a discussion of Katsura-Taft in the history debate between the U.S. and Korea, not to mention Japan and Korea. Apart from specialists, the majority of the Korean people are not very familiar with Katsura-Taft, and letting them know about it just weakens U.S. credibility. The only credible approach for the U.S. to take is to encourage Japan and Korea to improve their relations, without going into the substance of the historical debate."[69]
- "Korean intellectuals are all aware of Katsura-Taft agreement. But this is exclusively a matter between the U.S. and Korea. It has nothing to do with the Japan-Korea historical memory issues. Japan-Korea historical memory issues should be resolved exclusively between Japan and Korea."[70]
- "In the memory of Korean intellectuals and historians the Katsura-Taft agreement is clearly present. Oblivion by the Americans on this issue was conspicuous and even some in the embassy staff in Seoul had no clear understanding about it approximately until the period under Ambassador Thomas Hubbard, who served from 2001 to 2004. Yet, the Katsura-Taft agreement was only one factor of Korean criticism against the U.S. In the Japan-Korean context, this is a very remote issue when one thinks about the Japanese annexation."[71]

This approach is not considered to be realistic by high-level Japanese officials either:

> Asking the U.S. to become more cognizant of its historical position on the Katsura-Taft agreement may be logically correct, but in reality it is a distant objective and even a risky operation from the point of view of the Japan-U.S. alliance. But at least, in connection with the historical discourse between Japan and Korea, the U.S. may give advice that Japan-Korea relations should be considered within the context of broad East Asian international relations, and not exclusively through Japan-Korea bilateral relations. Korean scholars tend to see things from the exclusive perspective of Japan-Korea relations.[72]

---

[69] A retired South Korean businessman, December 13, 2007.
[70] A South Korean professor of international relations, December 11, 2007.
[71] A South Korean professor of politics, December 4, 2007.
[72] A senior Japanese diplomat in Tokyo, October 17, 2007.

Furthermore, evoking the U.S. role in the international situation leading to Korea's annexation may have the danger of encouraging some anti-Korean nationalists in Japan. They might argue that Korea should not blame Japan, because putting Korea under rigorous Japanese influence was internationally accepted at the beginning of the twentieth century, as proven by the second Anglo-Japanese alliance and the Katsura-Taft agreement. This is clearly neither Yang's intention nor my thinking. We both consider that readiness to express regrets over history on the part of such a superpower as the United States should make Japan more humble and enable it to realize the pain it inflicted on others. Yet, one can easily imagine that American recognition of some responsibility in its imperial policy in the late-nineteenth and early-twentieth century, working against Korean interests, may invigorate Japanese rightists to justify Japan's own imperial policy.

Another issue where the United States did play an integral part in the period immediately following Japan's defeat in World War II is the Takeshima/Dokdo issue. Japan and South Korea maintain different views concerning historical recognition, namely, how respective governments viewed sovereignty over these islands before their annexation by Japan in 1905. Their views also differ on the status of these islands from the point of view of international law, namely, how they were legally settled after Japan's defeat. On that second point, the U.S. government made at least three critical decisions. First, it excluded Takeshima from the administrative areas to be controlled by the occupation forces in the demarcation made by SCAPIN 677, dated January 29, 1946.[73] Second, in preparing a peace treaty with Japan, the U.S. government reexamined this issue and Dean Rusk, assistant secretary of state for Far Eastern affairs, notified the Korean ambassador on August 9, 1951, that Takeshima/Dokto "was according to our information never treated as part of Korea and, since about 1905, has been under the jurisdiction of the Oki Islands Branch Office of Shimane Prefecture of Japan."[74] Third, in the actual text of the San Francisco Peace Treaty, Takeshima was not included among the islands to which Japan renounced "all right, title and claim."[75]

---

[73] Hyon Deson, *Ryodo nationalism no tanjo* (Tokyo: Minerva shobo, 2006), p. 50.

[74] http://www.mofa.go.jp/region/asia-paci/takeshima/treatment.html (accessed March 39, 2009).

[75] Article 2 (a) of the San Francisco Peace Treaty reads "Japan, recognizing the independence of Korea, renounces all right, title and claim to Korea, including the islands of Quelpart, Port Hamilton and Dagelet."

Given this history, what can the United States do to protect its national interest, enhancing in parallel peace and stability in the region? Should it decide to intervene based on Rusk's position in 1951 and confirmed indirectly at San Francisco, it would certainly create an irreparable rift in the U.S.–South Korea alliance. Yet, should it reexamine its position from 1951 and take a more favorable position toward South Korea, nationalists in Japan may well explode to a level detrimental to the Japan-U.S. alliance. Thus, however real was the U.S. involvement in the emergence of the Takeshima/Dokto issue in 1945 through 1951, there does not seem to be an effective way for any U.S. participation in this issue at this point. The only approach that it might consider is to encourage Japan and South Korea to talk and exchange their views totally informally and quietly.

Yang's proposal for an integrated American approach does not seem to command support on either side. It might have some impact in enhancing better understanding on historical recognition between the United States and South Korea, but at least for now, there seems to be unanimous resistance on the South Korean side to mingling this issue with the Japan-Korea history issues. By the same token, there are also factors that make the Japanese response cautious. U.S. intervention does not seem to have any perspective at this point. The vision of improved historical recognition with South Korea and Japan, respectively, ultimately helping reconciliation between the two is a long-term objective. Time is needed for this approach to be taken seriously.

Conclusion

History issues between Japan and Korea are extremely complex. Not only in contention are the fundamentals of what happened during the thirty-five years of Japanese colonization and why it happened, but also there is the fundamental question of how the Koreans and the Japanese viewed history in the last sixty years during the process of nation building after World War II. The traditional wisdom was for the United States not to become involved in this historical discourse between Japan and Korea other than general encouragement for better relations, and given the complexity of the issue, this position may best be sustained today. But history moves and nothing remains the same. The Congressional resolution on comfort women in July 2007 might have opened a new door. Quiet advice that Washington experts on Japan gave to the Japanese side was based on U.S. values and knowledge of Japan's endeavor to overcome its past. It was based on a mediator-judge position and so far has been helpful in quelling emotions both in the United States and in Japan. This mediator-judge position, provided that it is deployed with utmost caution and sense of balance, may be effective again. Thorough study of historical facts, fair judgment, and utmost sensitivity not only to the content but also to the way U.S. views are expressed might allow the United States to take a balanced mediator-judge position, however difficult this might be.

Deeper historical knowledge might eventually create an opening for the United States to assume an insider position in East Asian history. Reconsidering its past as an integral part of Northeast Asian history could deepen mutual understanding between it, on the one hand, and South Korea and Japan, on the other, and help the two Asian countries to better understand each other. At this point, there is not much support in either state for this historically integrated approach, but for U.S. policy makers and opinion leaders, there may be some food for thought. The Obama administration, while basically advised to adhere to a non-interference policy, might give some careful thought to both the mediator-judge approach and an historically integrated approach.

5

Getting Away or Getting In?

U.S. Strategic Options in the Historical Controversy between Its Allies

Cheol Hee Park

South Korea and Japan are the two key allies for the United States in Northeast Asia. Each has been an ally for more than fifty years, and more than forty years have passed since the two countries normalized diplomatic relations in 1965. Considering the long period of working together under the U.S. umbrella, it would be expected that the two nations had themselves become allied. However, they still remain awkward partners, referring to the other as "geographically close but emotionally distant." What prevents them from developing a full-fledged partnership is the historical controversy lingering between them. More than half a century after the end of Japanese colonial domination, historical memory is a stumbling block preventing closer political ties. This does not serve their interests well and also fails to support U.S. aims for the region, solidifying security partnerships and forging a values-based coalition.

During the cold war period, historical animosity between South Korea and Japan was overshadowed to a considerable degree because the need for security and economic growth spurred the two countries to cooperate against the potential communist threat to both. Security imperatives made the two countries work together, albeit usually indirectly through the filter of the United States. Victor Cha aptly called the relationship "alignment despite antagonism."[1] Antagonism did not disappear even in the face of a common set of enemies; yet they found a way to collaborate through strong U.S. encouragement and also due to some domestic political reasons in each country. Anti-Japanese feeling erupted from time

---

[1] Victor Cha, *Alignment Despite Antagonism: The US-Korea-Japan Security Triangle* (Stanford: Stanford University Press, 1999).

to time, but it did not rupture their cooperative ties. Widespread antipathy toward Koreans in Japan also did not prevent the LDP leadership from pursuing cooperation. Japan and South Korea acted like "virtual allies," facilitated by Japanese conservative leaders restraining provocative behavior, made easier by the prevailing pacifist cultural orientation.[2] No less important, South Koreans, despite lingering anti-Japanese sentiment, accepted rapid Japanese economic development as a reality and treated Japan as a model.

This situation, however, did not continue after the cold war, as a new logic of historical controversy developed. In a democratized South Korea, popular voices for historical justice gained prominence, asking for a reevaluation of Japanese colonial rule and Korean collaborators during that period. Korean nationalism surged, with Japan its favorite target. At about the same time, in Japan, historical revisionism surfaced, gaining a wider following after the Gulf War contribution ended in disappointment.[3] In the early 1990s, the so-called comfort women issue became a visible controversy between Japan and Korea as well as other neighboring countries. This encouraged mobilization of right-wing voices in Japan intent on featuring their history in a new fashion. Rekindling the pride and prestige of their nation became the guiding spirit of the movement, which influenced ever-wider streams of Japanese conservatives.[4] These parallel streams of politically motivated intellectual movements provided the grounds for national debates in each country about taking a renewed look at their history, which negatively affected mutual perceptions. The United States did not meddle in this controversy, keeping silent in order not to be put in the awkward position of taking the side of one of its two allies.

After nearly two decades of this rift as the regional environment has been drastically transformed, is there reason for the United States to take a different approach? This chapter answers that question in four sections and a forward-looking conclusion. First, it identifies the domestic roots of the intensified historical controversy in the 1990s and after. After briefly contrasting the international and regional contexts in Europe and East

---

[2] Kenneth B. Pyle, *The Japanese Question: Power and Purpose in a New Era* (Washington DC: AEI Press, 1992); Thomas Berger, *Cultures of Anti-Militarism* (Baltimore: Johns Hopkins University Press, 1998); Peter J. Katzenstein, *Cultural Norms and National Security: Police and Military in Postwar Japan* (Ithaca: Cornell University Press, 1996).

[3] Kunimasa Takeshige, *Wangan senso to iu tenkanten* (Tokyo: Iwanami shoten, 1999).

[4] Oguma Eiji and Ueno Yoko, *Iyashi no nashonarizumu* (Tokyo: Keio University Press, 2003).

Asia, I consider how historical revisionism advocated by domestic political social movements developed and negatively affected political debates in each country. Second, I address the U.S position in this historical controversy, noting that it did not remain neutral despite appearances, nor could it, for the history controversy affected ties between its two key allies. I review its changing position over time, comparing the periods of Kim Dae-jung–Obuchi, Koizumi–Roh, Abe–Roh, and Fukuda–Roh. The third section discusses recent developments, including Fukuda Yasuo's active Asia diplomacy and Lee Myung-bak's impact, also taking note of China's "smile diplomacy" toward Japan. In this section, the meaning of comforting signs is assessed. Fourth, I focus on the theoretically possible and actually tried strategic options for the United States. There are costs and benefits for each option, which have different implications for a U.S. regional strategy in Northeast Asia, and I conclude with suggestions for practical and prudent ways to deal with the issue.

Domestic Sources of the Controversy: The Rise of Historical Revisionism

Neo-rightists emerged in Japan in substantial numbers beginning in the early 1990s and became politically prominent after the mid-1990s. In South Korea, new leftists rooted in social movements emerged as a new political force in the late 1990s. Even though neither group was in the political mainstream, they exerted an unprecedented influence on the discourse on history. What sparked the change in historical consciousness in Japan was, arguably, the response to Japan's contribution to the Gulf War. Unable to dispatch the Self-Defense Forces because of the constitutional constraint, Japan ended up contributing $13 billion to the war effort; however, its "checkbook diplomacy" and "one-country pacifism" were not fully appreciated in these new circumstances of forging a global order. This provided momentum for political change and new foreign policy initiatives aimed at making Japan into a "normal country."[5] A realist orientation emerged as a new alternative to pacifism.[6] This experience became the turning point in the rise of an intellectual movement that Japan should not be shamed by others. As a counter to the Japan

[5] Ozawa Ichiro, *Nihon kaizo keikaku* (Tokyo: Kodansha, 1993); Masayuki Tadokoro, "The End of Japan's Non-Decision Politics," *Asian Survey*, Vol. 34, No. 1 (November 1994), pp. 1002–15.

[6] Michael Green, *Japan's Reluctant Realism: Foreign Policy Challenges in an Era of Uncertain Power* (New York: Palgrave, 2001).

Teachers' Union, Nikkyoso, which long had inculcated pacifism, a group of opinion leaders argued for the importance of teaching Japanese pride and prestige.[7] Many who had felt the humiliation of being pressured by the United States, despite Japan's enormous contributions to the outside world, tried to revive Japanese pride by advocating the need to get over the history consciousness imposed upon them since the Tokyo Tribunal.[8] Unlike past discussions of history, which were strictly in terms of Japan's Asian neighbors or of U.S. *gaiatsu* (outside pressure) narrowly centered on trade disputes, the U.S. worldview now figured importantly in Japanese resentment.

In addition to the Gulf War, claims by South Korea, the Philippines, and other countries for acknowledging the existence of the comfort women during the past war also aroused new historical consciousness.[9] Based on testimony by former comfort women, victims pressured Japan to make an apology and pay compensation for its war crimes. The widespread practice of "sex slavery" was a shameful act for Japan to acknowledge, and the opinion leaders who advocated a new history perspective strongly denied the Japanese government's involvement in forced mobilization of the comfort women, deeming this issue to be no less than a direct assault against pride in their state.

In 1995, Iris Chang's best-selling book *The Rape of Nanking* claimed that Japan had carried out an inhumane massacre during the war.[10] This message was also considered a shameful affront by conservatives who made no clear distinction between their country before 1945 and afterward. To counter this claim, Kobayashi Yoshinori published the manga *Sensoron*, where he claimed that the Nanjing massacre was highly exaggerated.[11]

All told, I detect three streams of negative evaluation against Japan in the early 1990s, which induced a sense of shame about the country's past and a strong reaction to obliterate it by right-wing groups. One

---

[7] Fujioka Nobikatsu, Kobayashi Yoshinori, and Nishibe Susumu are some of them.

[8] For example, Fujioka appealed for a new history consciousness based on liberal histori-cism, *jiyushugi shikan*, rebutting the worldview imposed after the Tokyo Tribunal, which held that Japan's prewar system was the root cause of the evil and that the Japanese should be repentant about their own past.

[9] Jin Sung Chung, *Hyundai Ilbon eui sahwoi undongron* (Seoul: Nanam, 2001).

[10] Iris Chang, *The Rape of Nanking: The Forgotten Holocaust of World War II* (New York: Basic Books, 1997).

[11] Kobayashi Yoshinori, *Shin gomanizumu sengen SPECIAL: Sensoron* (Tokyo: Gentosha, 1998).

was a financial contribution to the Gulf War, which was not appreciated by external powers despite the huge amount of money Japan
gave to the multinational forces. Making a contribution with "troops
on the ground" through peacekeeping operations (PKO) became a new
trend in Japan after this.[12] The Japanese left, mired in "one country
pacifism," became a target of criticism and faded rapidly as a political
force. Another development was the rise of the comfort women issue on
the diplomatic front with South Korea, China, and other Asian countries, another shameful act the Japanese did not want to acknowledge as
their Asian neighbors demanded. Against the left wing's claim that Japan
should apologize more and fully compensate these women, the right-wing
element of Japanese society argued that neither the Japanese government
nor the military was directly involved in their mobilization. According to
the latter, the comfort women were voluntarily, not forcefully, mobilized
by local cooperative agents, and they were duly paid for their services.
Again, saving the pride of the Japanese was the most important aspect of
the right-wing claims. The other development was depicting Japan as a
cruel country that committed the unparalleled Nanjing massacre. Though
the right-wing group acknowledged the existence of a tragic event, they
argued that the number of victims was greatly exaggerated. According to
this claim, Japan conducted a just war without committing international
crimes, and in the process, it did what other imperialist countries did and
nothing more. The right wing heavily criticized the Japanese left-wing
arguments, also denying the claims of their Asian neighbors for wartime
criminal acts and making Japan a country that can say no to Asia. Seeking
to weaken and, if possible, silence collaborators within Japan along with
the Asian accusers, this group amassed in the Society for Making New
History Textbooks (*Atarashii kyokasho o tsukuru kai* or *Tsukurukai*).[13]

The upsurge of historical revisionism initiated by the right wing
encouraged Japanese political leaders to move in the same direction. It is
not coincidental at all that since the mid-1990s, we witness an increasing
frequency of provocative remarks by Japanese political leaders. Japanese
prime ministers did not necessarily take the same positions. Murayama
tried to avoid intense conflicts with Korea. He fired Minister Eto from his
cabinet after he made a careless remark that Japanese colonial rule was not

---

[12] Tanaka Akihiko, *Anzen hosho* (Tokyo: Yomiuri shimbunsha, 1997).
[13] Yoojin Koo, "Domestic Politics of Historical Consciousness in Japan: Focusing on the
Tsukurukai" (Seoul: Master of International Studies Thesis at the Graduate School of
International Studies at Seoul National University, August 2006).

all bad.[14] Obuchi Keizo made a historic declaration with Kim Dae-jung and tried his best to hold back the right-wing tendency in Japan. Mori Yoshiro provoked neighboring countries as well as progressives in Japan by his remarks about Japan being a "country of god,"[15] but he abstained from provoking China and Korea further. It is mostly under the Koizumi Junichiro cabinet that Japanese leadership circles relentlessly accepted the views suggested by the neo-rightists. Above all, Koizumi himself visited the Yasukuni Shrine every year despite mounting criticisms from Korea and China. Provoked by the remarks and actions of the Koizumi cabinet, Koreans responded emotionally. Unlike the past, when South Korea had initiated historical disputes, Japan did so from the mid-1990s.

In the case of South Korea, left-wing figures, who had long been oppressed by conservative governments, began raising their voices after the end of the cold war and the normalization of relations with Russia and China. This spurred changing thinking toward North Korea above all. Extremists among the student movement activists even accepted "Jucheism," the self-reliance principle advocated by the North Korean regime. These radical voices eventually resulted in the fragmentation of the student movement, but their actions and appeal for national reconciliation raised the voltage of aspirations for national unification or, minimally, for peaceful coexistence. The bold initiatives of Kim Dae-jung and Roh Moo-hyun for engaging the North may not have been possible without these calls for national reintegration raised by the left wing.

Progressive scholars in Korea seriously raised the question of national identity. For them, conservative and authoritarian governments over decades had mesmerized the entire Korean society by a distorted notion of identity.[16] The mainstream in Korean society had emerged from the ranks of pro-Japanese collaborators during the colonial period as well as collaborators with the authoritarian military governments in the postwar era. Cold war logic prevented them from being accused or indicted. According to some, these collaborators with Japanese colonial rule and the authoritarian regime should even be executed. The Research Institute for National Affairs, among others, took the lead to advance this logic, pursuing projects such as publishing in November 2009 a dictionary of

---

[14] *Dong-a ilbo*, November 14, 1995.

[15] Mori's remark that Japan is a country of god (*kami no kuni*) privileges the Shinto tradition, closely related to the Yasukuni Shrine. *Dong-a ilbo*, May 17, 2000.

[16] Jangjip Choi, *Minjuhwa ihu eui minjujueui* (Seoul: Humanitas, 2002).

pro-Japanese collaborators.[17] They also put pressure on the South Korean government to open up the secret files concerning diplomatic negotiations with Japan that occurred around 1965, wanting to know whether there was an undisclosed part involving an illegal political kickback to the Park Chung-hee government. This effort eventually led to the opening of the government archives on August 29, 2005. Left-wing efforts to expose misdemeanors of the past were not limited to pro-Japanese collaborators. They also questioned government involvement in the Kwangju uprisings in 1980, the arrest of North Korean spies in the 1970s, and other designated democratic movements under authoritarian regimes. This led to the establishment of several presidential committees by Roh.

Left-wing efforts did not necessarily target a single country or single regime. Their main goal was not to blame Japan, but the Koreans who had helped the colonial regime or authoritarian regimes. Resurrecting national identity based on pride and prestige paralleled what the right wing in Japan was seeking. While the Japanese new right was responding to outside pressure and domestic collaborators, the South Korean new left mainly questioned domestic collaborators. This does not mean, however, that they did not affect external relations. They turned the political timetable back. Rather than constructing a future agenda for national development, the left wingers traced back to the authoritarian past, colonial past, and even the late-nineteenth century a situation that they deplored. Clearing the history house became the issue of the day, especially during the Roh administration, which had strong ties to the progressive social movements and even established a special assistant in charge of civil society. Another effect was the growing salience of a nationalist agenda. In addition to inter-Korean reconciliation, these groups constantly raised the importance of national integrity in the diplomatic arena. When a conflict arose with Japan or another country, voices of nationalism grew stronger. In the controversy with China over the Koguryo period, these groups vehemently argued for the nationalist cause. When the Dokdo/Takeshima controversy became the focal point of contention between Korea and Japan, nationalists gained influence over political leaders.[18] Not all were leftists, but without the new left's contribution, nationalist causes might not have been high on the political agenda.

---

[17] It finally appeared in 2009 as Institute for Research in Collaborationist Activities (IRCA), *Chinil inmyung sajon* (Seoul: IRCA, 2009).

[18] The Office of President established a Special Task for Correct History (*barun yoksa kihoikdan*), which studied the history of the Japanese encroachment and regularly reported its findings before being integrated into the Northeast Asia History Foundation.

There is a tendency to excuse this dual outcome, even among scholars, by insisting that Korea is simply responding to external stimuli and Japan also is just responding to external criticism. However, analyzing only the external origins of the historical controversy can give a misguided impression that the other party is always the source of the problem when, in fact, domestic forces are affecting the development of historical controversy. In the case of Japan, the rising influence of the new right contributed to the intensifying tension over history issues inside Japan as well as with neighboring countries. In the case of South Korea, the new left contributed to bringing the past to the political forefront, directing media attention to the nationalist agenda. Given this situation, there remains a possibility that the historical controversy will reemerge despite the advent of prudent political leadership in both countries. In the past, U.S. involvement in the controversy became a factor as well, influenced by the way political leaders in the two allied states dealt with the rising nationalist forces.

The U.S. Stance on the Historical Controversy between Korea and Japan

Aware of the sensitivity of the historical controversy, the United States hardly ever took a strong position that could risk its relations with one side or the other. Also, active intervention raised the possibility of accusations being directed at U.S. historical responsibility in the postwar settlement. This does not necessarily mean, however, that it was an uninterested party or a neutral observer. Its position varied over time, depending on the strategic context in which the historical controversy was unfolding.

When Kim Dae-jung and Obuchi Keizo made a partnership declaration that bilateral ties should go beyond the historical controversy in pursuit of future-oriented relations, South Korea voluntarily put this aside as bilateral ties advanced rapidly. Both countries promised to open their cultural doors to the other. Also the idea of a South Korea–Japan free trade agreement (FTA) surfaced as a diplomatic goal. Furthermore, political turmoil related to the fisheries agreement was settled in 1998. An increasing proportion of Japanese came to have favorable perceptions about South Korea, which opened a new window of opportunity for improving bilateral ties,[19] as tourism also sharply increased.

---

[19] Japanese having a positive image of Korea increased from 48 percent in 1998 to 57 percent in 2002. http://www8.cao.go.jp/survey/h17/h17-gaikou/images/z07.gif (accessed

Despite the partnership declaration, South Korea–Japan relations faced hard times around April 2001 because of the history textbook controversy. The Fusosha-published textbook at the center of the turmoil included controversial descriptions; the South Korean government thus asked for revisions on specific points. The controversy over the textbook subsided only after the actual selection rate of the Fusosha textbook at schools recorded was only 0.037 percent at the end of August 2001. Thinking that interpretations of history are a domestic matter, the United States stood aloof to this controversy, remaining neutral.

Though new prime minister Koizumi's Yasukuni Shrine visit on August 13, 2001, aroused lots of criticism, it did not develop into an emotional conflict between the two states. Kim Dae-jung tried to avoid this after the heated debate over textbooks in the first half of 2001. Also, cohosting of the 2002 World Cup soccer game produced an amicable mood on both sides. That overshadowed Koizumi's next Yasukuni Shrine visit in April 2002. Later Koizumi surprised Koreans when he visited North Korea on September 17, 2002, signing the Pyongyang Declaration, which suggested the possibility of normalizing relations and brought strategic issues to the fore. Kim did not raise the history issue again until he stepped down in February 2003.

After his visit to Pyongyang, Koizumi became entangled in the unexpectedly emotional Japanese abductees issue as well as in responding to the newly unfolding tension over the secret nuclear weapons development program detected by the United States. South Korean politics were also embroiled in a controversy related to the deaths of two schoolgirls caused by an American tank, which became the most salient issue during the presidential campaign. Anti-American sentiment spiked, which helped Roh Moo-hyun to be elected in December. America was frustrated by Roh's anti-American rhetoric, contrasting it to the strong pro-American stance of Koizumi, who was fully aware of the deep impact of the September 11 terrorist attack. With such divergent responses, it is no wonder that the Bush administration leaned heavily toward Japan.

Until late 2004, Roh did not push Koizumi into a corner. Though Koizumi visited the Yasukuni Shrine annually, Roh gave more credit to Koizumi's efforts to normalize ties with North Korea. Shuttle diplomacy between the two countries seemed to be working. In a summit meeting on July 22, 2004, Roh even made a statement that he would not raise the

February 27, 2008). After a downturn, the figure rose to 63 percent in late 2009, as noted in Chapter 6.

history issue with Japan during his tenure. However, when North Korea showed no signs of resolving the abductees issue to the satisfaction of the Japanese public, the Koizumi cabinet toughened its stance, and Roh lost all hope for a Japan–North Korean rapprochement.

The South Korean approach to Japan was altered drastically after Shimane prefecture declared on February 22, 2005, that it would establish "Takeshima Day" in honor of the one hundredth anniversary of the annexation of Dokdo/Takeshima. The Roh government interpreted this as a centrally approved provocation to justify the colonial annexation of Korea, seeing this dispute as deeply entangled in the controversy over colonial rule. Roh and his aides took an inflexible position that the Japanese claim could never be accepted, and Roh declared a "diplomatic war" with Japan.[20] When the results of the middle school history textbook review were announced on April 5, 2005, pictures of Dokdo were featured on the front pages of a few history textbooks. This was viewed as another Japanese move to challenge the status quo of control over Dokdo by South Korea.[21] The United States did not intervene, seeing it as a matter of sovereignty claims between the two countries.

When in 2004–5 Japan pursued its strategic goal of bidding for a UN Security Council permanent seat, China strongly opposed this move and South Korea was reluctant to endorse it too. U.S. officials such as Richard Armitage had not hesitated to encourage Japan to seek this goal, which Koreans interpreted as unilateral support for Japan in the middle of the history controversy.[22] Reflecting policy lines suggested by the Armitage Report of 2000, the United States supported Koizumi's move as in line with its interests in the region and world.[23] Michael Green, who was in charge of East Asian affairs at the National Security Council, took the position that Japan's proactive and assertive diplomacy was in the

---

[20] The National Security Council announced a new hard-line policy toward Japan on March 17, 2005, and on March 23, Roh issued a strong message to the South Korean people, "Kukmin ege durineun geul."

[21] One year later, on April 14, 2006, Japan unilaterally notified the South Korean government that it would conduct investigations in the maritime area surrounding Dokdo, which brought about the possibility of a military conflict. Only after Vice Foreign Minister Yachi held an eight-hour meeting with his counterpart Yoo Myung-hwan on April 21, 2006, was this averted.

[22] See the Armitage interview by Kashiyama Yukio, *Sankei shimbun*, August 4, 2004. http://www.state.gov/s/d/former/armitage/re,arks/35190.htm (accessed February 27, 2008).

[23] Armitage Report 2000, "The United States and Japan: Advancing toward a Mature Partnership" (Washington, DC: INSS Special Report, 2000).

U.S. interest. The Armitage-Green line imposed a regional strategy that inclined the United States to close its eyes to the history issues.

Koizumi's Yasukuni Shrine visit in 2005 drew much wider attention both inside and outside Japan because it overlapped with the Security Council seat bid as well as the territorial dispute over Dokdo/Takeshima. By midyear, the Japanese domestic debate on the shrine became quite divisive. In a book published in April 2005, Tetsuya Takahashi pointed out the multilayered complexity of the Yasukuni problem.[24] In a speech delivered in May 2005 at the University of Tokyo, former South Korean president Kim Dae-jung took a very critical stance toward Yasukuni Shrine visits by Japanese political leaders. Wakamiya Yoshibumi of the *Asahi shimbun* and the chair of the *Yomiuri shimbun*, Watanabe Tsuneo, both clearly opposed visits to the shrine by a Japanese prime minister.[25] Conservative *Yomiuri shimbun* also organized a special task force to investigate Japan's responsibility for the war, resulting in two widely circulated books.[26]

In his second term, Bush turned to Condoleezza Rice as secretary of state, who argued for the importance of diplomacy and multilateralism instead of the unilateral approach advocated by neoconservatives. Chris Hill was appointed assistant secretary in charge of East Asian affairs and worked hard to negotiate the Joint Statement with North Korea in September 2005. The Rice-Hill team shifted the policy line to engagement with North Korea. Conservatives within the Bush administration preempted this by imposing financial sanctions on the North Korea–related Banco Delta Asia in September 2005 in contrast to Deputy Secretary of State Robert Zoellick's signal of a policy shift in October 2005, calling China a "responsible stakeholder." The moderates' State Department approach acquired stronger support after the Democratic Party secured a majority in Congress in November 2006. The Richard Cheney and Donald Rumsfeld line was eclipsed as sincere negotiations began with North Korea on the basis of consultations with South Korea, apparently adjusting the policy of one-sided attention to Japan.

Abe took office with the appearance of coping well with the changes in the Bush administration. Defying expectations that he would follow a U.S.-only policy, he picked Beijing and Seoul for his first foreign visits in

---

[24] Takahashi Tetsuya, *Yasukuni mondai* (Tokyo: Chikuma shinsho, 2005).

[25] The dialogue was published in *Ronza*, February 2006, and later published as a book. Watanabe Tsuneo and Wakamiya Yoshibumi, *Yasukuni to Koizumi Shusho* (Tokyo: Asahi shimbun, 2006).

[26] Yomiuri shimbun, *Kensho senso sekinin* (Tokyo: Yomiuri shimbunsha, 2006).

October 2006 to ameliorate tensions. It was a pleasant surprise to U.S. policy makers as well as to regional observers. Deemed the most hawkish LDP politician, he did not visit the Yasukuni Shrine, after insisting that he would not say whether or not he would do so once elected LDP president.[27] With his ambiguous stance, he avoided criticisms from both extremes of his party and also conflicts with South Korea and Japan that would consume his political energy without giving him much diplomatic credit.

Despite his adroit handling of the Yasukuni problem, Abe's remarks on the comfort women issue emerged as a focal point of controversy in 2007. On March 1, 2007, he said during the Diet session, "There may be enforcement in mobilizing the comfort women in a broader sense, but I do not think that the Japanese government or the military was directly involved in mobilizing them."[28] Not only was this controversial in South Korea and Japan,[29] it also sent a warning signal to the U.S. Congress, because Abe's remarks came just before he was supposed to visit Washington and speak before the Congress in April. Mike Honda, a U.S. representative from California, sponsored a resolution to criticize the Japanese government, specifically the Abe cabinet, which the House of Representatives unanimously adopted in July 2007. Though it was not a signal from the Bush administration, this resolution demonstrated U.S. alarm at the increasing right-wing tone in the Japanese Diet and government. While it did not necessarily support the South Korean position, Congress warned Japan not to go too far.

The unexpected resignation of Abe on September 12, 2007, made it possible for Fukuda, an advocate of Asian diplomacy, to be the new prime minister. His close foreign policy advisers were moderates who balanced Asian diplomacy with the U.S.-Japan alliance. Although they sought improved relations with South Korea, Fukuda did not take a strong initiative for at least two reasons. One was that even he was not fully trustful of Roh, who had a strong inclination to insert history issues into the negotiating agenda and who stuck to them even after Koizumi and Abe had stepped down. His inflexible position served as a hurdle against reorienting ties to a future-oriented relationship. The other concern was

[27] *Asahi shimbun*, August 5, 2006.
[28] *Asahi shimbun*, March 3, 2007.
[29] Making Koreans even angrier was a remark by Deputy Chief Cabinet Secretary Shimomura, "During the colonial times, there were Korean parents who voluntarily sold their daughters to the comfort stations." *Dong-a ilbo*, March 27, 2007.

that the South Korean presidential election was near.[30] The opposition candidate, Lee Myung-bak, was highly favored. Japan decided to wait a few months before pursuing reconciliation.

Comforting Signs after the End of 2007

Abe definitely ameliorated relations through his Seoul and Beijing visits. Despite lurking concern about the possibility of a Yasukuni Shrine visit, China appreciated his visit and began actively upgrading relations. Two premises were behind this move.[31] First, China expected Abe not to go to the shrine, since he would know that it would reignite the controversy. Second, China was ready to take an even harder stance if he visited the shrine after his friendly gesture toward China. Premier Wen Jiabao visited Japan on April 10 through 13, 2007, conducting "smile diplomacy."

After Fukuda assumed power in September 2007, the reelection of Hu Jintao at the Seventeenth Party Congress in October 2007, which consolidated his power, facilitated an upgraded approach. After a short visit to Washington in November 2007, Fukuda picked Beijing as the place for diplomatic advancement. He visited in late December and was welcomed by Chinese leaders in an open-hearted manner,[32] as the momentum built for Hu's expected visit to Tokyo the next spring. Lee Myung-bak's victory on December 19, 2007, signified a conservative revolt against Roh's foreign policy, including policy toward North Korea viewed as appeasement without reciprocity. The anti-American rhetoric of the Roh government, despite numerous ostensibly pro-American actions, embarrassed the conservatives. In regard to Japan, conservatives were tired of Roh's preoccupation with and search for a fundamental solution to the history controversy. Normalizing ties with Japan was the conservatives' aspiration.

During and after his election, Lee repeatedly made it clear that he would revitalize relations with the United States and Japan. Regarding the history controversy with Japan, he said, "I would not ask Japan to apologize again. Nor do I seek repeated repentance from Japan. I believe

---

[30] In a personal dialogue with the author on September 26, 2007, Chief Cabinet Secretary Machimura said, "It is not time for us to make a big diplomatic move with Korea, for the presidential election is so near."

[31] Liu Jiangyong, "China-Japan Relations: Interests and Principles," speech given at the Institute for Chinese Studies at Seoul National University on October 16, 2006.

[32] *Asahi shimbun*, December 28, 2007.

the Japanese themselves will handle the issue wisely."[33] He emphasized a future-oriented relationship and tighter economic cooperation, asking Japan to invest more so that South Korea could reduce its trade deficit with Japan. Fukuda positively responded to the idea of resuming "shuttle diplomacy," while promising to come to the inauguration ceremony on February 25, 2008, and inviting Lee to the G-8 summit in Hokkaido in early July 2008.

Lee's approach toward Japan contrasted to Roh's. He did not even mention it when he gave speeches on March 1, commemorating the independence movement, and on August 15, Independence Day, in 2008 and 2009. These are times when Koreans naturally recall the decades of occupation. Moreover, he put more weight on managing ties with the United States and Japan, in contrast to Roh's emphasis on deepening reconciliation with North Korea. Symbolic of his approach was the meeting arranged between the Taguchi family and Kim Hyun-hee, a former North Korean spy who had bombed a KAL plane in 1983 and was alleged to have learned Japanese from the Taguchis' abducted daughter. Before this occasion, South Korea abstained from touching the abduction issue, high on Japan's diplomatic agenda, for fear of a negative North Korean response. Also, Seoul and Tokyo agreed to upgrade their relationship in a way that goes beyond bilateral cooperation toward regional and global collaboration. On January 11, 2009, when Lee and Aso Taro met, they launched projects that signify what both sides referred to as a "new era of Korea-Japan partnership," even forming a joint research team to prepare a strategic report, which is targeted for September 2010, on drastically upgrading relations. Finally, Lee, unlike Roh, who kept pressuring Japan to repeat its apologies, avoided any rhetoric that could be perceived as political pressure on Japan. These changes contributed to ameliorating relations.

On August 30, 2009, the Japanese electorate pushed the LDP from power while bestowing it on the DPJ. Hatoyama Yukio became the first opposition leader to serve as prime minister with the popular endorsement of the Japanese voters. He highlighted his initiative for constructing an East Asian community despite U.S. suspicions. The Lee administration refrained from opposing it, considering Hatoyama's moderate outlook on the history issue. At a meeting with Lee, Hatoyama said, "I will sincerely embrace the Murayama declaration from the bottom of my heart.

---

[33] *Dong-a ilbo*, January 18, 2008.

My government is the one that can directly face the issue of the past."[34] On the basis of mutually shared perceptions about history, the two leaders promised to construct future-oriented cooperative ties.

The territorial controversy, however, remains an unending source of conflict. The Hatoyama administration tried to avoid the worst when it publicized guidelines for high school history textbooks on December 25, 2009. Unlike the previous year's inclusion of the name Takeshima in the text, mention of this name was intentionally dropped for fear of damaging relations.[35] When Takeshima was identified in July 2008, the Japanese side had argued that the two states have different opinions and that the Japanese public should deepen its understanding about its territory, leading Lee to recall the ambassador. In the midst of massive demonstrations against the reopening of the country to U.S. beef, the July 2008 controversy with Japan sparked a harsher response. Anticipating a positive relationship between the two countries under Hatoyama, Seoul's response was restrained at the end of 2009.

Despite ameliorating relations, the situation remains volatile. In Japan, new rightists are not fading away. If their voice is heard, Koreans will respond, reigniting the history controversy. In South Korea, with the advance of the conservative forces, the new left is fragmented, but its pursuit of historical justice remains popular and could again draw widespread support. While optimism is rising, inaction is not a solution.

U.S. Strategic Options as Possibilities and Actualities

Unlike the conventional wisdom that the United States is not a player on the history issue, my view is that it has explored several options in dealing with this controversy between its allies. Four options remain as logical possibilities: active disengagement, passive disengagement, passive engagement, and active engagement. At first glance, these strategies appear to be mutually exclusive, but, in reality, the United States has tried each, depending on the changing nature and intensity of the history controversy, and there are ways to combine two or more of them.

The first strategy is to close one's eyes and stand aloof from the controversy. This strategy is not simply to disengage, but to "actively disengage." This does not mean that U.S. officials would remain unaware of the controversy; rather, it is based on a judgment that the United States has little

---

[34] *Dong-a ilbo*, October 9, 2009.
[35] *Dong-a ilbo*, December 25, 2009.

to gain if it intervenes. If entrapped, it would face the dilemma that it might possibly take the side of one at the expense of the other, which is not desirable for the regional caretaker. Also, if seriously entrapped, it could face the prospect that its own responsibility in the immediate post-war period might emerge as a related controversy. The biggest dilemma is that there is no guarantee that U.S. involvement would lead to a positive outcome. In other words, the United States has much to lose while anticipating little benefit from becoming entangled in the history controversy. Thus, many diplomats advise it to close its eyes and remain on the sidelines. "Let them solve their problems by themselves," is the prevailing advice; yet there is a possibility the controversy could develop into a crisis between allies, from which the United States could hardly stay aloof. Also, if the United States took no interest when the relationship between its allies became more positive, it would avoid trouble, but also fail to seize an opportunity to achieve a long-term breakthrough.

This strategy was followed when the history textbook controversy occurred in 2001. The principle of non-intervention in domestic affairs was kept. South Korea and China, as victimized nations, questioned the accuracy of Japanese history narratives, but the United States had no intention of becoming involved. Instead of this spat being a temporary setback in the midst of improving relations since 1998, it was a harbinger of worse problems, especially in 2005. Active disengagement did not have a positive result.

The second strategy is fence-sitting and buying time until the dust settles. This is called passive disengagement since the United States closely tracks the controversy. The conflict over Dokdo/Takeshima is a case in point, since this territorial dispute has the potential to develop into a crisis seriously affecting security ties between two allies. Aware that the island is claimed by both countries, the United States cannot support either and does not envision any role that would deter them. Hence, it tracks the dispute and welcomes improved bilateral handling of it without daring to become involved.

The third strategy of passive engagement presumes Washington can try to play the role of coordinator, mediator, or moderator without favoring a particular position. It may ask both sides to calm down and sit at the table together to negotiate. Facilitating dialogue while avoiding an intense struggle is aimed at stopping any escalation in the conflict. Concretely, the United States can send a messenger to each country to urge caution. This might be done with low visibility or it might involve a public signal to both sides.

When conflicts intensified over Koizumi's Yasukuni Shrine visits, the United States sent envoys to Japan to urge it not to provoke its neighbors by repeating these visits. This was a passive strategy in the sense that such friendly advice was offered only after failing to react to the visit on several occasions. Arguably, the United States began to act because the right-wing element of Japanese society began directly challenging the U.S. role in the Tokyo Tribunal and raised the risk of arousing anti-American sentiment in Japan. If so, it engaged not because it agreed with the South Korean position but because U.S. interests might be directly challenged if the Japanese rightists were emboldened to proceed. Another interpretation is that in 2005 the deterioration of ties between the Japanese and both the South Korean and Chinese governments had become so serious that the United States was responding in order to stabilize matters, especially against the background of the North Korean nuclear crisis.

In the fourth strategy, that of active engagement, instead of standing on the sidelines or sitting on the fence, the United States would judge the issue as a referee and play the role of a solution finder. Unlike other strategies, the United States would be obliged to make a judgment about which side is right and which is wrong, or, at least, to state its own opinion about the history controversy. This option has rarely been chosen. Even though the U.S. government did not take this position, the U.S. Congress moved along this line when Abe made a statement about the comfort women issue in 2007. At the initiative of Representative Mike Honda, the House of Representatives passed a resolution that blames the Japanese government for not apologizing or educating its people on the issue. The resolution also urged the Japanese government to take a more active stance in compensating the comfort women. Yet, those who cherish the ideal of upgrading the alliance with Japan expressed serious concern that this kind of action may jeopardize relations, being aware that Japan was dissatisfied with the resolution.[36]

All in all, the United States has favored the passive engagement approach with a view to assuaging conflicts between its allies. If this strategy did not work, it opted for an active non-engagement strategy to keep the situation from worsening. Often, the United States has adopted a passive non-engagement policy while anxiously waiting for the two allies to resolve the conflict on their own. In this case, it appeared to condone Japan's actions by not taking a position. Active engagement has

[36] *Asahi shimbun*, June 27, 2009.

been a rarity in the history controversy between the allies, but in new circumstances it may receive more consideration.

Suggestions for the U.S. Strategy: Leading by Principle, Showing by Example

All the previously discussed strategic choices have merits and demerits. Avoiding unnecessary costs while getting maximum policy feedback is the goal when the United States engages in the history controversy. Here I would like to suggest a new way of dealing with this issue in a way that serves U.S. ideals and interests. Rather than directly involving itself in the controversy, the United States can send a signal to both parties so that the allies do not misunderstand its will. Signaling can be either preemptive or postcorrective. Instead of meddling in the controversy at some risk, it can lead by principle and show by example.

First, the United States is encouraged to practice diplomacy based on the norms and principles accepted by its multilateral partners. Promoting universal norms and cherishing democratic principles have long been ideals for American diplomacy. However, unilateral and offensive imposition of the norms may bring about negative responses even from allies. Instead, the United States can spread democracy by exemplary behavior and promote universally accepted human rights principles. Those norms and principles can be a yardstick that judges actions and non-actions of others as well as the United States itself. As long as it gives primacy to these liberal values, it does not have to take a position that either South Korea or Japan advocate. Instead, it can firmly stand by its own political and diplomatic ideals. Japanese right-wing voices for restoring the honor of imperial actions overseas should be criticized as advocates of a nondemocratic regime that abridged human rights. The comfort women issue can also be judged from the universal standard of protecting human rights regardless of the historical time. Sex slavery can hardly be justified from the human rights principle. The United States can argue that it is willing to defend democracy and human rights principles regardless of the nations and periods involved, including self-criticism as appropriate.

Second, the United States should send a signal to countries in Asia that both South Korea and Japan are valued allies that showcase the successful American engagement in the region. Thanks to American support and encouragement, both countries achieved democracy as well as economic development in the postwar era. Favoring one ally at the expense of the other does not serve U.S. interests. Sending a message that the U.S.-Japan alliance is the cornerstone of the alliance system in the region while the U.S.–South Korean alliance is a secondary concern not only distorts the strategic landscape in the region but also discourages a cooperative spirit among the allies. This was the case in May 2005, when Yachi Shotaro asserted, "Since the U.S. seems not to believe the Korean government, Japan cannot share information about North Korea with the Korean government."[37] Balanced alliance management that enables the United States to keep its interests intact in both states is critically important. When the two key allies in the region are duly managed, the United States will have more space for strategic maneuvering in Northeast Asia.

If the United States opts for Japan while downgrading the alliance with South Korea, the latter is likely to bandwagon with China, which will reduce the potential for flexible U.S. diplomacy in the region. If it gives more priority to South Korea while giving little attention to Japan, Japan is highly prone to pursue more independent and autonomous action that relies less on the United States. This would put Asia in jeopardy of an escalating arms race. Hence, managing the dual partnership in Northeast Asia with a sense of balance not only stabilizes the region but also serves U.S. interests. Finally, the United States had better be anchored in Asia with a spirit of promoting regional collaboration. A conflict-ridden Asia is not in long-term U.S. interests. To maintain its status as an offshore balancer, it can better constrain conflicts between allies in the region by working comfortably with other regional powers, including China. Geopolitics comes into play when the history controversy is mishandled. When the divide between South Korea and Japan intensifies, the country that gains most in the strategic landscape of Northeast Asia is China. If South Korea drifts away from Japan not because it willingly opts for China but because it reluctantly reacts to the history controversy, China obtains untold benefits. Hence, the United States has an incentive to hold the two allies together for its own interests, not out of benevolence.

[37] *Dong-a ilbo*, May 25, 2005.

6

U.S. Strategic Thinking on the Japanese–South Korean Historical Dispute

Gilbert Rozman

In 2005, Japanese–South Korean relations deteriorated in the face of differences over historical memories and a related territorial dispute. Similar downturns had occurred periodically over a quarter-century, and few expected these differences to be overcome or to lose their explosive potential. In 2009, new leadership in each country pledged to build a future-oriented relationship, avoiding any impasse over historical memories. With the DPJ, led by Hatoyama Yukio, replacing the revisionist-driven LDP, and Lee Myung-bak at the head of South Korean conservatives determined not to repeat Roh Moo-hyun's outbursts, hopes had again risen for full normalization of relations between two U.S. allies whose shared threat perceptions should draw them closer and facilitate triangular cooperation. While the new situation could reinforce U.S. optimism that history is fading as a problem and the best response is to maintain an attitude of non-involvement, another option is to seize the opportunity to play an active role by addressing history in a manner that could diminish its future impact. Reviewing past U.S. responses and new circumstances, this chapter scrutinizes developments in 2006 through 2009 to assess prospects for a breakthrough.

The United States has avoided involvement in the history issue that divides its two allies in Northeast Asia. Although Americans mostly sympathize with South Korea's position, sharing condemnation of Japan's militarism in the years leading to its defeat in August 1945, they attach low priority to addressing the issue. Geopolitically, it could be costly in alienating powerful Japanese politicians with whom the United States has made common cause. Few experts anticipate a shift in the foreseeable future,[1] given enduring interest in solidifying the alliance with Japan as the cornerstone of the long-term policy of constraining China's rise as the next superpower and also maintaining a forward military presence in a fast-changing region critical to global politics and economics. Yet, recently changing circumstances give cause for reconsidering how Washington may become more active in managing the history issue or, at least, in reshaping the context in which it arises. In this chapter, I explore these circumstances under four headings: (1) a snapshot of assumptions about national identities and their impact; (2) a chronology of U.S. attention to the history issue when it has arisen in Japanese–South Korean relations; (3) a review of the evolving context in 2006–8, including multifaceted values in Northeast Asia and multiple triangles, of which the U.S.–Japan–South Korean triangle is one; and (4) analysis of the changed context in 2009, as a new strategic environment altered the choices to be faced in Washington after a presidential election brought a new party to power in Japan and an elected South Korean president put his strong imprint on the way history is being treated.

Assumptions about National Identities and Their Impact

Three longstanding assumptions about national identities frame the foreign policy triangle of the United States, Japan, and South Korea. First, the United States is driven by principles, spreading its ideals and working with allies to base relations on trust rooted in frank discussion to deepen awareness of shared ideals. Second, Japan is a pragmatic nation that responded to defeat by setting ideology aside in favor of economic nationalism and political and military dependency on its ally to rally its citizens around shared objectives. Third, South Korea is a beleaguered state in a divided nation in the midst of four great powers, focusing on maximizing leverage on North Korea as it relies on its ally while positioning itself to draw support from the others. As Japan grew closer to U.S. human rights values as well as tightening its alliance and as South Korea democratized and faced new threats from a nuclear North Korea, cold war assumptions seemed even more applicable. With Bill Clinton assuming office focused on "human rights" and financial globalization

---

[1] Interviews with ten current and former State Department officials active in U.S. relations with Japan and South Korea reveal a strong consensus to avoid damaging relations by becoming involved in historical disputes; yet, there was also support for working together in search of a broader framework for reassessing these disputes.

in the face of "Asian values," and George W. Bush eager to "spread democracy" while demonizing the "axis of evil," values shared within the "alliance triangle" gained new prominence.[2]

Realities have defied the preceding assumptions not so much due to realist concerns regarding changing threats but because national identities proved to be different from what was assumed. In the cold war era, the United States had been frustrated in spreading its ideals to Japan and South Korea as well as in forging three-way ties that would supersede the clash over history between its two allies, but this was attributed to temporary factors: Japan's left-wing political forces were blocking the LDP from adopting a foreign policy of international responsibility, South Korea's dictators defied the "free world " principles of their ally, and older generations were seen as harboring memories that impeded efforts to heal the wounds of the colonial era. While memories obstructed efforts to improve Japanese–South Korean relations or any U.S. interest in playing an active role through three-way discussions of shared principles, optimism endured that the situation would improve. A democratic South Korea, the end of the cold war, the decline of the left, Japan's reawakening to the importance of U.S. ties, and North Korea's isolation and fixation on WMD all were expected to solidify the intra-alliance value consensus.

In 2005–8, U.S. engagement in a triangular discussion about values including history seemed more difficult than ever. Three discomforting generalizations lead to this conclusion. First, it had squandered moral authority with ill-timed or dubious invocations of values for foreign policy ventures, as a divided U.S. national identity had led to values being invoked in ways that conflicted with realist interests, undermining its international prestige. Claims to the moral high ground, even with Japan and South Korea, invited charges of hypocrisy. Anti-Americanism had spread around the world. George W. Bush had lost support among Americans. Given this legacy, caution was in order. Second, even as it accused Seoul as well as Beijing of playing the "history card" for foreign policy gain, Japan's leaders were also playing it in pursuit of a desired national identity and also as a substitute for a strategic approach toward Asia. Moreover, in 2007 the Japanese became more attuned to differences over history with the United States that increased the chances of spillover from disputes between it and South Korea. Because the U.S.-Japanese history gap is newly explosive, a dangerous downward spiral may play into the

---

[2] Gilbert Rozman, "Japan and South Korea: Should the U.S. Be Worried about Their New Spat in 2001?" *Pacific Review*, Vol. 15, No. 1 (2002), pp. 1–28.

hands of fervent nationalists. Third, events in 2005–7 suggested that the acute South Korean divide between conservatives and progressives on national identity, the unpredictability of relations with North Korea, the dearth of strategic debate over Japan's future role in the region, and the potential volatility of history issues linked to past U.S. activities recommend against opening the Pandora's Box of history. This was the thinking only a few years ago.

Given this reasoning, it was easy to caution U.S. officials not to risk the major bulwark of stability in Northeast Asia – the U.S. dual alliances – on the improbability that a triangular framework could be achieved, in which Japanese–South Korean ties would be strengthened and the United States would enhance the role of values in these alliances. This conclusion held even among those aware that there is a price to pay at a time of recurrent nationalist arousal for not putting to rest simmering resentments over history. All three pairings in the triangle suffer. Arguably, Japan is the biggest loser. It will be unlikely to overcome strategic isolation in Asia, will continue to be marginalized in dealings over the Korean peninsula, and will be in danger of losing more respect in the international community, including the United States. It had the most compelling reason for rethinking its approach to history; until it did so, the United States and South Korea had best show patience, even if disadvantaged by this outcome. The U.S. alliance with Japan is not as sturdy without frank reconciliation over historical differences that percolate below the surface, and its ties with South Korea in a triangle where Japan is favored are diminished. Moreover, a values consensus for shaping a new regional framework is harder to reach. Finally, South Korean foreign policy can be distorted by allowing the history issue to reduce realist maneuvering among the great powers. The status quo is not satisfactory, but that does not justify an idealistic approach that could do more harm than good.

By 2010, a very different environment was taking shape. In the wake of Bush's counterproductive manipulation of values for an extreme agenda, Koizumi and Abe stirring nationalist emotions that isolated Japan in Asia, and Roh's unbalanced, emotional approach to Japan, a new set of leaders has refrained from similar behavior. First, Lee set his sights on improving ties with both the United States and Japan, taking a realist view of inter-Korean relations. Already, he drew close to Bush in meetings in 2008, but signs of convergence in thinking intensified when Obama visited Seoul in November 2009, making this the high point of his travel in Asia in contrast to his troubled summit with Hatoyama in Tokyo. Second, Obama made engagement the centerpiece of a foreign policy that reframed realist and value differences to avoid posturing and maximize multilateral cooperation. After reassuring Lee that Obama's attempts to draw Kim Jong-il into talks would not marginalize his country, Obama proved his mettle in December 2009 by sending Stephen Bosworth to Pyongyang in order to revive these multiparty talks without removing UN sanctions or reducing pressure for denuclearization. Third, Hatoyama, in his first months in office, shook up the status quo more than any other leader had since the end of the U.S. occupation, calling into question the alliance in ways that provoked a searching review and promoting an East Asian community with China and South Korea despite doubts. His attempt to draw closer to South Korea but not the United States occurred against the backdrop of an assertive China. After its October 1 sixtieth anniversary "liberation" ceremony, an October summit with Kim Jong-il centered on boosting economic ties, a chilly November hosting of Obama, December confrontational tactics at the Copenhagen climate change summit, and signs of opposition to tough sanctions against Iran promised by Obama, China revealed a new boldness worrisome to the other three states. Yet, in an October three-way summit and later meetings, China tried to forge an East Asian community, actively striving to pull Japan and South Korea away from their ally.

The China challenge coupled with the North Korean threat increases the realist rationale for Japan and South Korea to draw closer, but there is also another rationale in which historical memory plays a part. After all, the formation of a community assumes shared values. In their October summit, leaders of China, Japan, and South Korea agreed to write a joint history, recognizing the importance not only of narrowing this divide but also of building the foundation in longstanding historical interactions for future ties. Responding to the challenge in November, Obama called for an Asia-Pacific community. This too draws attention to the need for a shared history, especially among the three states in the U.S. alliance system. Narrowing the history gap of Tokyo and Seoul can serve this aim and contribute to a balanced historical outlook on the East Asian community too.

The stark challenges ahead in Northeast Asia argue for addressing the history disputes between Japan and South Korea as part of a broader context when conditions are suitable. Far-reaching changes in the security environment are eliciting political changes in each country that contribute to fresh debates about national identity. A more consistent, respected U.S. foreign agenda is regaining moral authority that was lost. Japan's internal debate about history is intersecting with recent groping for a more sustainable strategic agenda in Asia. South Korea is moving beyond the tumultuous reactions to U.S. and North Korean unilateral moves to achieve a new level of agreement over foreign policy and the identity issues that underscore it. Thus, U.S. preparations for a regional approach inclusive of values and history may now gain genuine support in the other two countries.

Past U.S. Attention to the History Issue: Lessons to Be Learned

For a half-century, U.S. policy makers have wrestled with the challenge of turning the two bilateral alliances in Northeast Asia into a whole greater than the sum of its parts. Whereas in Europe NATO drew allies together, ties to Japan and South Korea were of a hub and two spokes, for which even the concept of a "virtual triangle" only slowly gained credibility.[3] If U.S. efforts, in stages, made limited progress, they repeatedly failed to realize the expectations of new administrations, whether Lyndon Johnson at the time of the Vietnam War, Richard Nixon in search of Asianization during that war, Jimmy Carter anxious to apply a human rights approach to South Korea and achieve reconciliation in the region, Ronald Reagan intent on containing the Soviet Union's aggressive moves in Asia, Bill Clinton struggling with the first nuclear crisis over North Korea, or George W. Bush in opposition to China as a strategic competitor and to North Korea as part of the "axis of evil" and later in search of coordination in the Six-Party Talks and alliance upgrades to meet new security challenges. Forging a genuine alliance triangle proved to be an elusive goal not only because neither Japan nor South Korea was willing to anchor its foreign policy on a realist assessment of regional dangers, but also because the two took sharply opposing views of historical issues perceived as critical to their identities.

One of the most compelling arguments against U.S. involvement is that, with nationalist emotions on both sides focused on a history long inflammable, such involvement might trigger a downward spiral of accusations and counteraccusations targeted at historical behavior by the United States. The Japanese have generally exercised caution in pointing to the "barbaric" U.S. atomic bombing of Hiroshima and Nagasaki, the Tokyo Tribunal "victor's justice," or the "provocative sanctions" that preceded Pearl Harbor, but widespread dissatisfaction with these and other past U.S. actions coupled with traces of "anti-Americanism" amid

---

[3] Victor Cha, *Alignment Despite Antagonism: The Korea-Japan Security Triangle* (Stanford: Stanford University Press, 1999).

continuing dependency could trigger a chain reaction. Similarly, South Koreans in positions of power long refrained from voicing misgivings about alleged U.S. willingness to sacrifice their country in favor of U.S. interests, as in the mutual acquiescence to colonialism after the Russo–Japanese War, the division of the peninsula with the Soviet Union to conclude World War II, the wartime atrocities committed by U.S. as well as South Korean troops during the Korean War, and the alleged approval of Chun Doo-hwan's bloody crackdown at Kwangju. By inserting itself into bilateral recriminations over history, Washington may open the door to both sides venting their long-suppressed grievances toward it. In turn, heightened American public sensitivity to the beleaguered position of their country may make a backlash more likely if matters at the core of American pride are called into question. This includes self-satisfaction over help given to these two states, as allies and friends, in the shift to democracy, human rights, and all-around modernization.

Even if U.S. leaders had reason to become involved in the history issue, they could not avoid considering how to do so effectively. Is an informal role more likely to be productive than formal, open assertion of the U.S. position? Is there a broader context that can be invoked in order to reduce emotionalism and center the debate on common interests that overshadow historical differences? How would it justify its involvement to satisfy the public in both South Korea and Japan and to avoid a backlash at home if any acknowledgment of past U.S. shortcomings is required? What can we learn from past U.S. efforts to deal with these matters, such as Ambassador Walter Mondale's visit to a Tokyo bombing anniversary remembrance, cancellation of the Smithsonian Museum's Enola Gay display, and Deputy Secretary of State Robert Zoellick's inquiries about how U.S. help might cool the emotions between Koizumi and Roh over the Yasukuni Shrine visits and the territorial dispute. Northeast Asian specialists in the State Department recognize the intractability of the history issue and advised against U.S. involvement. From time to time, a high official will inquire, with the European model of reconciliation in mind, about an active U.S. role to promote some sort of compromise. What such newcomers to the issue may overlook is the danger that this would rekindle the embers of historical resentment centered on perceived U.S. injustices. This is the message gleaned from officials privy to past discussions, but it does not mean that no way forward exists.

Experts agree that Congress should not pass resolutions of the sort that angered Japan in July and Turkey in October 2007. Complicating relations with allies makes the job of the executive branch more difficult. If Congress may at times take a stand to contrast with an executive position that is seen as damaging the national interest, the feel-good moralizing of 2007 had no such justification. Yet, the executive branch too should not so undermine the moral authority of the United States that Congress is driven to act. It should not stand by as Japanese leaders such as Abe call into question the moral fabric of Japan's postwar reconciliation, taking instead a more forthright stance to putting regional alliance ties, in which values matter, on a secure footing. U.S. officials who loudly trumpet universal values do not meet the expectations of many by dismissing history issues, as did those who demonized North Korea without prioritizing consensus.

In a twenty-five–year span, four U.S. presidents – two Democrats and two Republicans – took office with a strong commitment to asserting values along with their notions of American national identity into foreign policy. The effects in Northeast Asia proved to be negative: Jimmy Carter's human rights approach to South Korea and idealistic rush to achieve reconciliation with North Korea; Ronald Reagan's alienation of China with his initial Taiwan-centered approach and indifference to Chun Doo-hwan's domestic image because of an obsession with countering the Soviet "evil empire"; Bill Clinton's human rights approach to China and initial haste to consider a preemptive strike as an option with North Korea; and George W. Bush's "axis of evil" approach to North Korea coupled with democratization as a kind of panacea. If at times informal, quiet diplomacy might have served a more constructive purpose, each leader paraded his value-based diplomacy before Asians with scant appreciation of the complicated mixture of values in regional affairs. That does not mean that future presidents should eschew any mention of values, but it does alert us to the importance of starting with awareness of priorities in the region and tailoring discussions of values to the leadership and exigencies currently present. "Do no harm" takes precedence before doing some good can be prudently explored.

Obama already established in his first year that he is the president least fearful of addressing values issues in a complex way. Already before and during his November visit to Tokyo, he faced the question of whether he would visit Hiroshima without dismissing the possibility. His close rapport with Lee suggests that the two are better positioned than prior leadership tandems to delve deeply into the history of relations without the South Korean side needing to pander to a nationalist base. Obama's troubled start with the DPJ raises the likelihood that the alliance will undergo reexamination, justifying U.S. preparation to view it in a broad historical context and to involve both the Japanese and South Koreans in a reassessment of the cold war. Neither country has a suitably positive image of what they accomplished as U.S. allies, allowing a sense of abnormality as a defeated power or the absence of democracy to overshadow a shared experience that deserves to be recalled as overwhelmingly positive in building trust for continued alliance relations.

Multiple Triangles in 2006–2008

The East Asian alliance triangle operates in the context of multiple triangles: the strategic triangle of U.S.-Soviet-Chinese relations of the cold war that now is reviving to some extent with greater Russian assertiveness; the Sino–Soviet–North Korean triangle that was paramount for North Korea and under Vladimir Putin drew Russian interest; the core historical triangle of Sino–Japanese–South Korea relations still plagued by Japan's past misconduct even as it produces economic integration conducive to regionalism; the Japanese–South Korea–North Korea triangle that could play a role in the economics of reunification; the triangle of the U.S.-South Korea–North Korea now intertwined with the nuclear crisis; and the Sino–South Korea–North Korea triangle most critical for peninsular integration. Just one of eight triangles relevant to Korean affairs, the U.S.-Japanese–South Korean triangle, deserves more attention for its regional impact.

The alliance triangle is more than a military arrangement between one hub and two spokes and a virtual political alliance in which one weak leg contrasts with two very strong legs pivoting on the United States. It also has a significant cultural component that operates in the context of the multiple regional triangles. As the strategic triangle evolved in the 1950s through the 1980s, the alliance triangle hung solidly as an anchor for U.S. power in Asia with an ideological component contrasting with totalitarianism. The alliance triangle also set the foundation for facing the cultural issues in the core historical triangle even though the United States is outside the East Asian sphere and its emergent regionalism through ASEAN + 3, the East Asian Summit, and recent steps by China, Japan, and South Korea to institutionalize three-way ties. As Japan struggles to coordinate policies to South and North Korea, completing normalization of relations in all respects a century after its annexation of the peninsula in 1910, the shadow of the United States falls across its path.

In 2007, the alliance triangle remained, on the surface, much as it had been in recent years, but, beneath the surface, powerful tremors were shaking its very foundation. The Abe-Bush April summit brought more solemn pledges of a close attachment between two allies drawing ever closer; yet the atmosphere was more troubled than in Koizumi's farewell "Graceland" summit the previous summer when the two leaders were in accord, even in their populist embrace of Elvis Presley's singing. If Roh and Bush were able to continue regular consultations that led to an FTA and mutual assurance of implementation of the February 13 Joint Agreement in the Six-Party Talks, the vast gulf between policies toward North Korea and Japan was not narrowing. They did not hold a summit to celebrate their FTA, and at the APEC meetings in Sydney, the news centered on Bush's insistence on denuclearization as a prerequisite in the face of Roh's appeal to advance quickly to a peace regime as he set the agenda for a summit with Kim Jong-il. Meanwhile, Abe and Roh had little follow-up to their perfunctory summit in October 2006, as each leader continued to be vilified in the other country as worse than any previous leader since normalization in 1965. Japan's media left little doubt of their hope for a conservative victory in the presidential elections, while Abe's departure was a relief to South Koreans bombarded with attacks against his revisionist outlook on history. Many in Japan accuse South Koreans of never being satisfied with Japan's apologies on history, despairing that they should even bother to seek common ground and arguing that Seoul reneged on its side of the Obuchi-Kim agreement on history. As evidence, they contrast Hu Jintao's effort to reach an accommodation with Abe during his year in office to Roh's assumption that any such attempt would be useless. Earlier South Korean politicians had been schooled in Japanese and had a good understanding of their counterparts, and they had steered ties through various minefields; however, with the April 2004 National Assembly elections, the careers of the last of these politicians ended. The loss of confidence in Japan in the management of relations added to the sense of hopelessness. This situation was soon to change rapidly.

Views of the U.S. role in the postwar era start from perceptions of how the war ended, which drew attention in 2007 when Defense Minister Kyuma Fumio spoke of the U.S. atomic bombs as if there had been no way to avoid dropping them, causing his firing amid charges that he was talking like a member of the U.S. government. Publication of Tsuyoshi Hasegawa's book in Japanese soon after the English-language edition appeared provided scholarly depth to the discussion of the bombs, as did his *Chuo koron* article reflecting on the Kyuma remarks and the debate that followed.[4] South Koreans too have shown renewed interest in whether the Truman administration ended the war responsibly. Debates swirled on how to evaluate the U.S. occupation of Japan, the Tokyo Tribunal, the San Francisco Peace Treaty, and the circumstances that led to the Korean War.

Abductions, especially of young girls, are powerful symbols of outrage. When Abe in 2007 was poised to carry Japan's revisionist agenda further with words of denial about the sex slaves whom Japan had mobilized, largely from Korea, Abe was rallying the Japanese people against the North Korean abductions of youngsters from Japanese soil. In this situation, the U.S. response to Japan was more vigorous, pressuring Abe to drop revisionist treatment of a matter that would enrage Koreans by linking support for his abductions issue to it.[5] This drew a new connection, keeping the most sensitive value issues in the region from eclipsing the U.S. agenda, but it did not narrow the values gap.

An unexpected test for U.S. involvement in the history issue arose in 2007 when the House of Representatives spent a long time considering Mike Honda's resolution critical of Japan's handling of the comfort women issue, which finally passed on July 30. Abe's April U.S. visit occurred under the cloud of this resolution. Introduced in January with wording that called on Japan to accept total responsibility for its wartime conduct and formally apologize and make restitution, the resolution was debated on February 15 at a subcommittee hearing. Yet, only after Abe's statements before the press in Tokyo on March 1 that no proof existed that the Japanese military had resorted to force and that the Kono Yohei 1993 statement of apology was deficient did the U.S. mass media become aroused, with the *New York Times* and *Washington Post* taking the lead, even denouncing the hypocrisy of harshly criticizing North Korea for its abductions while having abducted tens of thousands in this fashion.[6] Having remained aloof to historical issues between Japan and its neighbors, Washington suddenly acknowledged their trilateral nature. If some in Japan saw this as the China and Korea lobbies at work,[7] others paid

---

[4] Togo Kazuhiko, *Rekishi to gaiko*, pp. 213–14; Hasegawa Tsuyoshi, "Migi kara no genbaku hihan ga motarasu Nichibei domei no kiki," *Chuo koron*, No. 9 (2007), pp. 192–9.

[5] *Japan Times*, November 9, 2007.

[6] Tan Romi, " 'Jogun weianfu to China robi' no shinjitsu," *Gekkan gendai* (June 2007), pp. 84–5.

[7] Ibid., pp. 86–8.

attention to Honda's words, recognizing the widening impact of history issues on regional security.[8]

A new concern in Japan is that lobbying may be influencing U.S. policy, initially through the Congress. Some charged that lobbying by Chinese and Korean communities backed by generous donations to political campaigns accounted for the success of the Honda resolution.[9] Norman Hsu, who was arrested as a fugitive and convicted after serving as a major fundraiser and donor to politicians, drew attention from those inclined to see an Asian American conspiracy after being identified as hosting a birthday party for Honda in his district and bundling donations to various Democrats from many Chinese Americans.[10] Such suspicions cast a dark shadow on the way the history issue was handled.

When in October 2007 the United States House of Representatives debated a resolution on genocide against Armenians, *Sankei shimbun* pointed to the damage this threatened to cause in relations with Turkey, the only U.S. Islamic ally and a state on which the United States depends for supplying its troops in Iraq.[11] There was no need to mention that a similar resolution critical of Japan's historical conduct months earlier also jeopardized vital alliance ties in a manner defiant of realism as well as morally dubious. Another article linked U.S. betrayal of a "loyal ally" to immigrant communities concentrated in the districts of certain congressmen.[12] It follows that Japan should do as Turkey has done in asserting its own importance to the United States. This reasoning leaves no doubt that the honor of the postwar is tied to pride in wartime behavior, grouping Japan's sole ally with the Asian states that must be resisted and told of history's likely adverse impact.

Some on the Japanese right consider that they had made a tacit agreement with officials in the United States that closer alliance ties and mutual trust mean avoiding the history issue. With the Honda resolution and the departure from the Bush administration of many of those considered pro-Japan, questions were raised about whether this bargain was sticking. Influential LDP adviser Okazaki Hisahiko suggested that it was not, warning that pro-China and anti-Japan groups are gaining influence. This shift from the first term of George W. Bush was linked to the problems of the Iraq War and signs of a retreat from Asia leaving Japan isolated and a

[8] Tokudone Kinue, "Beigeingiin Michael Honda ni kiku," *Ronza* (June 2007), pp. 76–82.
[9] *Sankei shimbun*, August 31, 2007, p. 6.
[10] *Sankei shimbun*, October 13, 2007, p. 7.
[11] *Sankei shimbun*, October 16, 2007, p. 6.
[12] *Sankei shimbun*, October 28, 2007, p. 11.

vacuum that China is filling.[13] Newly isolated, Japan must pursue a more independent foreign policy, conservatives and progressives argued.

The Japanese were unduly harsh on South Korean motives for troubling bilateral relations, concentrating on "appeasement" to the North and the danger of Japan under a weak leader becoming entangled in it as a cash-dispensing machine abandoning its own national interests, such as the abductees.[14] At the same time, South Koreans exaggerated the driving forces behind Japan's actions toward Dokdo/Takeshima as if it were part of a far-reaching change in foreign policy that could threaten security in the region. Roh and Koizumi as well as Abe did not take steps to overcome these extreme interpretations.

Abe's final international moves as prime minister exposed the values dilemma he faced. At the APEC summit in early September 2007, he made it clear that the abductions issue was Japan's number one issue and suggested that his trip would be a success to the extent that other countries recognized its importance, while other states optimistically maneuvered for the endgame of the nuclear crisis. At the same time, as Great Britain under its new prime minister, Gordon Brown, pulled back from full support of George W. Bush on Iraq and APEC host Australia had entered an election process in which Prime Minister John Howard seemed likely to lose along with unconditional support for the United States in Iraq, Abe seemed to be Bush's last avid backer. Given the impression that Bush had abandoned Abe on the North Korean issue and that the Minshuto leader, Ozawa Ichiro, would refuse to let the Upper House, which his party now controlled, extend the law allowing Japan to provide logistical support to the United States and NATO in Afghanistan, Abe appeared helpless in dealing with Japan's ally. As the United States heralded the new atmosphere in normalization talks with the North in Geneva, Japan could only respond to its failed talks in Mongolia with an extension of unilateral sanctions. Yet, in order to improve the atmosphere for the Mongolian working group, Abe had agreed to devote the first day of the two-day meeting to discussing how the unhappy past between the two sides might be settled. He brought history back to bilateral talks, as many assumed that this meant large-scale economic compensation plus a perfunctory apology of the sort issued before.[15]

[13] *Sankei shimbun*, August 30, 2007, p. 13.
[14] *Sankei shimbun*, October 14, 2007, p. 3.
[15] *Asahi shimbun*, September 5, 2007, p. 7.

Values have been rising to the forefront in Japanese and South Korean diplomacy in spite of the seriousness of the nuclear crisis. Abe Shinzo stressed advancing relations with countries that have shared values, while his foreign minister, Aso Taro, spoke of a "values diplomacy" (*kachi no gaiko*) along with the "arc of freedom and prosperity." This is a big switch from Japan's distancing itself from U.S. values–based diplomacy and insisting on Japanese values as well as Asian values, blaming the Tokyo Tribunal for hypocritical application of so-called universal values after the war. Yet, as Tanaka Akihiko observes, this raises the issue of how to reconcile Japan's approach to the historical consciousness question (*rekishi ninshiki mondai*) with its new advocacy of universal values.[16] As Fukuda toned down talk of both historical and universal values (the Yasukuni Shrine, comfort women, and the arc of freedom and prosperity faded from sight), confusion reigned over whether a U.S.-Japanese value consensus existed.

The U.S. response could be affected by joint nationalism of the two Koreas. Some in Japan argued that this was happening already, for example, in the complementary moves at the United Nations to gain recognition for the name East Sea along with or in place of the Japan Sea. As preparations for the inter-Korean summit proceeded, there was some speculation in Japan that the two regimes would find common ground by pressing Japan together on such themes,[17] fusing nationalism through history and territory issues. After all, when Japanese raises the abduction issue with North Korea, it responds with demands for making amends for Japan's colonial past, while South Koreans cannot avoid being torn between two competing value systems. With Lee's election, concern dropped of inter-Korean nationalism trumping shared democratic values.

Briefly the apology issue was reversed on October 24, 2007, when a South Korean government committee acknowledged for the first time that the South had kidnapped Kim Dae-jung in August 1973, violating Japan's sovereignty. When the ambassador to Japan on October 30 expressed regrets, Fukuda was quick to accept this as sufficient and stress future relations. Indeed, Japan's failure to defend Kim Dae-jung's human rights in a case of abduction with parallels to what happened to those taken to North Korea led some to call for a Japanese government apology.[18]

---

[16] Tanaka Akihiko, "Iu wa yasuku okinau wa kataki (bukkakan gaiko)," *Foresight* (July 2007), p. 27.

[17] *Sankei shimbun*, August 31, 2007, p. 2.

[18] *Asahi shimbun*, October 25, 2007, p. 3; November 29, 2007, p. 18.

Kim had fueled this criticism by charging that Japan had abandoned its responsibility to protect him, not insisting on his return to Japan after he had been abducted, and, when he was sentenced to death years later, not pleading for his life.[19] Yet, a more common media response was to demand a formal South Korean apology for violating Japan's sovereignty,[20] unlikely as it would be given the way Japan has handled the demands of its past victims for apologies.

The Japanese right wing not only criticized Kim Dae-jung and Roh Moo-hyun and their progressive policies, especially toward North Korea, but also attacked both South Korean conservatives and Japanese pragmatists in search of a shared regional strategy as well as Chris Hill and the Bush administration after the shift at the end of 2006. The abduction issue became their most successful lever in claiming to be purer than others in defending sovereignty and national identity.[21] With Yasukuni stubbornness losing its luster since Koizumi left office and Abe had failed on the comfort women issue, attention shifted to abductions as a surrogate for firmness on the history issue. Since this theme involves the Korean peninsula and tests coordination with the United States and South Korea most of all, it became linked to the struggle over history. Without removing this cudgel from the hands of those wielding it as a weapon against consensus, progress on the history issue is unlikely. With Abe's tenure judged a failure and Fukuda, however short his tenure, able to raise the credibility of a moderate course, prospects had improved for a favorable reception to an initiative from Seoul backed by Washington.

Japanese commentators recognized the shift toward pragmatism in South Korean thinking in 2007, from politics to economics and from change to stability. As the sense of danger over the North lessened, the divide between pro- and anti-America no longer drew so much attention, and regional loyalties were diminishing, a more mature democracy was recognized.[22] In this context, Lee Myung-bak's desire to improve relations with the United States and Japan drew considerable attention. Despite awareness that he along with the other candidates paid attention to the issues of Yasukuni Shrine and historical consciousness, there was a basis for cooperation on realist grounds and on values.[23]

---

[19] *Asahi shimbun*, October 31, 2007, p. 30.
[20] *Mainichi shimbun*, October 25, 2007, p. 5.
[21] *Sankei shimbun*, October 17, 2007, p. 15.
[22] *Mainichi shimbun*, November 26, 2007, p. 7.
[23] *Asahi shimbun*, November 26, 2007, p. 2.

With Fukuda's pragmatic Asian diplomacy on display at the ASEAN
+ 3 and EAS meetings in Singapore in November and his visit to China
in December, most eyes in Japan were fixed above all on the presidential
election in South Korea. On the one hand, it would signal the end of Roh
Moo-hyun's leadership, which was roundly blamed for the deterioration
of bilateral relations. On the other, increasingly it became clear that the
election would usher in a conservative era, when Japan would have an
opportunity to rebuild ties. Apart from anticipating a different tone from
Lee Myung-bak, the Japanese were faced with a need to reflect on what
they should do and how the United States entered the picture. The mood
at the start of 2008 held promise for initiatives that encompass values
issues.

Some observers, especially in Japan, conclude that values are drawing
the Japanese and South Koreans closer, if only politicians would find a
way to capitalize on this. In 1998–2004, the Japanese took the lead in
pointing to improving cultural ties, including the removal of restrictions
on cultural imports from Japan, the surge in Japanese tourism to South
Korea, and the wave of Korean dramas attracting Japanese television
viewers. In 2005–6, when Japanese visitors to South Korea dipped and
political relations soured, less attention was given to this cultural boom.
Yet, the gradual improvement in relations after Abe's 2006 visit to Seoul
renewed interest in the surge in tourism, as South Korean tourists soon
outnumbered Japanese tourists after visa-free visits were reciprocated.[24]
Politicians can build on expanded cultural relations to overcome the
lingering tensions over history.

As presented by Kim Dae-jung in a talk at Ritsumeikan University,
the South Korean position is unsustainable, lumping together increased
military preparations in Japan, constitutional revision, and textbook distortions about the past as markers of educational failings that lead to
ignorance about Japan's historical behavior.[25] It confuses revisionism
with realism, denying Japan the right to take measured responses to the
rapidly changing security environment in East Asia. To make progress on
the history issue, South Koreans must acknowledge Japan's defense needs
and forge with the United States an understanding acceptable to realists
in Japan rather than hoping for some magical return to the idealist era
when the Japanese accepted some degree of pacifism or, at least, passive dependence on the United States alliance. Lee Myung-bak is doing

[24] *Nihon keizai shimbun*, evening, October 17, 2007, p. 15.
[25] *Asahi shimbun*, October 31, 2007, p. 12.

that, appreciating the value of the Trilateral Coordination and Oversight Group (TCOG) as a forum that Roh had let atrophy since 2004.

The death of Kim Dae-jung on August 18, 2009, brought testimonials to his long-time affection for Japan. He had spent his first two decades studying in Japanese under Japan's rule, stayed in Japan after his defeat in the 1971 presidential election until South Korean agents kidnapped him in 1973, and in October 1998 achieved the historic breakthrough that opened his country to Japanese culture and led to the "Korea boom" in Japan.[26] More than anyone else, he deserves credit for changing the momentum in relations, reducing distrust as a leader after contributing to it indirectly through his struggle for democracy.[27] Yet, Kim's decision to pursue Pyongyang even without reciprocity or real coordination with Washington and Seoul, compounded by Japanese leaders' insensitivity on matters linked to history, put obstacles in the way of this rapprochement, which intensified under Roh. With Kim at odds with Lee and Japan poised to turn power over to the DPJ, Kim's legacy fell short of setting a course for reconciliation. In 2010, as the Japanese and Koreans made preparations for the one hundredth anniversary of the annexation of Korea, it would again be difficult to avoid historical memories despite new leaders on both sides eager to do so.

History rises to the forefront when priorities become confused. Indeed, those most eager to stress history are apt to latch onto emotional issues as a means to cast doubt on a balanced foreign policy. Such is what occurred when *Sankei shimbun*, at a time of some momentum in the Six-Party Talks, insisted that Fukuda must inform Bush during his November 2007 visit that the most important thing for Japan is the abduction question and warn him that the alliance would be seriously eroded if the United States were to go forward with plans to remove North Korea from the list of states that support terror even contingent on its steps toward disablement and declaration of its nuclear assets.[28] This paper and the groups it represents were shifting the blame to the United States as well as to certain politicians and media in Japan, who supposedly were leaving additional abduction victims without any hope of rescue. In opposition to Fukuda's weak policy toward Asia, Japan's right wing was pointing to the United States as the latest culprit (after North Korea, China, and South Korea). Policies to the North had become the final rallying point in order to

[26] *Yomiuri shimbun*, August 19, 2009, p. 7.
[27] *Asahi shimbun*, August 19, 2009, p. 3.
[28] *Sankei shimbun*, November 15, 2007, pp. 3, 19.

salvage the case for historical revisionism linked to the symbol of victimized Japanese; with the South already regarded as beyond redemption,
it was now the turn of the United States to incur the wrath of the right
wing.

The increased vehemence and fervent search for new targets suggest
that ultranationalists had become more desperate. Bush's shift to mod-
eration coupled with the loss of popularity in the United States of the
hard-line foreign policy that he had advocated left Japan's strategy of
2004–6 at a dead end, as had occurred twenty years earlier when Ronald
Reagan switched direction on the Soviet Union and, fifteen years before
that, when Richard Nixon had changed his approach to China. This was
compounded when Fukuda took office ready to seek reconciliation in
Asia. Finally, the victory of Lee actually dealt a blow to LDP extremists
since he is much more difficult to demonize than was Roh. To capitalize
on these signs of marginalization for Japan's most nationalist elements,
China moved quickly in summit diplomacy, intensively wooing the DPJ
after it took power.

In July 2008, the territorial dispute flared again as Japan announced
new textbook guidelines to inculcate recognition of the disputed territory as its own, similar to the way it has been treating the four islands
occupied by Russia. South Koreans reacted angrily, withdrawing their
ambassador and filling the media with outraged commentaries. When it
was discovered that the U.S. Board on Geographic Names had changed its
website to define the territory as "undesignated sovereignty," the uproar
threatened to widen in the aftermath of two months of frenzied criticism and candlelight vigils against Lee for allowing the resumption of
U.S. beef imports. When the U.S. side explained that this was not a policy change but just a technical standardization measure, it meant little
in the face of offended Koreans who saw this as one more instance of
failure to give offense to Japan or recognize the nature of Japan's imperialism. Even with a conservative president who had stressed stronger
ties, America was not meeting the values test until Bush reversed the
change with the aim of avoiding involvement in explosive historical
issues.

The varied Japanese press coverage of this development, delayed so
as not to interfere with Japan's hosting of the G-8, demonstrated that
Fukuda's weak support base made him vulnerable to LDP nationalists
who branded him as pro-China, soft on the abductions in the face of U.S.
pressure, and lacking Abe's commitment to sovereignty. Even the wording
on the island dispute drew a rebuke because it had been softened from

what had been proposed by the Ministry of Education and Science.[29] Such right-wing pressure endured under LDP rule but lessened dramatically after the DPJ took power.

South Koreans value the alliance with the United States for many reasons, among them its potential to set limits on China's rise and to dull Japan's aspirations as a military power. The changing thrust of the alliance, focusing on Taiwan and encouraging Japan's rise, has put a strain on the South. In these circumstances, it is important for Japan to offer reassurances, winning more trust from South Koreans. Instead, changes in textbooks, such as in July 2008 elevating insistence on Takeshima/Dokdo's return to the status of the Northern Territories, have aggravated distrust. For South Koreans, calling for the return of this island is equivalent to justifying Japan's invasion and annexation, even denying their right to independence. If progressives, led by Roh, appeared to lose balance in handling this issue and to precipitate a downward spiral in relations, conservatives under Lee were poised to wipe the slate clean and give priority to future-oriented relations. Yet, Japan's announcement that textbooks would now emphasize the territorial claim undercut Lee's plans. Indifferent to the effect on their most promising South Korean political partner and on recently improving public opinion toward their country, the Japanese let revisionist values trump idealist or realist ones. Despite its low military budget – far lower as a percentage of gross national product (GNP) than that of China or South Korea – and still reactive diplomacy, Japan allowed the image to spread that it, rather than China, was the impatient, assertive nationalist state.

New Leadership and the Changing Strategic Environment in 2009

In September 2009, the new cabinet formed by Hatoyama was described as pro–South Korean, as ten of its eighteen members belonged to the Diet Japan–South Korea union. Yet, these were mostly center-left members, different from LDP conservative members of the same union.[30] To find common ground with the conservative leadership in Seoul would require more than prudence over history issues and rights for the Zainichi Koreans living in Japan. Saying that Japan has to have the courage to face up to history, Hatoyama did not necessarily intend to stop Japan's momentum in putting territorial claims to Takeshima/Dokdo in textbooks. A shared

---

[29] *Sankei shimbun*, July 15, 2008, p. 2.
[30] *Sankei shimbun*, September 18, 2009, p. 8.

view of triangles involving Washington and Beijing was essential as well as agreement on how to address a belligerent Pyongyang.

The Japanese had become fearful of entrapment as a result of the Security Treaty with the United States. While Americans considered it a one-sided arrangement that let Japan escape the risk and responsibility of addressing dangers that both countries shared, this specter persisted. Despite the fact that regarding the two serious neighboring threats to security – North Korean military action and a Chinese attack on Taiwan – many Japanese felt that they were more endangered than Americans, the image of entrapment did not recede. It coincided with the no-less-potent image of Japan-passing, or ignoring Japan's views, evoked in U.S. ties with China on these very issues. Insufficient feelings of international responsibility, linked to failures in history education, including about the cold war, lead to such narrow thinking. While most attention has centered on the history gap in regard to relations with Asian neighbors, the gap with the United States may be no less serious. The duplicity of pretending to adhere to the "three nos" – not building, possessing, or allowing nuclear weapons to be brought into the country – when a secret agreement with the United States (which after half a century the DPJ is finally revealing) permitted the U.S. military to bring such weapons into Japan is indicative of troubled logic under the shadow of the "nuclear allergy."[31]

Although the Japanese left wing collapsed by 1996 when the LDP reasserted its rule, its thinking about the cold war, the U.S. alliance, and Asianism remained entrenched. The DPJ emerged at the end of the 1990s as a broad opposition party, but its core group comprised many who retained this worldview and others cynically prepared to appeal to it, especially as Koizumi veered sharply in the other direction. When the revisionists with doubts about the U.S. role in history sought benefit in drawing closer to Japan's ally but not embracing or adequately explaining its international responsibilities, this widened the opening for the left to expose the failure of the revisionists' strategy and respond with a different one.

As South Korean expectations rose for a DPJ victory that promised to avoid the historical provocations long associated with LDP rule, optimism gave way to doubt as the impact on Japanese-U.S. relations became clearer.[32] Disputes over specific flashpoints linked to history had masked

---

[31] *Asahi shimbun*, August 15, 2009, p. 3.
[32] *Sankei shimbun*, August 28, 2009, p. 8.

a deeper divide over history, involving the United States. When U.S. officials greeted Hatoyama's more inviting East Asian policies by noting that when tensions had been raised with its neighbors the U.S. response had been unfavorable, they also stressed the need for parallel moves by the two states to strengthen ties in the region.[33] This could be interpreted as a warning that cutting a deal with China without coordination would be harmful to U.S. interests and the alliance. South Korean leaders shared this concern that the DPJ view steeped in history could undercut the South's security.

In seeking to "leave the United States," to establish "equal relations" with it, and add the role of "balancer," Hatoyama brought to mind Roh Moo-hyun. Ozawa's notion of a "normal Japan" when he was with the LDP in the early 1990s had become associated with the one-sided Kanemaru mission, seeking a breakthrough with North Korea on terms worrisome to both South Korea and the United States, followed by Ozawa's own trip. Critical of the way Roh had failed to demand reciprocity from the North or to link assistance to the way it cooperated in denuclearization, South Koreans and some Japanese feared Ozawa's impact.[34]

In 2001–3, South Koreans had worried about U.S. unilateralism leaving their sunshine policy irrelevant after hopes had just been raised. In 2006–9, the Japanese were concerned about U.S. multilateralism, marginalizing their concerns, such as the abductions issue, in the aftermath of raised expectations for the personalized Koizumi-Bush alliance. In each case, they turned to leaders intent on rebalancing relations by diminishing dependence on the United States and strengthening ties in the region. Yet, the result was rising concern about Japanese–South Korean relations. Although Roh in 2003–4 stressed improved ties to Japan, nervousness was growing and then erupted in 2005 as relations frayed. As soon as Hatoyama took office in 2009, similar nervousness spread in South Korea despite his early assurances, also due to fear of a setback in the other state's ties to the United States.

China's strategy toward the DPJ was clear even before Hatoyama took office. It stressed the prospects for relations based on "fraternity" and "community" (Hatoyama's idealistic concepts), downplaying notions of a G-2 where Japan had to choose sides by insisting that China remained a developing country in need of learning from the economic great power,

---

[33] *Asahi shimbun*, October 2, 2009, p. 4.
[34] *Sankei shimbun*, September 12, 2009, p. 8.

Japan.[35] Some suspected that "fraternity," despite its link to the French Revolution, not only is not a universal value, but also is a vague pretext for overlooking human rights violations.[36] Not only would China stop criticism of Japan for its revisionism, Japan would feel similarly obliged to wipe the historical slate clean in regard to authoritarianism and concerns about a return to sinocentrism, in essence accepting a subordinate role under Chinese leadership.

The October 10, 2009, trilateral meeting in Shanghai marked the tenth anniversary of cooperation, as Hatoyama asserted that Japan had been too dependent on the United States and would now stress that Asia be more guided by his notion of "fraternity" (*yuai*) and in pursuit of an East Asian community. Lee responded cautiously, warning of preconditions that had to be met as commentaries noted that Hatoyama had failed to clarify his thinking in his September 23 meeting with Obama and seemed to rule out U.S. involvement.[37] In contrast to the June 28 meeting between Lee and Aso, which showcased their agreement on taking a tough posture toward North Korea and relying on the United States while also deepening coordination with China,[38] Hatoyama's visit to Seoul and three-way meeting in Shanghai gave the appearance of moving beyond history to community while leaving South Koreans unsettled about other questions of history and the meaning of community.

Ozawa Ichiro, the kingmaker in the DPJ, visited Seoul in December 2009, seeking to boost bilateral relations. He and Lee Myung-bak agreed that 2010 should be a new starting point for the two states, as Ozawa welcomed the idea of a visit by the Emperor.[39] While apologizing for Japan's wrongdoings in the period of colonialization, Ozawa spoke hopefully of preparations in the Diet to give ethnic Koreans living in Japan the long-sought right to vote in local elections.[40] A remarkable shift had occurred in Japanese views of this relationship. The annual poll on foreign relations by the Japanese Cabinet Office revealed that the number of Japanese who regarded ties with South Korea as smooth had jumped by 17 percent to 66.5 percent, as a record 63 percent indicated that they

---

[35] *Nihon keizai shimbun*, September 5, 2009, p. 8.

[36] *Sankei shimbun*, September 9, 2009, p. 1.

[37] *Sankei shimbun*, October 11, 2009, p. 1.

[38] *Sankei shimbun*, June 29, 2009, p. 1.

[39] "Ozawa: Visit to S. Korea by Emperor a 'Good Thing,'" *Yomiuri shimbun*, December 13, 2009.

[40] "Ozawa Apologizes for Wartime Atrocities," *Korea Herald*, December 14, 2009.

feel friendly toward that country.[41] With the DPJ courting South Korea and the Japanese looking much more favorably on the country, there was new hope for consolidating ties.

South Korean views of Japan also were easing. Following Lee Myung-bak's call for the Emperor to visit, 64 percent approved while only 31 percent were opposed. Also, unlike the 63 percent who said in March 2005 that they hated Japan when relations were at a low point, the number of South Koreans who said this in late 2009 was 36 percent.[42] Japanese government restraint would be crucial to sustain this trend. The Emperor's visit could build momentum, but a breakthrough on distrust over history required more.

While some South Koreans took note of the more forthcoming Japanese attitude toward their country, this was clouded by the rebalancing of Sino-Japanese relations in the fall of 2009 as U.S.-Japanese relations were shaken. The dual visits of Xi Jinping to Japan and Ozawa to China – both wielding clout in future ties – drew attention at year's end. As in the cold war era, no matter how much South Koreans emphasized the danger from Japanese conservatives, the real danger came from the progressives who had sought rapprochement with North Korea and, as seen by Hatoyama, still have a rosy view of China-centered Asianism. Without a shared understanding of the joint cause of the cold war U.S. alliances, progressives in Japan and South Korea are ill prepared to view the other nation in realist terms. A shared three-way history focusing on universal values, but not cynically invoking them as Japan did in 2005–6, should boost trust.

Conclusion

Since at least 1950, a major purpose of the U.S. military presence in Japan has been to deter North Korean ambitions to seize South Korea by force. Optimally, this means not only coordination between U.S. troops stationed in Japan and South Korea, but also cooperation between Japan and South Korea. Reconciliation would make that easier, and historical memories persist as the principal barrier to achieve that. It took until 1965 for diplomatic relations to be normalized, to the 1980s for political ties to be regularized, and to 1998 to reach agreement on removing barriers

---

[41] "Japanese Feel Friendlier than Ever toward Korea," *Chosun ilbo*, December 14, 2009.
[42] *Donga ilbo*, January 1, 2010.

to normal cultural exchanges. Yet, at the start of 2010 there was still doubt that Emperor Akihito would pay the first visit ever of a Japanese emperor to this close neighbor. The fact that he could visit even China in 1992 suggests how strange it is that this symbol of normal ties has yet to materialize.

A joint history project in 2002–5 failed in the midst of the renewed imbroglio of 2005. A second committee from 2007 has some prospects for progress, but few faced the 2010 centennial of annexation optimistically. Given the lack of Japanese consensus on its past in Asia, linked to vagueness on how to address Japan's place in global history, signs were not positive, even under DPJ leadership downplaying history, for a joint textbook. If the Emperor could soon visit South Korea, however, followed by restraint not shown in Sino-Japanese relations after 1992, a foundation amenable to U.S. involvement could take shape. Given the regional environment, quickly capitalizing on a security consensus with a high-profile imperial visit offers the most promising timing.

Recalling how a downturn in U.S.-Japanese relations was overcome in 1995 by his initiative, Joseph Nye suggested to the Japanese as another downturn was anticipated that it would be a good idea for Obama to visit Hiroshima during his November 2009 visit to Japan to help to build a more equal relationship.[43] As in the proposed Emperor's visit to Seoul, this held out hope of a symbolic jump-start to overcoming a historical divide. Such a visit would raise many questions, which some have assumed have been well buried, and would require a far-reaching follow-up strategy alert to its national identity implications. An Obama visit would be even more welcome after the alliance anxiety under Hatoyama.

Contradictory themes leave in doubt the core of Japan's national identity. With the incomparably instrumental Yoshida Doctrine in effect for more than one-third of a century, Japan was known as supremely pragmatic; yet later revisionist thinking seriously undercut this. Longstanding images of a state obsessed with its economic rise yielded to amazement at the power of its cultural identity, seen in the outpouring of writings on Nihonjinron and still in evidence. Seeming satisfaction with dependency on the United States, whose values and causes pose little challenge to Japan, lost credibility in the face of evidence that it anxiously seeks autonomy. The struggle between internationalism and Asianism bedevils strategists, forming the context in which history battles are fought.

---

43 *Nihon keizai shimbun*, September 9, 2009.

The meaning of Asianism became inseparable from colonialism in 1905–10, when Japan made the decision to annex Korea. An opportunity to put it behind came in 1985–90, at the peak of Japanese confidence. The failed Asianism could then have been decried in favor of a new Asianism; instead, a minister aroused public opinion in the midst of South Korea's democratization by claiming the South Korean side was responsible for the annexation too.[44] In 2005–10, China's rise and the search for an East Asian community have rekindled debate. Yet, struggling to interpret the history of U.S.-Japanese ties, Japan is still at a loss to clarify Asianism without finally reaching consensus on internationalism.[45] Revisionists bungled their chance under Abe, and idealists may reach an impasse under Hatoyama. Centrists alone stand a chance of reconciling these two poles in Japanese thinking.

While U.S. and South Korean cooperation is critical, Japan is the key actor in overcoming the history divide. If Obama and Lee Myung-bak create a favorable environment while Chinese and North Korean assertiveness sets limits on rosy idealism, a triangular vision linked to shared history is more likely to arise. Along with security triangulation, history triangulation could be part of the U.S. regional agenda if Japan's DPJ opts to become a centrist political force rather than cater to its left wing as the LDP long catered to its right wing. A visit by Emperor Akihito to Seoul and visits by Obama to Hiroshima and the DPJ leader to Pearl Harbor could give impetus to a joint history. After long preferring to keep history hidden in the shadows, leaders on all sides may find that the timing is more favorable to bring it into the open and to preempt future moves to use it in ways harmful to alliance needs.

[44] Togo Kazuhiko, *Rekishi to gaiko*, p. 120.
[45] Gilbert Rozman, "Internationalism and Asianism in Japanese Strategic Thought from Meiji to Heisei," *Japanese Journal of Political Science*, Vol. 9, No. 2 (Spring 2008), pp. 209–32.

PART III

HISTORICAL MEMORIES, SINO–SOUTH KOREAN
RELATIONS, AND U.S. VALUES

Sino–South Korean Differences over Koguryo and the U.S. Role

Jin Linbo

After three years of fierce fighting in the Korean War and a forty-year cold war confrontation, the PRC and the ROK put an end to their antagonism and established formal diplomatic ties in August 1992. Stimulated by fast-growing economic and strategic common interests, relations between these states have made remarkable progress in almost all fields, and the two countries announced "the establishment of an all-around cooperative partnership" in 2003, only one decade after normalization.[1] Economically, China had not only become the ROK's largest destination for foreign direct investment (FDI) since 2001, but also surpassed the United States as South Korea's largest trading partner by 2004; strategically, the two countries have shared increasingly converging security interests in maintaining peace and stability on the Korean peninsula, especially diplomatic cooperation in dealing with the nuclear weapons program pursued by the DPRK since 2002; and socially, the number of visits between the two countries' leaders and peoples has also grown remarkably since normalization.

During the first decade of diplomatic relations, mutual fever between the two nations – the "South Korea wave" in China and the "China fever" in South Korea – elevated bilateral ties at the grass-roots as well as the official level. Expectations were raised that the two may draw even closer, to the extent of becoming strategic allies on a par with the alliance

---

[1] Department of Policy Planning, Ministry of Foreign Affairs of the People's Republic of China, *China's Foreign Affairs 2005* (Beijing: World Affairs Press, 2005), p. 268.

between the United States and South Korea.[2] Such hopes reached a peak
early in the tenure of Roh Moo-hyun, but from 2004, they were dashed
by the totally unexpected emergence of an obscure history issue in Korean
consciousness. High expectations for relations turned abruptly into disappointment and even deep skepticism when contested academic arguments
over the history of the Koguryo state (37 BC–AD 668), which is often
referred to as one of the ancient "Three Kingdoms of Korea" along with
Paekche and Silla, suddenly became a hot diplomatic issue involving the
two governments and peoples in the summer of 2004. This controversy
dealt a powerful blow to warming relations, and bilateral ties lost the
momentum of previous years. South Korea's China image changed dramatically. A survey by major newspapers showed that China's preference
rate fell abruptly from 61 percent before the Koguryo spat to 29 percent in 2005. Thanks to swift actions taken by both governments, the
immediate tensions in 2004 soon eased, leaving the controversy to percolate primarily in the realm of academic debate, though the fact that it
remained unresolved and was not replaced by a more reassuring symbol
of shared values left bilateral relations unsettled.

In the short term, given the fact that deepening economic interdependence and converging security interests continue, it seems unlikely that
this controversy will erupt again with similar severity as a political issue
or diplomatic row that could further damage relations, but in the long
run, since the different views on the history of Koguryo are deeply rooted
in the two academic communities and have the potential to intensify again
as an academic dispute, the impact and the repercussions of the controversy could cast a dark shadow on relations. As far as mutual images
are concerned, the eruption of this controversy might be regarded as a
"turning point," putting values in the forefront in a way that undercuts
what was laboriously achieved in other areas.[3] Especially the Koguryo
dispute might even mean, as Peter Hays Gries put it, the end of the decade-
long South Korean love affair and a dramatic shift from infatuation to

---

[2] Concerns over this rapidly improving relationship were explicitly expressed within both
the United States and the Republic of Korea from mid-1990s. For further reference,
see Zbigniew Brzezinski, Lee Hamilton, and Richard Lugar, eds., *Foreign Policy into
the 21st Century: The United States Leadership Challenge* (Washington, DC: CSIS,
1996), p. 49; Hong Soon-young, "What Does China Mean to South Korea?" *Dong-
a ilbo*, February 13, 2004; Korea Foundation, ed., *Korea Focus* (March–April 2004),
pp. 36–8.
[3] See Scott Snyder, "A Turning Point for China-Korea Relations?" *Comparative Connections* (Fall 2004), pp. 109–14.

suspicion.[4] It remains to be seen whether the mutual suspicions will be dispelled through exchanges between academics or will spread as part of a wider sense of unease in two nations with different approaches to national identity.

Even after the two governments' successful management of the Koguryo spat, the mutual suspicion was far from being eliminated. In fact, South Korea's suspicion contains not merely skepticism over China's revisionist interpretation of Koguryo, but something close to strategic distrust toward rising China. Chun Jin-sung has argued that South Korea's dispute with China is not a symbolic one over a sense of pride in history, but it is confronting "the ghost of hegemonism hovering over Northeast Asia."[5] Such concern about a possible hegemonic giant neighbor would unavoidably contribute to the existence of a negative image of rising China.

Meanwhile, South Korea's excessive reaction to the Koguryo issue at both the governmental and societal level has catalyzed growing unpleasant feelings, criticism, and even resentment toward South Korea, especially visible among Chinese netizens, and heightened suspicions about South Korea's true motivation among Chinese academics and officials. Although there was no public survey conducted in China before and after the Koguryo incident, negative views of both the state and the people of the ROK by netizens have clearly increased. Many comments brag about China's historical cultural superiority while disparaging South Korea's cultural dependency on ancient China and arrogance about its cultural roots after achieving economic success. Such sentiments were publicly expressed in fora linked to the Olympic Games in August 2008. When the Olympics torch relay encountered some anti-Chinese activists in Seoul in April, a great number of Chinese students in South Korea gathered to safeguard it, some wielding bamboo sticks while clashing with South Korean human rights activists and riot police. The South Korean government took stern measures against the Chinese students and some civic groups accused the Chinese ambassador Ning Fuqui of abetting student violence and requested a police investigation. Three months later, when South Korean broadcaster SBS aired a secretly recorded clip of a rehearsal of the opening ceremony for the Beijing Olympic Games, Chinese media

---

4 Peter Hays Gries, "The Koguryo Controversy, National Identity, and Sino-Korean Relations Today," *East Asia*, Vol. 22, No. 4 (Winter 2005), p. 4.

5 Chun Jin-sung, "Our Dispute with China Isn't about Ancient History," http://english. chosun.com/site/data/html_dir/2007/02/27/2007022761035.html (accessed November 25, 2009).

severely criticized South Korea, and China's image of the ROK further deteriorated. When conservative Lee Myung-bak was elected, his pro-American stance and repeated stress on the importance of the U.S. alliance caused some concerns in China about the ROK's foreign policy and relationship with China. Confronted with this situation, the two governments made efforts to improve the somewhat estranged bilateral relations. In May 2008, Lee and Hu Jintao met in Beijing and agreed to upgrade relations from a "comprehensive cooperative partnership" to the highest status of a "strategic cooperative partnership," which indicates much more political and security cooperation. There is no doubt that the two governments' diplomatic efforts have had a positive effect on bilateral ties. They also may be expected to reduce the negative impact of the Koguryo controversy on Sino-Korean relations in the years ahead.

In this chapter, I take a Chinese perspective on the Koguryo controversy and on how values influence Sino–South Korean relations with ramifications for U.S. policy in the region. This chapter sheds light on the academic as well as the political backdrop of the eruption of the controversy and examines its causes and consequences. Largely due to a lack of sufficient published materials in China, this is not a detailed exploration of the subject. Instead, it provides a rough sketch of the academic background of China's Northeast Project, which has been the focal point of the controversy, and adds general analysis regarding its impact and the ramifications for bilateral relations. Finally, I propose ways for China and South Korea to manage their differences and discuss how this may influence the environment in which U.S. policy operates.

China's Northeast Project

Generally speaking, different views on Koguryo have long existed in the Chinese and ROK scholarly communities, but it was not until China's Northeast Project, a national research project, led by the Center of China's Borderland History and Geography Research under the Chinese Academy of Social Sciences (CASS), was launched in 2002 and the "history war" between China and South Korea intensified in the summer of 2004 that the controversy drew broad attention from the two governments and publics. According to the general introduction on the center's website, what was officially called "A Series of Research Projects on the History and Current Status of the Northeast Borderland" was a five-year joint research project co-organized by CASS and China's three Northeast provinces (Heilongjiang, Jilin, and Liaoning) authorized by the central government and formally launched in February 2002. The project has a wide range of research subjects that include studies of the Northeast borderland's history, especially the history of ancient kingdoms such as Kojoson (2333 AD–BC 108), Koguryo (37 BC–AD 668), and Parhae (698 BC–AD 926); Sino-Korean and Sino-Russian relations; and strategies for maintaining social stability in this borderland area. The purpose of the project was clearly defined as coping with "a variety of challenges facing the Northeast region," especially the "politically motivated distortion of the region's history by a number of foreign scholars, organizations and politicians in some countries" in recent years. The introduction stressed that one primary task of the project is to "find answers to historically disputed issues, current hotspot issues and theoretically knotty problems that relate to the Northeast region through overhauling the academic findings of the past."[6]

From the preceding, it is obvious that although the views expressed by the individual participants may not necessarily represent the view of the Chinese government, the Northeast Project is government-sponsored academic research designed not only to cover knotty historical matters but also to address current issues concerning the region with a view to dealing with outside challenges and maintaining social stability in China's borderland area. It is unimaginable that any academic project similar to the Northeast Project could be organized and implemented without the government's political and financial auspices, but also the purpose of the project was clearly justified as reactive and defensive in nature. However, from the South Korean perspective, both the form and the content of the project appear offensive and threatening to South Korea's national identity and even its future security. Some editorial writers in South Korea criticized the view taken by the project as a modern-day "Sino-centric view of history."[7] Some even went so far as to characterize its launching as "an example of China-centered great-power chauvinism."[8] Such a huge perception gap between China and South Korea may help to explain why this project and the Chinese government's ratification of it aroused extensive criticism inside South Korea.

---

[6] See "The Introduction of the Northeast Project," the official website of the Center of China's Borderland History and Geography Research (CASS), http://chinaborderland.cass.cn/more_news_dbgc(n).asp (accessed January 15, 2008).

[7] Korea Foundation, ed., *Korea Focus* (March–April 2004), p. 49; Lee Yun Jae, "History War among Korea, China, and Japan," *Kyunghyang shinmun*, February 16, 2004.

[8] Korea Foundation, ed., *Korea Focus* (January–February 2004), p. 38; Park Woo-jung, "Goguryeo, China and Dokdo, Japan?" *Hankyoreh*, January 12, 2004.

In June 2003, nearly one and a half years after the project's inauguration, three key members using the pen name of Bianzhong published a long and well-prepared article concerning its research findings in *Guangming Daily*, a national newspaper influential within the academic community. Entitled "On Several Issues concerning Koguryo History Studies," it argues the following:

- Historiographical and archaeological materials reveal that ethnologically the people of ancient Koguryo were an ethnic minority that belonged to ancient China and their activities had never extended beyond the current territory of China's Northeast region before or during China's Zhou and Qin dynasties.
- Long before the founding of the Koguryo kingdom China's Han Dynasty had already set up the Four Commanderies and implemented effective administration in the area where the Koguryo people were living.
- During most of its 705-year-long rule the Koguryo kingdom was actually a subordinate state that fell under the jurisdiction of Chinese dynasties. After its collapse, most of its population were absorbed into China and only a small part were absorbed into Silla, centered in the southern part of the Korean peninsula.
- Based on the preceding historical facts, it is reasonable to say that the ancient "Koguryo Kingdom was an ethnic local government in China's Northeast region."[9]

Furthermore, the article asserts that although another kingdom called Koryo (918–1392) emerged on the Korean peninsula 250 years after the collapse of Koguryo and unified the Korean peninsula in AD 935 and China's historiographies after the Song Dynasty mistakenly described Koryo as the heir of Koguryo partially due to the loss of historical materials caused by the wars at that time, reexamination of the historical facts show that there was no relationship of inheritance between Koguryo and Koryo; that is, Koryo, which has evolved into present-day Korea, has nothing to do with Koguryo, and, accordingly, the history of the ancient Koguryo kingdom, which had closer ties with China than with Korea, should not be regarded as an integral part of Korean history.

These arguments presented in Bianzhong's article signaled a complete change in the mainstream Chinese view in Koguryo studies, especially in

---

[9] See Bianzhong, "Shilun Gaogouli lishi yanjiu de jige wenti," *Guangming ribao*, June 24, 2003.

comparison with the decades before the 1980s, and both the content and the form of the article were quite shocking for the South Korean mass media and academic community, which had long been accustomed to a Chinese view that did not appear to be challenged at home or controversial abroad. During the better part of the first three decades of the PRC under Mao Zedong's leadership, almost all publications, including the history textbooks for middle and high school and university students, dealing with the subject upheld the view that Koguryo was a component of Korean rather than Chinese history.[10] This reality, however, does not necessarily mean that the Chinese historians at the time fully accepted this predominant view. In general, before China adopted Deng Xiaoping's "reform and opening" policies in 1978, academic research in the social sciences was profoundly affected by or even thoroughly subordinated to the political and ideological needs of the times, and mostly was conducted through uniform approaches and unanimous conclusions. In addition to the overall internal political and social environment, an external factor – namely, China's need to strengthen its relationship with the DPRK – had made only the internationalist-toned Koguryo research obligatory, while objective academic studies were impossible and even politically incorrect and dangerous, especially during the Cultural Revolution.

In the 1980s, some change occurred. Encouraged by the reform movement and increasing openness, many Chinese academics started reexamining their research subjects through relatively independent and multiple scholarly approaches. Under the new circumstances, some unorthodox and nationalist-toned descriptions of Koguryo history gradually appeared in history textbooks for university students and in increasing numbers of academic articles. According to research by Ma Dezheng, a key drafter of the Bianzhong article and primary architect of the Northeast Project, the trajectory of changes can be clearly detected in history textbooks for university students from the late 1970s. As early as 1978, the beginning of China's "reform and opening" era, a textbook on ancient and medieval world history coedited by fourteen Chinese universities described the Koguryo kingdom as a transnational borderland state that was founded in China. From the mid-1980s, there were further explicit changes in the depictions of Koguryo in history textbooks for college students. Two textbooks published respectively by People's Educational Press in 1985 and

---

[10] I have so far not found the exceptional case that treated the history of Koguryo kingdom differently, but further investigation into publications is needed to better understand the content and process of change in the Chinese mainstream view.

People's Press in 1990 took a further step by asserting that Koguryo was a Chinese Ji'an-based ancient kingdom. In the 1990s, the same view as in Bianzhong's article was adopted by an increasing number of university-used textbooks. For example, in a textbook on world history published by People's Press in 1997, the Koguryo kingdom was treated completely as "a vassal state and local government under Chinese dynasties."[11]

The changes in college history textbooks well reflected the changeover in the mainstream scholarly community. From the mid-1980s, increasing numbers of Chinese historians clarified their position on Koguryo's "Chineseness." For instance, as early as 1986, a Chinese historian suggested that Koguryo is separate from the history of the Three Kingdoms on the Korean peninsula, and later he argued that the people of Koguryo had the same lineage as the Chinese in the Northeast region, while the Korean people were part of the Silla lineage.[12] In fact, entering the 1990s, there was a sharp increase in the number of articles that regard the Koguryo people as one of the ethnic groups of ancient China, the Koguryo kingdom as a local government under Chinese jurisdiction, and Koguryo as an inseparable part of Chinese, not Korean, history. As a result, the revised view overwhelmed the traditional view, which treated Koguryo as Korean rather than Chinese; it became the mainstream view around the mid-1990s, long before the eruption of the diplomatic dispute in the summer of 2004. Moreover, as the trend continued, the revised mainstream view on Koguryo would unavoidably, in due course, affect the Chinese government's position on the matter.

Notwithstanding the fact that the shift in the mainstream view of the academic community was largely generated by domestic factors, especially the political and social changes in China after the end of the 1970s, it seems that the launching of the Northeast Project and consequently the eruption of the Koguryo controversy as a serious diplomatic row between China and South Korea were also accelerated by many external factors. Two developments seem particularly significant: One was the DPRK's application to UNESCO for registering the Koguryo tomb murals as North Korea's first world heritage site; and another was the irredentist discourse and proposals pushed by some nationalist politicians and scholars in South Korea. The DPRK's application for world heritage

---

[11] Ma Dazheng, "Luelun Gaogouli lishi yanjiu zhong de jige xangguan wenti," in Ma Dazheng, ed., *Gudai Zhongguo Gaogouli lishi conglun* (Harbin: Heilongjiang jiaoyu chubanshe, 2001).

[12] Sun Jinji, *Dongbei minzu yuanliu* (Harbin: Heilongjiang renmin chubanshe, 1986).

status was a problem for China with significant short-term and long-term political implications for not only territorial and security interests, but also its future relations with both the DPRK and the ROK. Also, South Korea's support for the application and the visible linkage between various nationalist moves against China there in North Korea's application put pressure on Chinese policy makers to devise a better plan to cope with the complicated situation.

Under the circumstances, it seemed that only a joint application would provide an ideal way to tackle this from the Chinese perspective. If North Korea would agree to submit its application to UNESCO jointly with China, it would be easier to address the issue in a relatively noncontroversial way. With such reasoning in mind and with some hope, China not only directly consulted with but also sought to persuade the DPRK through officials in UNESCO, but in the end it failed to get the DPRK's consent.[13] As a matter of fact, North Korea's unilateral application in 2001 forced the Chinese government, which had heretofore shied away from commenting on Koguryo-related questions, to clarify its official position on the matter publicly. Consequently, China submitted its own application to UNESCO in 2003, which demonstrated that the government had adopted the mainstream academic view about Koguryo's "Chineseness." This appeared to some, at least, as the only realistic option left, and both applications of the PRC and the DPRK were approved at the twenty-eighth session of the World Heritage Committee of UNESCO held in Suzhou, China, on July 1, 2004. According to *China Daily*'s report right after the meeting, the committee recommended to the two governments future cooperation on the Koguryo relics, and in his response, China's cultural minister Sun Jiazheng said, "the Chinese government encourages domestic archaeologists and scholars to undertake all possible cooperation with their peers in the DPRK."[14] Thus, the world heritage application issue seemed to have ended happily, but Chinese concerns were far from being dispelled. For China, increased nationalistic sentiments against it and irredentist arguments over its Northeast provinces in South Korea remained a potential threat to borderland security.

Before normalization of relations with China, Koguryo was not a popular subject for South Korean historians, but since the mid-1990s there has been a proliferation of research and exhibitions on Koguryo history

---

[13] This is based on interviews with Chinese government officials, which were conducted by the author in November 2007.

[14] "Koguryo Sites Put onto Heritage List," *China Daily*, July 2, 2004.

and cultural heritage. For many Chinese scholars, the Korean attachment to the former lands of the Koguryo kingdom has much to do with territorial ambitions toward China's Northeast provinces, parts of which have been regarded by some Korean nationalists as "falsely separated from the organic national community." Ultranationalists – progressives and conservatives – have even made claims for the "restoration of the lost former territories."[15] At the same time, South Korean attempts to gain some sort of jurisdiction over ethnic Koreans living in the Northeast also infuriated the Chinese government and local authorities. Some South Korean politicians called for granting special rights of residency in South Korea to Korean Chinese in China, and a special bill on the matter was submitted to the National Assembly in 2001. From the Chinese perspective the present-day ethnic Koreans residing there are immigrants from the peninsula from the mid-nineteenth century (some scholars argue that they began to arrive at the end of the Ming Dynasty) and especially during the period of Japanese colonial rule, and they have little to do with the ancient people of Koguryo. Accordingly, the nationalistic moves in South Korea trying to forge a link between the two peoples were seen as posing grave harm to China's security interests and thus prompted action.[16] In this regard, the launching of the Northeast Project was just a countermeasure taken against nationalist provocations, though it was a quite restrained and defensive reaction for many who perceived these moves in South Korea as not only a potential danger to China's territorial integrity and long-term security but also as a real threat to social stability in today's Northeast. As the introduction to the Northeast Project stated, its primary task was to "cope with the dangerous political attempts taking place in some countries," obviously referring to South Korea. Against this background, China took further defensive measures in addition to its ratification of this project.

In April 2004, the Chinese Foreign Ministry deleted the name of Koguryo from the Korean history section on its website without issuing any notice. The deletion, which has been viewed by South Korea as an official "distortion of history" by the Chinese government, incited harsh criticisms along with the Northeast Project. In early August, China deleted all references to Korean history prior to 1948 on its website in

---

[15] Yonson Ahn, "Competing Nationalism: the Mobilization of History and Archaeology in the Korea–China Wars over Koguryo/Gaogouli," *Japan Focus*, http://japanfocus.org/products/details/1837 (accessed January 18, 2008).

[16] Ma Dazheng, "Luelun Gaoguli lishi yanjiu zhong de jige xangguan wenti."

order to mitigate the growing anti-Chinese sentiment; however, this further infuriated South Korea and triggered the "sharpest crisis" in this diplomatic relationship. Facing unprecedented reactions from the South Korean government and its people, the government dispatched vice foreign minister Wu Dawei (former ambassador to the ROK) to Seoul to find common ground. After nine hours of talks, Foreign Minister Ban Ki-moon announced that the two sides had reached a five-point verbal understanding in which both agreed to make joint efforts to prevent the history issue from harming relations and to find a fair solution to the dispute through early academic exchanges.[17] Although the verbal understanding was taken by many in South Korea as "unsatisfactory" or a "stopgap measure for China to dodge the escalating anti-Chinese sentiment in Korea,"[18] it was to some extent welcomed in China simply because of the desire to put an early end to the harmful political tensions between the two countries. As Ban told reporters in Seoul, China's concern over its borderland was a driver in the talks. "Although this is not included in the points of understanding, China showed acute reactions to claims by some Korean politicians and scholars that the Chinese far-eastern provinces should be returned to Korea," and, "China called for the government to restrain them."[19] Ban's remarks, in fact, partially explained China's intentions in launching the Northeast Project.

The Impact of the Koguryo Controversy

Although the Koguryo controversy appeared to have been successfully removed from the list of hot disputes between China and South Korea, there can be no doubt that the controversy did a great deal of harm to relations, aside from the fact that it remains unresolved as an academic dispute with future political implications. The most visible negative effect is the sharp deterioration in mutual images, especially South Korea's image of China. In fact, after initial awareness of the dispute, public opinion toward each other started showing a downturn tendency. Some opinion

---

[17] Seo Hyun-jin, "China-Korea Truce in Ancient-Kingdom Feud," *Asia Times Online*, August 25, 2004, http://www.atimes.com/atimes/korea/FH25Dg01.html (accessed January 31, 2008).

[18] Bruce Klingner, "China Shock for South Korea," *Asia Times Online*, September 11, 2004, http://www.atimes.com/atimes/korea/FI11Dg03.html (accessed September 11, 2004).

[19] James Brooke, "China Fears Once and Future Kingdom," *New York Times*, August 25, 2004.

polls conducted in South Korea even indicate that "China-phobia" soon surpassed "China fever" as the country's mainstream view. In a survey conducted in April 2004, four months before the controversy became a hot issue, 63 percent of South Korea's ruling party members identified China as South Korea's most important diplomatic partner, but in an August poll of South Korean parliamentarians 80 percent named the United States and only 5.7 percent chose China.[20] The survey reflected the fact that the controversy revealed a heretofore unobserved level of deep suspicions toward China that alleviated intensified anti-American sentiment. Kang Jun-yong argued that "Korea-China relations do not play out in accordance with an alliance framework, but rather that the two countries are engaged in a cooperative relationship," because, "China has always adopted self-oriented strategic approaches that are based on its own perceived interests," and, "views Korean peninsula-related issues within a framework of its relations with the United States."[21]

During the summer of 2004, South Korea experienced an unprecedented "China bashing" movement. Editorial writers warned South Koreans about "Sino-centrism" and the return of a "Middle Kingdom" to dominate Asia's land mass. Some parliamentarians urged their country to "ally with Tibetans, Mongolians, Vietnamese and other peoples surrounding China to refute Sino-centrism."[22] One small group of National Assembly members even prepared a bill to nullify a 1909 treaty known as the Kando Convention that established the boundary between China and the present-day North Korea. South Korea's resentments resulted mainly from two arguments: one linked with Korean national identity, the other with the territorial and security conditions of a unified Korea that may emerge in the near future. With regard to the former, the South Korean Foreign Ministry asserted on August 5, 2004, that "the history of Koguryo is the root of the Korean people and is an issue of paramount importance related to our national identity."[23] This echoes a widely shared perception that China's revised view on Koguryo was actually an insult to Korean

[20] Snyder, "A Turning Point for China-Korea Relations?" p. 115.
[21] Kang Jun Young, "China's Northeast Asia Project and Its Diplomatic Implications," *Kukmin Daily*, August 24, 2004; Korea Foundation, ed., *Korea Focus* (September–October 2004), p. 46.
[22] James Brooke, "Reviving a Korean Kingdom," *International Herald Tribune*, August 25, 2004.
[23] Spokesperson of MOFAT, "China's Distortion of the History of Koguryo," August 5, 2004, http://www.mofat.go.kr/english/press/pressrelease/index.jsp (accessed October 29, 2007).

national identity and should not be tolerated. Peter Gries explained why Koreans feel so strongly about Koguryo, emphasizing two reasons:

> First, Koguryo is central to the stories that Koreans today tell about their relationship with China, and China is the first and arguably foremost other against whom Koreans define who they are. Second, Koguryo is a symbol of heroic Korean resistance against foreign invaders. It is central to a virile and masculine Korean nationalism; robbing Korea of Koguryo, therefore, is like robbing Korean nationalists of their manhood. "China's Koguryo," in other words, translates into an emasculated, feminized Korea.[24]

As far as Korean security is concerned, many nationalist politicians and scholars believe that safeguarding Koguryo's "Koreanness" is vital for maintaining the territorial integrity and security of a future united Korea. They assume that China's revised view on Koguryo and the actions taken by China have to do with unrevealed security considerations and even territorial ambitions on the peninsula. For instance, Kang Jun Yong contends that, in general, the launching of the Northeast Project was affected by the new developments in Northeast Asia, such as the emergence of the North Korean nuclear crisis, the adjustment of the South Korea–U.S. alliance, and the U.S. efforts to upgrade Japan's strategic importance in the region, but China's main focus was on preparations for the eventual collapse of the North Korea regime and control over the Jiandao region where the ethnic Koreans reside. It follows that China plans to use the project to "counter the possibility that ethnic Koreans in the region may launch a separatist movement after the two Koreas are unified or that a unified Korea may stake a claim to areas of the Jiandao region."[25] Kim Woo-jun argued, "if Koguryo is incorrectly interpreted by China as China's old kingdom, the North Korean region becomes China's historical territory. And this can serve as justification for future Chinese intervention," while Kim Moon-so, a National Assembly member of the Grand National Party, contended that "the Chinese government's apparent history distortion is evidently intended to prepare for a territorial dispute after unification of the North and South Korea."[26] Choi Kwang-sik went so far as to assert that "China's history distortions are far more serious than the issue of Japanese distortion of history textbooks," because they are led by the Chinese government itself, and, "if these distortions

---

[24] Gries, "The Koguryo Controversy, National Identity, and Sino-Korean Relations Today," p. 8.

[25] Kang, "China's Northeast Asia Project and Its Diplomatic Implications," p. 45.

[26] Seo, "China-Korea Truce in Ancient-Kingdom Feud."

are left uncorrected, they could result in undercutting the span of Korean history to less than 2,000 years and delimiting the size of Korea's territory to an area south of the Han River." Meanwhile, since this argument was made before the approval of North Korea's World Heritage application, Choi also warned that "if China were to succeed in placing the Koguryo tumuli located in Manchuria on the Heritage List as Chinese, it could lead to a serious misunderstanding of the Korean kingdom as indeed a part of Chinese history," and urged South Korea to help North Korea's application be approved, adding that a successful defense of the history of Koguryo will "serve as an excellent case of inter-Korean teamwork," because, "the history of Koguryo is not a history belonging to either South or North Korea exclusively, it is the history of the entire Korean people."[27]

Choi's argument indicates that there are visible triangular interactions involving China and the two Koreas over the Koguryo dispute. Generally speaking, Koguryo has been treated in both South and North as an ancestral state and symbol for distinguishing Korea from China and for uniting the Korean peninsula. Compared to South Korea, the North has attached much more importance to eulogizing the "Koreanness" as well as the "greatness" of the Koguryo kingdom. Therefore, in North Korean media, Chinese claims over Koguryo have been strongly denounced as "a pathetic attempt to manipulate history for its own interests" or "intentionally distorting historical facts through biased perspectives."[28] In confronting China's claims over the heritage of Koguryo, the two Koreas actively cooperated with each other. As Ri Ui Ha, head of the North Korean delegation participating in the World Heritage Committee's conference in 2004, commented right after the meeting, "Koguryo culture is the Korean nation's common heritage which unites our national blood vessels." Furthermore, the North-South cooperation was even viewed as "a spiritual and cultural basis of the reunification" by both North and South Korea.[29]

The shared thinking and practical cooperation between the two Koreas regarding Koguryo's "Koreanness" does not mean, however, that the North Korea factor has already turned completely into a negative and detrimental element in China–South Korea relations. On the contrary,

---

[27] Choi Kwang-sik, "What Lies behind the Northeast Asia Project?" http://www.korea.net/News/Issues/issueDetailView.asp?board_no=15177 (accessed January 27, 2008).

[28] Yonson, "Competing Nationalism."

[29] Yonson Ahn, "The Contested Heritage of Koguryo/Gaogouli and China-Korea Conflict," http://japanfocus.org/products/details/2631 (accessed January 27, 2008).

settling the North Korean nuclear issue through the framework of Six-Party Talks remains one of the most important common interests for political and security cooperation. Ever since the division of the Korean peninsula became a reality, the North Korea factor has been the most influential in shaping China's strategic thinking and policies toward South Korea and, therefore, affecting the state of relations. Since normalization of relations, the North Korea factor has exerted mostly a positive impact on China–South Korea relations. It is more than obvious that the emergence of the second North Korean nuclear crisis has offered a welcome opportunity for both China and South Korea to recognize their increasingly converging political and security interests and to enhance their relations through diplomatic consultations for resolving the problem. It was especially the case when South Korea implemented the sunshine policy under Kim Dae-jung and Roh Moo-hyun.

Of course, it is natural that there are also differences between China and South Korea in dealing with North Korea–related issues, such as how to handle North Korean defectors within China, simply because the two countries' strategic objectives and policies toward the North could not overlap completely. Yet, neither side views these differences as grave obstacles for the further development of bilateral relations. For China, its policy framework toward the two Koreas was already established in the early 1990s. Historically, based on geographic proximity and strong political and cultural linkages, China has characterized its relationship with the peninsula as "as close as lips and teeth" and attached great importance to maintaining close ties with it ever since the West extended its military power to East Asia. Before the Sino–Japanese War in 1894–5, China had great sway over Korean issues, but it failed to develop effective strategic thinking and concrete policy measures to maintain its influence. In cold war circumstances, China had no other choice but to implement an unbalanced and much constrained policy toward the peninsula for more than four decades. It was only after the end of the cold war and the establishment of diplomatic relations with South Korea that China's strategic thinking toward the peninsula gradually evolved in a more balanced, sophisticated way, shaped in accord with the following principles: maintaining peace and stability on the peninsula; realizing the final goal of denuclearization; resolving the North Korea nuclear issue through Six-Party Talks; paying close attention to North Korea's security concerns; pursuing balanced policies toward the North and the South; and promoting exchanges between the two that may lead to the eventual reunification of the peninsula. Under these principles, it seems unlikely that China would pursue an unfriendly policy based on expanding nationalism or hegemonic behavior, though its involvement with the two Koreas will be increasingly characterized by putting more emphasis on safeguarding and enlarging reasonable national interests. At the same time, China's general foreign policy stance of "non-alignment, non-confrontation, and non-targeting at any third party" is likely to be maintained in dealing with peninsular issues.

Policy Implications for China and South Korea and the U.S. Role

The eruption of the Koguryo controversy is rooted in profound social, political, and academic causes that have loomed large from the mid-1990s in both countries. It is especially evident that the changeover of the mainstream view on Koguryo in the Chinese academic community has mainly resulted from the large-scale national economic reforms begun in the late 1970s and the burgeoning of at least somewhat nationalist-toned academic approaches pursued by increasing numbers of scholars since the 1980s. Although some scholars still hold their position of regarding Koguryo as part of Korean history, their arguments are no longer supported by the majority of Chinese historians. This basic trend is unlikely to be reversed in the foreseeable future, a reality difficult for many Korean scholars to accept. Nevertheless, this does not necessarily mean that Chinese academics would reject the possibility of sharing the history and heritage of Koguryo with both Koreas. As a powerful ancient state, this kingdom had close ties with both China and the Korean peninsula, and its history and heritage need not be viewed within a narrow present-day nation-state framework. As Yonson Ahn points out, the nation-state framework as constructed through the lens of nationalism clouds understanding of Koguryo as a shared cultural legacy, one that encompasses and expresses the variety and permeability of political and cultural boundaries. Therefore, the focus needs to be placed on the multiple relationships and mutual observations that a transnational approach makes possible for positing the Koguryo heritage in cross-continental relations as a heritage of East Asia that is not the exclusive property of a single nation, but which spread across a wide area, eventually leaving its imprint on realms that include contemporary northeast China, North Korea, South Korea, and beyond to Japan.[30] In fact, there are many cases in other parts of the world where the history of an ancient state has been shared by

[30] Ibid.

two modern-day countries. As Park Doo-Bok suggested, Koreans need to "develop a broad-minded understanding of history that is based on shared ownership rather than adopting a rigid dichotomous attitude toward the history of Koguryo."[31] This calls for both China and South Korea casting away their nationalistic arguments and learning to share the history of Koguryo, perhaps the only way to resolve the dispute.

The Koguryo controversy severely damaged bilateral relations not only in 2004 but also thereafter. Nevertheless, the two governments proceeded with confidence to repair the damage and advance their official relationship with renewed efforts. As for China, motivated by strong political will to develop an amicable and cooperative relationship with South Korea, it is likely to maintain a restrained and discreet stance to eschew any direct collision on Koguryo-related issues. Immediately after the two governments reached the five-point verbal understanding on Koguryo in August 2004, the number four leader, Jia Qinglin, chair of the China People's Political Consultative Conference, visited South Korea. By admitting that bilateral relations had been affected by Koguryo, Jia added that Hu Jintao sought to prevent any more conflicts over the issue arising. In a meeting with ROK reporters in April 2007, Wen Jiabao further explained China's official position: The two sides should stick to the principle of "separating research from politics and reality from history" and avoid any negative impact on bilateral relations.[32] These remarks show that China wants to concentrate its energy on developing a comprehensive and cooperative partnership before complete resolution of the issue is achieved. This position seems to be shared by South Korea, whose emphasis on positive ties has contributed to the relatively stable development of relations after diplomatic tensions over Koguryo in 2004.

After Lee Myung-bak was elected, his pro-American stance and emphasis on the importance of the U.S. alliance and close relations with Japan caused some concern. It could have contributed to a worsening image of South Korea and led to further deterioration of ties. Confronted with this unfavorable situation, the two governments strove to improve their somewhat estranged relations. In January 2008, the Chinese government sent Vice Foreign Minister Wan Yi to Seoul to meet Lee, who stressed that relations with China are the most important for South Korea, and his incoming government would not strengthen ties with the United

---

[31] Park Doo-Bok, "History of Goguryeo Calls for Fact-based Approach," *Dong-a ilbo*, January 27, 2004; Korea Foundation, ed., *Korea Focus* (January–February 2004), p. 35.

[32] "Wen: No Territorial Problems between China, ROK," *China Daily*, April 6, 2007.

States and Japan at the expense of relations with China. South Korea's positive stance and political willingness to implement "pragmatic diplomacy" largely eased Chinese concerns. Meeting South Korean Special Envoy Park Geun-hye in Beijing in the same month, Hu Jintao expressed China's willingness to upgrade bilateral ties to a new level. In May 2008, Hu and Lee agreed to upgrade relations from a "comprehensive cooperative partnership" to the highest status of "strategic cooperative partnership," which indicates much greater political and security consultation and cooperation.[33]

There is no doubt that these diplomatic efforts have given positive momentum to the development of bilateral ties. With all the differences in political, security, and cultural areas, the high expectations for further economic cooperation including a possible FTA in the near future and more cultural exchanges have not shown any downward tendency. As South Korea's largest partner in trade and investment, China's continued high-rate economic development has provided many opportunities. In 2008, bilateral trade reached $186.1 billion, continuing its fast growth. China remained South Korea's largest trading partner and overseas investment destination, and South Korea became China's third largest trading partner. Sixty thousand South Korean students accounted for 36 percent of all foreign students registered in China, and there were 34,000 Chinese students in South Korea, accounting for 58 percent of all students in the ROK. These achievements indicate that despite the remaining negative impact of the Koguryo dispute, relations still are developing in a relatively stable manner. Yet, given the fact that the dispute has much to do with mutual strategic distrust, the continued remarkable development of relations in all fields, especially the top-level commitment to strengthening strategic consultation and cooperation, would also be expected to help reduce the dispute's negative impact in the years ahead. It would be mutually beneficial if the two countries can keep the unresolved dispute under control and make their warming relations sustainable in the decades to come.

The condition of Sino-South Korean relations not only unavoidably affects the security environment in Northeast Asia as a whole, but also their relations with other countries, especially the big powers. As South Korea's closest ally, the United States is the top stakeholder, explaining why it was worried about the excessively close Sino–South Korean ties

---

[33] Chinese Foreign Ministry, "China-South Korea Relations," http://www.fmprc.gov. cn/chn/pds/gjhdq/gj/yz/1206_12/sbgx/ (accessed January 1, 2010).

under Roh Moo-hyun. South Korea basically views itself as a nation between two big powers,[34] naturally weighing which country is more important for maximizing its long- and short-term interests. It is also natural for both of these powers to pay close attention to South Korea's relations with their countries.

When the Koguryo history dispute becomes a negative factor in Sino-Korean relations, there seems to be no positive role for the United States to play. Careful avoidance of any involvement in values-related issues such as "history wars" among East Asian countries is in its interest, at least for the time being. Such a passive stance, however, is unlikely to produce a positive outcome for long-term U.S. interests, because its indifference would create a situation in which China, South Korea, and other regional powers may turn to exclusive nationalism and regionalism and pay less attention to regional stability and the U.S. role. Given its interest in peace and stability and in managing North Korea's WMD challenge, there may be a constructive role for the United States in diminishing nationalist inclinations related to history. As a sophisticated global power, it is positioned to play such a role. Recent public opinion surveys show that there is high recognition of U.S. economic, cultural, and human capital soft power in many Asian countries. American influence in the region remains very strong, especially among citizens of the major powers. This gives the Obama administration a strong base to build upon.[35] Under current circumstances, positive involvement in academic or possible official discussions of the Koguryo history controversy is unlikely to be rejected by South Korea or China if the United States is prepared to play a balanced and constructive role with a view to stabilizing the long-term security environment in Northeast Asia. With North Korea possibly inclined to divide China, South Korea, and the United States in the context of the Six-Party Talks and to use nationalist symbols to influence South Korean behavior, minimizing the Sino–South Korean divide over the Koguryo dispute can be positive development in building trust.

---

[34] See Jae Ho Chung, "South Korea between Eagle and Dragon: Perceptual Ambivalence and Strategic Dilemma," *Asian Survey*, Vol. 46, No. 5 (September/October 2001), pp. 777–96.

[35] Chicago Council on Global Affairs, *Soft Power in Asia: Results of a 2008 Multinational Survey of Public Opinion*, 2009 Edition (Chicago: Chicago Council on Global Affairs, 2009), pp. 7–8.

8

New Grounds for Contestation

South Korea's Koguryo-Era Historical Dramas and Sino-Korean Relations

Scott Snyder

The emergence of the controversy in 2003 and 2004 over whether the Koguryo kingdom (37 BC–668 AD) was properly a precursor to or influence on the development of the modern Chinese or Korean state has marked an important shift in Korean public perceptions of China that could have political ramifications for the future of the Sino-Korean relationship. Competing North Korean and Chinese applications to register Koguryo-era tombs as a UNESCO "world heritage" site gained media attention in South Korea and raised South Korean public concerns about Chinese efforts launched in 2003 to pursue historical and archaeological research on Koguryo history as part of its multiyear, state-sponsored Northeast Project. This campaign was part of China's effort to strengthen the historical basis for claiming that ethnic minority areas within China would be historically identified with China through "internalization of border areas" (*bianjiang neidihua*).[1]

Chinese Foreign Ministry efforts to revise the Korean history section of its own website in the summer of 2004 stirred up a firestorm of controversy in South Korea (but virtually no media coverage or public awareness in China), necessitating the negotiation of a five-point oral agreement between China and South Korea in December of that year over how to manage the conflict. It also stimulated public demands for South

[1] Jae Ho Chung, "Dragon in the Eyes of South Korea: Analyzing South Korean Perceptions of China," in Jonathan D. Pollack, ed., *Korea: The East Asian Pivot* (Newport, RI: Naval War College Press, 2005), pp. 253–66.

The author would like to thank Yoo Jean Shim and SoRhym Lee for their research assistance and See-Won Byun for editorial assistance.

Korean government–led efforts to promote archaeological and historical research on Koguryo to match the Chinese Northeast Project that would be used to validate claims that Koguryo was indeed "Korean" and not "Chinese."[2] In the summer of 2004, a series of articles by Choi Kwang-shik of Korea University in the *Korean Times* "on China's distortion of the history of the ancient Korean kingdom on Koguryo" criticized its motivations, refuted its claims, and called for inter-Korean as well as international cooperation.[3] Although the five-point agreement stabilized the immediate situation, the Koguryo question remains a chronic problem in Sino-Korean relations.

The emergence of the Koguryo kingdom as a point of contention between Korean and Chinese historians, archaeologists, politicians, and publics may strike third-party observers as ironic since it is anachronistic to believe that the Koguryo people themselves would have thought in terms of a modern nation-state in ways that would identify them as either "Korean" or "Chinese." But given the role of the state in the shaping of national identity as an instrument for promoting political legitimacy in Asia since the end of World War II, it is not terribly surprising that such efforts, when focused on a kingdom such as Koguryo, the boundaries of which overlapped the existing border, might result in contradictory interpretations. Although China has done well in recent years to resolve disputes over most of its land-based borders, Asia is littered with competing historical narratives regarding the identification of islands. Much of the current competition over claims to the legacy of the Koguryo kingdom has been fed by the recognition on both sides that the border issue will only be resolved in the context of Korean reunification. In anticipation of that prospect, both sides will continue to mobilize politicians, historians, archeologists, and, as we explore in this chapter, directors, producers, actors, and curators in support of their respective claims.

Although the Chinese-Korean verbal agreement in 2004 provided guidelines for managing the conflict, Koguryo has not faded from South Korea's public consciousness. Instead, the private sector and individual activists have attempted to raise consciousness of the Koguryo issue

---

[2] Peter Hays Gries, "The Koguryo Controversy, National Identity, and Sino-Korean Relations Today," *East Asia*, Vol. 22, No. 4 (Winter 2005), pp. 3–17; Snyder, "A Turning Point for China-Korea Relations?"

[3] Choi Kwang-shik, "What Is behind China's Attempt to Distort the Past?" *Korea Times*, August 31, 2004, http://univ.ac.kr/do/MessageBoard/ArticleRead.do?id=497165 (accessed December 14, 2009).

with passive cooperation from the South Korean government. In the process, the dispute and its management have served to highlight differences
between South Korea and China in the state–society relationship. The
emergence of Koguryo as the background and subject of a series of historical dramas on South Korean television has fueled popular consciousness
of Koguryo in ways that have ramifications both for Korean national
identity and for how South Korea thinks of and deals with China.[4] The
battle has also led to conflicts between individual Chinese and Koreans
in spheres that are beyond state control or that draw state actors into
conflicts with each other. One example was the protest signs held up by
South Korean female short-track skaters in the 2007 Asian Winter Games
in Changchun, China that said "Mount Baekdu (located on the China–
North Korea border) is our land," a protest that led to South Korean
official apologies since South Korean territory is neither contiguous with
the Baekdu/Changbai mountain nor does South Korea have any basis
for a claim to the mountain.[5] Indeed, a small group of radical Korean
nationalists have since the early 1900s dreamed of taking over Yanbian,
China's ethnic Korean autonomous prefecture, currently home to two-
fifths of China's ethnic Korean population, referring to the Northeast
Chinese region as a "third Korea."[6]

The South Korean approach contrasts with the Chinese approach to
Koguryo, which remains primarily controlled by state actors, state fund-
ing, and state direction. South Korean media and civil society actors have
played a leading role in the effort and the use of "soft" instruments of
persuasion and promotion of cultural efforts to raise Korean public identification with and popular consciousness about Koguryo. This effort has
superseded historical and archaeological duels over competing claims as a
dominant influence in shaping public views of both the Koguryo kingdom
and Chinese historical claims to it.

As a way of promoting Korean identity, South Korean private actors
have also played a role in encouraging DPRK government-led efforts
to highlight Koguryo. In the process, the two Koreas have emphasized
the issue as a vehicle for promoting inter-Korean cooperation, with the
Chinese government as an implicit target of criticism for standing in the

---

[4] "Ah! Koguryo...," *Munwha ilbo*, February 8, 2007.
[5] Andrew Leonard, "The 'History War' in Northeast Asia," Salon.com, March 14, 2007;
Scott Snyder, "China-Korea Relations: A Dark Turn in Political Relations," *Comparative
Connections*, Vol. 9, No. 1 (Winter 2007), pp. 107–16.
[6] Andrei Lankov, "The Gentle Decline of the 'Third Korea,'" *Asia Times*, August 16, 2007,
http://www.atimes.com/atimes/China/IH16Ad01.html (accessed December 14, 2009).

way. But state-led cooperation of this sort has only engendered suspicion on the part of Chinese counterparts, further affirming the presumption that Korean nationalism may lead to Sino–Korean conflict or pose a political challenge for China in the context of Korean reunification. In turn, China fears that a unified Korea may claim a "Greater Korea," including the Yanbian area, where, in addition to about 3 million ethnic Koreans, at least tens of thousands of North Korean refugees reside.[7] Korean experts also point to China's "one country, one people" policy adopted in 1980 as a reflection of historical assertions and a broader effort to integrate all Chinese, including ethnic minorities, within its borders.[8] Manipulating competing claims to Koguryo is a potential tool for expressing preferences or exercising political retaliation in future Sino–Korean political disputes.

This chapter analyzes the significance and influence of the rise of Koguryo-themed historical dramas on South Korean public consciousness of Koguryo and the implications for South Korean perceptions of China. In addition, it assesses North Korean willingness to cooperate with South Korean efforts to highlight the history of Koguryo through the holding of public exhibitions in Pyongyang during 2007. Based on this analysis, I draw conclusions about civil society–led efforts to promote consciousness of Koguryo and their implications for the future of Koguryo as an issue in Korea-China relations.

Korean Historical Dramatizations of Koguryo

The 2004 Koguryo history controversy made a deep impression on South Korean opinion, reverberating among the public and serving as a catalyst for the production and airing of a series of Koguryo-themed historical dramas during 2006 and 2007. The initial effects were reflected clearly in public opinion polls. In 2004, only 6 percent of National Assemblymen viewed China as their most important diplomatic partner, compared to 55 percent who had rated China a more important partner than the United States only four months earlier.[9] This shift contributed to the

---

7 Andrei Lankov, "Two Countries, Two Systems, One Porous Border," *Asia Times*, August 14, 2007, http://www.atimes.com/atimes/China/IH14Ad01.html (accessed December 14, 2009).

8 Choi, "What Is behind China's Attempt to Distort the Past?"

9 "China or the United States?" *Korea Herald*, April 28, 2004; Lee Joo-hee, "Lawmakers Pick U.S. as Top Ally; Many Pessimistic on Economic Outlook for Second Half: Herald Survey," *Korea Herald*, August 16, 2004; Snyder, "A Turning Point for China-Korea Relations?"

decision by all major broadcasters to air historical dramas that centered on the Korean heroes of the Koguryo era.

Each of the four dramas that aired in 2006 and 2007 was a historically based reconstruction of some facet of the Koguryo period that attempted to stimulate pride in Korean history and heroes from that era. The very fact that a wave of Koguryo-themed dramas would saturate the Korean media was bound to have an influence on popular Korean identification with the Koguryo period. In 2007, it was estimated that up to 90 percent of the Korean viewing public watched at least one of these dramas,[10] all of which were aired in prime time slots and had the potential to influence perceptions of China.

MBC's drama *Jumong*, the name of the founder of Koguryo, King Dongmyeongseong, was aired in eighty-one episodes from May 15, 2006 to March 6, 2007, receiving over 40 percent viewership ratings. Originally planned for fifty episodes, its popularity led to an extension, which, some argued, hurt the quality of the program. *Jumong* has also enjoyed successful exports to foreign countries, contributing to the perpetuation of the "Korean wave"; however, its popularity in China was criticized by some Korean netizens as evidence that the drama's storyline might be manipulated by the Chinese to further their own historical claims to the Koguryo kingdom.[11] This drama begins with the fall of Gojoseon following a long battle with the Han Chinese nation. Jumong's father, Hae Mo-su, a legendary soldier, joins forces with Geumwa, a crown prince of the Buyeo kingdom, but they are separated after a fierce battle and Hae Mo-su is nursed back to health by a princess of the Haebaek tribe, who eventually becomes the wife of Geumwa, the crown prince of Buyeo. Jumong is raised as a Buyeo prince and eventually meets his real father, who teaches him the fighting skills necessary to reconsolidate territory and establish the kingdom of Koguryo in BC 37.[12]

SBS produced *Yeongae Somun*, based on a prominent Koguryo-era General Yeon Gae Somun, who killed the penultimate Koguryo king in a coup d'etat in BC 642. The drama aired in one hundred episodes from July 8, 2006, to June 17, 2007. It was widely anticipated, but it was criticized by Korean netizens for emphasizing the Chinese Sui kingdom

---

[10] "Ah! Koguryo. . . . "

[11] "Hallyu Reaches Other Side of the World," *Korea Times*, October 30, 2007, http://www.imbc.com/broad/tv/drama/jumong/opinion/index.html (accessed January 5 and 8, 2008).

[12] A summary is available at http://twitchfilm.net/archives/006653.html (accessed January 6, 2008); or http://www.esiamdvd.com/filmreviewsnews/koreantvdramahistorical.php (accessed January 5, 2008).

to the extent that some viewers started to call it the "Sui Kingdom Historical Drama."[13] Ratings dropped to about 10 percent, although by the end of the series viewership had returned to around 20 percent. It takes place during the seventh century, almost six centuries after *Jumong*, in the waning days of the kingdom, when factional intrigues engulfed the Koguryo leadership as Sui and Tang invaders increasingly challenged them. The drama captures the factionalism and divisions that characterized a kingdom in decline as it fought a series of battles against Sui and Tang Dynasty invading forces. Although Koguryo was able to repel Sui invaders, it eventually succumbed to the Tang, who joined hands with the Shilla army after the death of Yeongae Somun. A controversial aspect of focusing on Yeongae Somun is that the plot elevates him while diminishing General Yang Manch'un, who is known in history texts as having shot the Tang Emperor in the eye with an arrow.[14]

KBS produced *Daejoyoung*, based on the life of General Dae Jo-young, who witnessed the downfall of Koguryo and established the successor kingdom, Parhae.[15] Aired in over one hundred episodes between September 16, 2006, and December 23, 2007, *Daejoyoung* was praised for being the most true to historical events of the four dramas, while *Jumong* and *Yeongae Somun* were challenged from various quarters regarding their historical accuracy. *Daejoyoung* covers many of the same events as *Yeongae Somun* at the end of the seventh century, including the intrigues surrounding the Tang-Shilla alliance to destroy Koguryo, while also describing how Parhae was established and relations were managed with the Tang and Shilla rulers, thus establishing links between the Koguryo and Parhae kingdoms. It provides a sense of continuity between Koguryo and Parhae, emphasizing the latter's Koguryo origins.

MBC also produced a science fiction–like drama, *Taewang Sasingi*, based loosely on the story of Kwanggaeto, the greatest king of the era who expanded Koguryo territory into Manchuria. Starring the actor at the forefront of the "Korean wave," Bae Yongjoon (lead star of the Korean love drama *Winter Sonata*), *Taewang Sasingi* ran in twenty-four

---

[13] "From 'Jumong' to 'Daejoyoung,' Let's Review the Koguryo-Era Dramas," http://www.ohmynews.com/NWS_Web/view/at_pg.aspx?CNTN_CD=A0000799641 (accessed January 6, 2008).

[14] See Hwang You-mee, "Big-Budget Historical Dramas Popular," *Korea Herald*, July 10, 2006; http://www.koreandrama.org/?p=312 (accessed January 6, 2008). Summaries are available in Korean at http://wizard2.sbs.co.kr/resource/template/contents/07_review_list.jsp?vProgId=1000239&vVodId=V0000328662&vMenuId=1004373 (accessed on January 6, 2008).

[15] On Daejoyoung, see http://www.kbs.co.kr/drama/daejoyoung/ (accessed on January 8, 2008).

episodes from September 11 to December 5, 2007, but scored audience ratings in the low 30 percent range for most of its run.[16] Despite high expectations and an all-star cast, the science fiction approach and its relative brevity left viewers somewhat disappointed,[17] especially since the Koguryo controversy aroused great interest in the life and times of King Kwanggaeto. In a contest sponsored by the Bank of Korea in 2007 to select the Korean figure for the 100,000 won bill, King Kwanggaeto was the top choice, but he was officially excluded from the list out of concern for the likely negative diplomatic reaction from China.[18] His popularity is further illustration of the impact that Koguryo-era dramas have had on Korean historical consciousness during 2006–7, and the feeling that his story has not yet been properly told may stimulate an additional Koguryo-era historical drama despite the expected response from China.

Koguryo-Era Historical Dramas: Intent and Impact

Any historical drama inevitably attempts to mix historical fact with drama and imagination to produce a compelling script and action. Viewers are aware that they are watching a drama, but the historical background and setting impute to the drama a certain level of credibility, while the dramas shape the public's historical knowledge in a far more vivid manner than textbooks or original documents concerning the era in question. The historical drama also may take on aspects of a morality tale; the producer and directors can impute values and cultural pride through the telling of the story. In the case of the three main Koguryo-era historical dramas, all these elements influenced the viewer.

An English-language synopsis for *Jumong* describes the drama as follows:

> You are about to go back to the time of Koguryo, a time which was bigger than now. "A time when our nation was the most beautiful," "A time when our nation was the center of the world." ... The most surprising time in history has come back 2000 years later, a time when the nation made China fall down to their knees and when we fought other nations without any fear.[19]

---

[16] See http://www.esiamdvd.com/filmreviewsnews/koreantvdramahistorical.php (accessed January 5, 2008).

[17] "From 'Jumong' to 'Daejoyoung,' Let's Review the Koguryo-Era Dramas."

[18] "Popularity of Goguryeo King Puzzles BOK," *Korea Herald*, August 9, 2007.

[19] See http://content.mbc.co.kr/e_mbc/drama.asp?idx=223 (accessed January 6, 2008).

The lead actor, Choi Soo-jong of *Daejoyoung*, described the lead character as a great hero who overcame threats from China: "I once again realized that we are a small but strong nation.... Since historical dramas are not documentaries, certain parts are different from the facts. Nevertheless, what *Daejoyeong* wants to emphasize is the process of finding our national identity through Parhae, like America's pioneer spirit." Director Kim Jong-sun also emphasized that, "I hope our young viewers could discover pride for our nation through *Daejoyoung*."[20] Likewise, the writer of *Yeongae Somun*, Lee Hwan-gyeong, argued that the importance of his work was the restoration of "lost history." "I felt frustrated by the Korean government's inactive response toward the Chinese' distorted historical viewpoint over Koguryo. Through this drama, I hope to change people's mind and tackle China's unreasonable claims over Koguryo."[21]

In the absence of polling regarding the impact of the dramas, one way of assessing their influence is through a review of various blogs or netizen reactions. These blogs are available either in the form of "fan clubs" established at popular South Korean portal sites in response to the dramas or on the sites of the broadcasters themselves. They give some indication of the ways in which Korean viewers responded to each of the three dramas, and particularly to the interaction between the heroes and their Chinese interlocutors from the Han (*Jumong*), Sui (*Yeongae Somun*), and Tang (*Daejoyoung*) dynasties. One clear effect has been to heighten consciousness, especially among middle and high school students, about the importance of studying history.[22] Viewer comments reveal the following themes:

• Some were sensitive to deviations from the versions of history they had learned in school, especially when they made the "Korean" historical figures look weak.

Viewers were particularly upset by historical inaccuracies that were introduced in order to enhance the dramatic quality of the storyline. For instance, the *Jumong* drama delayed advances in iron-making technology

---

[20] Donga.com article about Daejoyoung, September 14, 2006, http://english.donga .com/srv/service.php3?biid=2006091499418 (accessed January 5, 2008).

[21] See http://www.esiamdvd.com/filmreviewsnews/koreantvdramahistorical.php (accessed January 5, 2008); Hwang, "Big-Budget Historical Dramas Popular"; "Historical Dramas Strain Sino-Korean Relations," July 3, 2006, http://blog.naver.com/margenda/ 140025925952 (accessed January 8, 2008).

[22] See Lim Ji-hye, "Middle School Student Essay: 'Palhae Daejoyoung,'" No. 1299, November 11, 2006, at http://www.kbs.co.kr/drama/daejoyoung/netizen/bbs/index.html (accessed November 11, 2006).

in its representation of Buyeo technology compared to Han Dynasty weaponry, sparking comments from viewers that the producers should not take liberties or distort historical facts, especially in ways that portrayed the Korean protagonists as weaker than they really were, simply for the sake of a plot line.[23] Another posting on *Jumong* was concerned that the producers had portrayed the Buyeo kingdom as a Han vassal state, warning that, "if we ourselves acknowledge that Buyeo is a vassal state of Han China and if it comes out that the prince was sent to China, the Chinese will say, 'Look at that, if it is right that Buyeo was a vassal state of the Han nation and if a king from Buyeo named Jumong established Koguryo, then Koguryo must also be a vassal state of China.'"[24] Viewers of *Yeongae Somun* were frustrated with the drama's portrayal of the Sui Dynasty invaders and the successes that they had against Koguryo, leading some to criticize the authors for making a drama that might actually support aspects of the argument that the history of the period belongs to China.

Suh Jun-soo's posting gave both an appreciation and a critique of the influence of dramas on historical understanding, part of the intent of the producers that was validated in the vast majority of responses:

> ... the current Koguryo-era historical dramas can of course provide some response to China's efforts to distort history through the Northeast Project, but I think it is not right to solve historical problems through promotion of nationalism. The actual history of the Tang Dynasty is not just about how China was brought together to be unified, but also about how the Han established a diverse and multi-ethnic kingdom.... Departing from a simplistic view of this being a China–Korea historical dispute, I think it is the role of a historical drama to be more objective and balanced in its interpretation of that historical period. In many ways *Daejoyoung* was better than the other historical dramas in that aspect.[25]

- Many expected the main characters to be leaders with a grand vision for the "nation." There was also disappointment with the failures of the heroes, even if the storyline was true to historical facts.

---

[23] Lee Bo-lam, "Han Soldiers Didn't Have Iron Technology; That Was a Characteristic of the Koguryo Kingdom," February 23, 2007, http://www.imbc.com/broad/tv/drama/jumong/opinion/index.html (accessed January 7, 2008). Also see http://twitchfilm.net/site/view/sageuk-world-no-1-jumong-ep-19/, June 26, 2006 (accessed January 7, 2008).

[24] See Kim Su-young, http://www.imbc.com/broad/tv/drama/jumong/opinion/index.html, "You've Made Buyo Look Like a Vassal State of the Han Kingdom...," October 12, 2006 (accessed January 7, 2008).

[25] See Suh Joon-soo, "Some Areas of Regret," October 7, 2006, http://www.kbs.co.kr/drama/daejoyoung/netizen/bbs/index.html (accessed January 7, 2008).

Viewers expressed irritation with the incorporation of romantic motives or plot lines into the portrayal of heroic figures who were involved in the larger business of consolidating power or creating a new kingdom. Some commentators criticized the portrayal of Jumong as foolish or felt that Jumong's love story either got in the way of the history or was incompatible with the image befitting the founder of a nation. Viewers found the title character of *Yeongae Somun* to have been weak and were disappointed by attempts to weave love stories into the narrative.[26] Both the *Yeongae Somun* and *Daejoyoung* plots involved romantic weaknesses that provided an opening for Sui and Tang manipulation.

- Viewers expected the dramas to make a strong defense of Korea's historical position in an effort to refute claims made by China's Northeast Project.

In response to early episodes of *Jumong*, Cha Yang-won wrote, "Come on! In the face of the reality that the Chinese continue to pile up historical distortions as part of their Northeast Project, if the dramas that we make are too weak, then what will we be able to use to counter the misunderstandings of the Chinese?"[27] *Daejoyoung* viewer Kim Tong-jin had the following reaction to the roles of Yeongae Somun and Daejoyoung at the time of Koguryo's fall:

> Although it is just a drama, it really made me cry for the reality of our division. . . . I was really upset when Yeongae Somun was told that "History is in the hands of the ultimate victor." My heart ached so much that I didn't want to watch *Daejoyoung* because our Koguryo history is becoming part of Chinese history as a result of China's Northeast Project. My heart is broken at the thought that in one hundred or two hundred years our descendants will read textbooks that have changed Koguryo history into Chinese history.[28]

One problem that *Yeongae Somun* faced with Korean viewers was the perception that it spent too much time covering the Sui invasion of Koguryo and the capital of Pyongyang. Kim Gil-sung wrote, "If I look at *Yeongae Somun* right now, I'm too stressed out. Instead of extending the

[26] See Chin Dong-ok, "Taejoyoung Is Too Weak," January 4, 2007, http://www.kbs.co.kr/drama/daejoyoung/netizen/bbs/index.html (accessed January 7, 2008).

[27] See Ch'a Young-won, "If You Are Going to Do It on Such a Small Scale, Get Rid of the Fight Scenes!" September 5, 2006, http://www.imbc.com/broad/tv/drama/jumong/opinion/index.html (accessed January 7, 2008).

[28] See Kim Tong-jin, "Let's Find Our Forgotten History," December 2, 2006, http://www.kbs.co.kr/drama/daejoyoung/netizen/bbs/index.html (accessed January 7, 2008).

Sui kingdom historical story, what about Yeongae Somun? Of course,
I know that Yeongae Somun and the Sui kingdom are connected, but
the story of Yeongae Somun is only about 15 percent, so this is really
irritating."[29]

• The dramas collectively stimulated curiosity and speculation about
  what Korea would be like if historical events had developed in a different direction.

A review of all four dramas on the *Oh My News!* website speculated that,
"If you are Korean, you can't help but wonder how events might have
developed if Korea had been unified under Koguryo instead of under the
leadership of the Silla Dynasty. To that extent there is high Korean interest in the Koguryo kingdom."[30] This question was also reflected in the
blog entries that covered events in connection with the fall of Koguryo,[31]
notably the failures of Yeongae Somun and Daejoyoung against the Sui
and Tang dynasty forces. For instance, *Daejoyoung* viewer Choe Young-
sun expressed disappointment following the end of the drama that she
did not get to see the fall of the Tang Dynasty.[32] The raising of such
a question, however, is doubly provocative, given that one reason why
Koguryo-era history had not been emphasized is that such stories might
embellish the legitimacy of North Korea. The airing of Koguryo-era historical dramas is a powerful indicator of the extent to which the inter-
Korean relationship has changed. In fact, the director of *Yeongae Somun*
sought North Korean assistance in filming some parts of that drama.
Speculation might follow into whether Koguryo might have been better
positioned to lead a larger Korean Empire that would have been more
aggressive against the Chinese and to what extent Korean unification was
achieved as a result of outside collaboration with the Tang. After all,
the Shilla Dynasty, which had occupied the southern part of the peninsula, benefited from collaboration with Tang in its successful quest to
defeat the Paekche and Koguryo kingdoms in order to unify the Korean
peninsula.

---

[29] Ibid.
[30] "From 'Jumong' to 'Daejoyoung.' Let's Review the Koguryo-Era Dramas."
[31] See Kwak Ch'oongyoung, "We Need Heroes for Our Times!" September 30, 2006,
     http://www.kbs.co.kr/drama/daejoyoung/netizen/bbs/index.html (accessed January 7,
     2008).
[32] http://www.kbs.co.kr/drama/daejoyoung/netizen/bbs/index.html, Entry No. 71074,
     January 2, 2008 (accessed January 7, 2008).

Inter-Korean Cooperation and Cultural Representations of Koguryo

Aside from the production of South Korean dramas, an exhibition of photographs of Koguryo-era murals from North Korea's UNESCO world heritage site that had been making its way through Japan and South Korea in 2005–7 also opened at the Korean Central History Museum in Pyongyang from October 8 through November 10, 2007. It was cosponsored by Kyodo News Agency and South Korea's Yonhap News Agency, with cooperation from the DPRK's Central News Agency, the Association for Cultural Relations with Foreign Countries, and the DPRK-Japan Exchange Association. Of the 107 Koguryo tombs that have been discovered, 76 are located in or around Pyongyang.[33]

The exhibition opened immediately following the 2007 inter-Korean summit and was characterized by North Korean officials as a way of improving inter-Korean relations. North Korean official Hong Son-ok described the exhibition opening as an event that "will further boost our people's struggle to achieve a unified powerhouse nation and promote the improvement of [North] Korea and Japan relations based on a drastic clearance of their past." The Yonhap News Agency president stated that "The murals of the Koguryo kingdom, which controlled the northern part of the Korean peninsula and Manchuria, are an element that links the people of South and North Korea."[34]

In 2004, Choi Kwang-shik described the Koguryo problem as "not one for South or North Korea, but one for all Korean people, this being an opportunity for the two countries to cooperate with each other."[35] In addition to joint inter-Korean efforts against Chinese actions, he called for increasing technical support to upgrade North Korea's Koguryo sites and surrounding areas, expanding South Korea's information network, given the level of China's personnel and material support. Choi also called for holding international forums, such as one in March 2004, to promote Koguryo history with experts from other countries, such as Japan, the United States, and Russia. He also indicated that China's Northeast,

[33] "Photo Exhibition of Ancient Korean Murals to Open in Pyongyang," Kyodo News Agency, October 8, 2007; "Yonhap's President Leaves for North Korea for Joint Exhibition on Ancient Korean Kingdom," Yonhap News Agency, October 8, 2007.

[34] Kim Hyun, "N. Korea Sees Koguryo Legacy as Way to Promote Inter-Korean Relations," Yonhap, October 11, 2007.

[35] Choi Kwang-shik, "Two Koreas Should Join Forces to Rectify China's Folly," *Korea Times*, August 31, 2009.

drawing increasing interest since Sino–South Korean diplomatic normalization in 1992, was the subject of heated debate in a 1993 meeting
between Chinese and North Korean academics. Choi added that moves
to address potential problems arising from Korean unification, in response
to the ROK National Assembly's establishment in 2001 of a law to deal
with ethnic Koreans in China, reflect Beijing's underlying concerns over
the long-term questions of unification. "Seen in the long-term, China's
moves can be seen as a proactive measure to deal with a potential border
dispute that could arise if South and North Korea were to be unified. Or
else, it is a preemptive act in preparation for possible power changes in
North Korea by fortifying its position in the northeastern region."[36]

Chinese Reactions to Korea's Production of Koguryo-Era Historical Dramas

Most Chinese reactions to South Korean concerns about China's Northeast Project have been state-led. After the Ministry of Foreign Affairs
deleted from its website all references to pre-1948 Korean history instead
of making the revisions requested by Seoul, China also blocked public
access to any online discussions of the issue. Officials were particularly
sensitive as a result of the fact that all three networks decided to produce
Koguryo-era historical dramas at the same time that the South Korean
government had decided to launch a response to the Northeast Project.
During the 2006 Shanghai Television Festival, Chinese broadcasting officials reacted sensitively to MBC posters and other material promoting
Jumong. Apparently, officials had previously reacted to efforts by South
Korean broadcasters to promote the "Korean wave" primarily due to concerns that those imports would further exacerbate China's trade deficit
with South Korea, but the promotion of Koguryo-era dramas was particularly sensitive issue for officials, who saw it as a direct challenge to
China's own Northeast Project.[37]

The Chinese government has shunned historical textbooks that provide
evidence for or highlight texts that emphasize Korean versions or claims
to Koguryo-era history. Two novels, entitled *Song of Sword* and *Ahbe's
Family*, were rejected, along with one classic early Korean history text,

---

[36] Choi, "What Is behind China's Attempt to Distort the Past?"
[37] See "Broadcasting Stations Discover Diplomatic Problems Related to the Koguryo
History Dramas," *Yonhap*, June 22, 2006; Robert Koehler, http://www.rjkoehler
.com/2006/06/22/china-suspicious-about-koreas-goguryeo-history-dramas/ (accessed
January 7, 2008).

Samguk yusa (Legends of the Three Kingdoms). According to Woosuk University historian Cho Bup-jong, "Chinese historians are reluctant to accept the term 'three kingdoms' because they define the ancient history of Korea as that of two kingdoms, Shilla and Baekje, not three that include Koguryo."[38]

Another response is sponsorship of a Chinese historical drama entitled *Legend of Xue Rengui*, named after the Tang general who led the invasion and conquest of Koguryo. In the drama, Xue defeats a rebellious army from Boliao who had hoped to establish their own "Boliao kingdom." Given that there is no historical location called Boliao, South Koreans criticized what they saw as intentional attempts to subvert the historical integrity of the Koguryo claims by mixing place names and subverting historical details, promoting the idea that Koguryo was a regional government under the Tang as part of the broader aim of the Northeast Project.[39]

As mentioned previously, *Jumong* has done well in export markets, including Hong Kong and China. One apparent reason is that Chinese drama fans did not distinguish the difference between "Koguryo kingdom" and "Korean kingdom," and did not realize that the content was politically sensitive until Chinese "history experts" noted the controversy. The government has also reportedly blocked the airing of *Taewang Sasingi* on Chinese public stations, but it is available to viewers online. Although some Chinese bloggers have expressed concerns about the dangers of Korean nationalism, other sites have reportedly emphasized that Korean objections to Chinese history should remind Chinese to be proud of their own history and cultural heritage and take good care of it.

Although very little official commentary about the Koguryo controversy has been published in Chinese journals, Kao Yen has published two articles warning of the rise of "radical nationalism on the Korean peninsula" and arguing that traditionally, Koreans had long accepted a subservient role in recognition of the superiority of Chinese civilization, and that the best prospects for peace in Northeast Asia would come with reaffirmation of this traditional role. Along with Japanese right-wing nationalism, the author argues that

> ... another kind of nationalistic extremism originates with the two parties of North and South Korea on the Korean peninsula, manifesting itself

---

[38] "Chinese Publishers Recoil from Historical Korean Books," *Chosun ilbo*, July 30, 2007.
[39] "Koguryo Udie Iss-nin-ga?" *Hangyore Sinmun*, May 11, 2007; author's personal communication with Chinese drama fan, January 7, 2008.

in arrogance and stubborn, extreme behavior. The latest North Korean nuclear incident exemplifies the dangers of narrow nationalism to regional peace... in the present stage, the key to Chinese action lies in the need to defend Northeast Asia and even the truth of Chinese history, and this historical truth will naturally reveal the various historical rights and interests of China on the Korean peninsula. Therefore, the understanding of history is the core issue in the conflict between radical nationalism on the Korean peninsula and the national interests of China at the current stage.[40]

Kao's view is that historically the Korean peninsula occupied a "subservient position and not a leading role," and that both North and South Korean attempts to secure independence are factors for instability since "the Korean peninsula was not a genuinely independent nation historically but instead part of a Chinese East Asian entity that was highly systematized." Thus, one key to peace on the peninsula is for the Koreas to accept their traditional role within the context of a broader "Chinese civilization." Kao interprets this historical relationship as

> ... a structure of appendage to China's imperialistic system. ... In the event of resistance arising from a reluctance to accept China's reign, the Korean peninsula would have lost the foundation of its survival, that is, the endorsement by the Chinese hinterland for its independent survival. Precisely for this reason, during the Han and Tang dynasties the Korean Peninsula was twice incorporated into Chinese territory to remove all counter-resistance, and Koguryo, which arose in the northeastern part of China and extended its influence toward the Korean peninsula, was completely eradicated because of its confrontation with the Chinese dynastic court. Eventually, it merged with Chinese civilization to become one of the ancestral sources of the northern Chinese people, instead of continuing its survival as a country or a nationality. The history of Koguryo provides a counter-lesson for the northern Korean Peninsula about how it should get along with China in peaceful co-existence."[41]

Conclusion

With China replacing the United States as South Korea's biggest trade partner in 2003, the Koguryo dispute revealed South Korea's growing wariness about a future more closely aligned with China.[42] The upgrading

---

[40] Kao Yen, "Radical Nationalism Rears Its Head in Northeast Asia," *Kuang Chiao Ching* (Hong Kong; in Chinese) No. 413 (February 16–March 7–15, 2007), pp. 32–5 (Open source center, Doc. No. CPP20070307710001).

[41] Ibid.

[42] Bruce Klingner, "China Shock for South Korea," *Asia Times*, September 11, 2004, http://www.atimes.com/atimes/Korea/FI11Dg03.html (accessed December 14, 2009).

of the Sino–South Korean relationship to a "strategic cooperative partnership" in 2008 affirmed rapidly expanding bilateral trade ties, projected to reach $200 billion by 2010 and already representing a fifth of South Korea's foreign trade, but the political side of the relationship remains challenged by unresolved differences over such issues as history and North Korea.[43] These limits on the extent of this partnership were seen in the clashes surrounding the Beijing Olympics torch relay in Seoul at the time of the April 2008 Hu-Lee summit, pitting Chinese students and South Korean human rights activists demonstrating against China's handling of Tibet and treatment of North Korean refugees.[44]

This review of the flurry of Koguryo-era historical dramas, the intent behind their production, and the public response to them suggests that the Koguryo issue is unlikely to be easily resolved, especially as Korean consciousness of contested histories continues to be heightened as a result of such dramas. Both the launching of these productions and the public responses suggest that the contest over Koguryo has moved beyond the control of the two governments and into the private sector, where public opinion over the original 2004 dispute created demand for such dramas, which in turn further heightened public consciousness as well as political sensitivities surrounding management of the dispute.

The initial South Korean response to the Koguryo issue and the continuing focus on it is driven in part by the asymmetry inherent in the relationship and the asymmetrical response to the dispute itself. While there has been a firestorm in South Korean public opinion combined with ongoing efforts to raise consciousness about and identification with Koguryo, the Chinese response has been minimal. There have been few Chinese efforts to mobilize opinion on the issue, and most Chinese are not even aware of Korean sensitivities surrounding this issue. A recent *China Daily* article promoting tourism in Jilin Province again stirred strong online reactions among South Koreans, suggesting that China has "admitted Koguryo is Korean" based on the article's statement that "The ancient Korean kingdom established its capital in Ji'an more than 2,000 years ago."[45]

---

[43] Scott Snyder, "Establishing a "Strategic Cooperative Partnership," *Comparative Connections*, Vol. 10, No. 2 (July 2008), http://csis.org/files/media/csis/pubs/0802qchina_korea.pdf (accessed December 14, 2009).

[44] Kurt Achin, "Massive Chinese Crowds Overwhelm Olympic Torch Protests in South Korea," *Voice of America*, April 27, 2008.

[45] "From Waterfalls to Ancient Capitals – Jilin Parades Its Top Beauty Spots," *China Daily*, October 22, 2009, http://www.chinadaily.com.cn/life/2009–10/22/content_8831798.htm (accessed December 14, 2009).

The handling of Koguryo as a diplomatic and political issue and the way in which the dispute has developed further underscores the different systems in South Korea and China, which in turn have made management of the dispute more difficult. On the Chinese side, the fact that the Northeast Project is government-sponsored has served to heighten public sensitivities regarding the issue in South Korea, while Chinese counterparts had difficulty understanding how the mobilization of civil society and public opinion to focus on this issue could be a response to grass-roots demand rather than led politically and financially by the government. History issues between the two sides also expose the gap between the historical nature of Sino-Korean relations and current challenges. In the words of one South Korean diplomat:

> ... after a hundred years of hiatus, Korea and China met again in 1992, but this meeting in one hundred years is a different kind of meeting – a qualitatively different meeting than the way our relations were a hundred years ago. Before the nineteenth century, China had been the center of the world for the Korean mindset. But when we met in 1992, a lot had changed. We were richer than China; we were equipped with different ideas; and this is also important; we are the ally of a superpower, which is the United States, and our way of thinking came from a different direction, from the West. When we met again we were a completely different nation.[46]

The history issue dramatizes the tensions that accompany a gap in expectations and understanding between the traditional Sino-Korean relationship of the past and the desire on the part of South Koreans to forge a new relationship on very different terms.

The migration of the Koguryo dispute into the sphere of media and popular culture has also highlighted questions surrounding the utility and limits of "soft power" both as a tool of diplomacy and as a flashpoint for potential political conflict. Koguryo historical dramas have had a major influence on Korean perceptions of their own history and attachment to Koguryo, but the audience for this message was probably ultimately Korean-only. The attractiveness of Korean dramas as a "Korean wave" cultural export has been celebrated as a potential tool that would enhance South Korean stature and power abroad, but such tools faced real limits due to Chinese concerns that the dramas would send the wrong message to Chinese viewers. The popularity of the dramas, to the extent that they were appreciated as entertainment, also provided opportunities to circumvent Chinese state control. Yet, such products are not likely to have

---

[46] Author interview in Seoul, October 18, 2007.

a direct influence on Chinese views of Koguryo in the face of contrary and competing messages sponsored by the Chinese state.

Finally, the production of historical dramas and their influence on Korean identification with Koguryo have probably served to promote the politicization of the dispute and enhanced the likelihood that Koguryo will remain an intractable dispute for the foreseeable future. The spread of the dispute to the cultural sphere is likely to ensure that periodic flare-ups will occur as South Korean grass-roots perceptions clash with Chinese government-led parameters for addressing the issue. The two governments will have to spend more time and effort on managing an issue that is unlikely to be easily resolved.

9

U.S. Strategic Thinking on Sino–South Korean Differences over History

Gilbert Rozman

History serves as a contentious arena for explaining the world as it is and as it is desired. In October 2009, Chinese, Japanese, and South Koreans made plans to write a joint textbook recognizing the shared history of their countries and helping to realize an East Asian community. In the tradition of new regimes steeped in the Confucian heritage, a didactic history would serve a legitimating purpose. Yet, it could also pose a challenge to U.S.-centered histories of the twentieth-century struggle for freedom and to efforts to look ahead toward globalization based on universal values. China's thinking about the past is at the center of this struggle between rival histories, and its recent disputes with South Korea over an ancient kingdom are instructive for understanding what is at stake.

The Hu Jintao era reveals an increasingly assertive China in international affairs, striving to counter U.S. power around the globe while drawing neighboring states closer in a regional community. Much has been written about China's use of economic power and its buildup of military power, as its search for soft power also has not been ignored. Yet, discussions of soft power have little to say about the way China handles historical memories, even with the two countries most often associated with its Confucian tradition and its twentieth-century wars. To the extent history is covered, it is centered on Japan's need to apologize and reassure the Chinese people. Missing is how China deals with issues from its own imperial assertiveness. The Koguryo dispute with South Korea has revived interest in this with implications for China's ambitions toward Japan and other neighbors. In the background looms the potential emergence of sinocentrism as an organizing principle excluding the United States and countering what is depicted as hegemonism.

As Jae Ho Chung observes, Koguryo is but one in a series of Chinese projects to present a far-reaching historical review conducive to present-day sovereignty objectives. The Southwest Project subsumes Tibetan history in Chinese local history. Ma Dezheng, a Xinjiang expert, was given charge of the Northeast Project, suggesting links to thinking about China's Northwest region too.[1] Writings on dynastic history and China in transition after 1911 and under communist rule have become increasingly targeted at reinforcing territorial claims and strengthening the legitimacy of Communist Party rule. With little notice outside China, the doctrinaire histories of the Maoist era are being revised with more factual accuracy but also with distorted interpretations to make a more persuasive case to nationalist audiences of today. China is making history a battleground, putting Korea on the front lines in a struggle that is likely to intensify, as it challenges U.S. views ranging from the age of imperialism to the struggle between socialism and the free world. The Koguryo issue in the 2000s alerts us to the role of history in sinocentrism.

While the dispute with South Korea over how to characterize this ancient kingdom has drawn little attention in the rest of the world, it has had a dramatic effect in transforming the thinking of citizens and politicians in South Korea toward China and, indirectly, toward the United States and regional relations. It offers a window on lingering struggles over national identity or history in the region that supersede single-minded preoccupation with Japan's wartime conduct. Played out in academic textbooks, television dramas, and the mass media, this controversy has aroused the South Korean public at the same time that China's stubbornly provocative approach informs us about its strategy for regional leadership and the reverberations inside China when a controversy of this sort flares. By reviewing the Koguryo dispute, we better understand how Sino–South Korean relations are unfolding and how the United States might anticipate the impact of sinocentrism and develop its own approach to historical memory as an appealing alternative to China's.

In 2004–8, with attention drawn to the rivalry between Japan and China and to tensions between the United States and South Korea as well as Japan and South Korea, few foreign policy observers took much notice of burgeoning competition between South Korea and China. Even when controversy between the two erupted over divergent views of the historic

---

[1] Jae Ho Chung, "China's 'Soft' Clash with South Korea: The History War and Beyond," *Asian Survey*, Vol. 49, No. 3 (May/June 2009), pp. 468–83.

state of Koguryo, it was readily dismissed as of little consequence. To the extent that questions have been raised about conflicting strategies in Beijing and Seoul, the focus has been rival plans for investment and commerce in order to gain access to natural resources and achieve an economic foothold in the poverty-stricken North. Yet, we would be remiss to overlook how the Koguryo dispute fits into the broader struggle over the future of the Korean peninsula, in which politics and culture matter as well as economics. The United States is already caught in the crossfire between clashing agendas for steering North Korea away from its profound isolation, and it is likely to realize that one part of the struggle involves interpreting the long-term course of Sino-Korean history.

The Koguryo controversy lingers today as a source of doubt in South Korea over the future of a united Korea's relations with China. Behind differences in interpretation regarding how to categorize the state that 1,350 to 2,050 years ago straddled today's border of Northeast China and North Korea lie uncertainties about Korean reunification, future territorial claims, China's prospective influence on the peninsula, and efforts to firm up national identities. Ordinarily, the United States, as is its wont in similar situations, would refrain from taking any position since there exists no direct controversy over any apparent policy issue. On the surface, this is an arcane matter of reinterpreting a distant historical state; yet, if views of history become intertwined with struggles linked to security, this may become a test of regional transformation, in which history matters.

The scholarly literature on this dispute is not extensive. A 2005 article by Peter Gries assessed the immediate impact when the issue arose.[2] A 2009 article by Jae Ho Chung took a broader perspective on how the dispute contributed to more negative views of China in South Korea.[3] In Chinese, the dispute is little covered, even in histories such as a 2005 edited book from Changchun.[4] In Korean, the mass media offers mostly short items narrowly treating how the issue had arisen, as well as specialized historical works, including Lee Sungun's 2005 book on the period of Koguryo.[5] An exception is U Silha's 2004 book that disabuses Koreans of the notion that the issue arose through local research when he can demonstrate clearly that the Northeast Project reflected a decision of the

[2] Peter Hays Gries, "The Koguryo Controversy, National Identity, and Sino-Korean Relations Today," *East Asia*, Winter 2005, pp. 3–17.
[3] Chung, "China's 'Soft' Clash with South Korea, pp. 468–83.
[4] Jiang Weigong, ed., *Gaojuli yanjiu chubian* (Changchun: Jilin daxue chubanshe, 2005).
[5] I Sungun, *Koguryo yoksa, kwayon nugu e yoksa inga?* (Seoul: NuriMedia, 2005).

top leadership.[6] Such sources do not say much about the broad context in which the issue has emerged or any possible U.S. role. They only hint at the bigger challenge from China's thinking about the history of relations between states, regionally and globally.

The National Identity Context

The Confucian tradition closely linked regime legitimacy in East Asian states to reasoning about historical precedents. Failure to achieve even minimal consensus on what constitute appropriate apology and closure for Japan's aggression through 1945 left an open wound to fester in national identity debates. Of late, China's rapid rise and the prospect of Korean reunification raise long-submerged questions about not only spheres of influence, but also legitimacy rooted in history. The Koguryo controversy arose amid a whirlwind of historical consciousness as nations seek clarification of their uncertain national identities after the cold war and in response to globalization as well as regional economic integration. High levels of nationalism raise the stakes for historical disputes.

Nationalism in South Korea intensified under Park Chung-hee with emphasis on pride in the early history of Koreans striving to unify their country and establish a strong, independent state. Koguryo figured importantly in that narrative, as it fended off various Chinese dynasties with designs on Korean territory and finally joined in the unification that produced the Koryo state. With South Koreans intent on overcoming the division of their country, identification with the northern state of Koguryo served to clarify the case for commonalities in the Korean nation and for historic precedent in overcoming division. Democratization and the end of the cold war heightened nationalist sentiments about the prospects of reunification, as contacts widened first with the Koreans living inside China on the border of North Korea and within the territory once belonging to Koguryo. The way national identity has been constructed leaves Koreans highly sensitive to this theme.

Chinese nationalism changed in nature in the 1980s as increased decentralization and academic freedom gave voice to local interests, reflected most in provincial academic circles. With the collapse of the Soviet Union amid loss of territory, leaders encouraged the field of border studies that reinforced a sense of state identity. In Northeast China, an established,

---

[6] U Shilha, *Dongbuk gongchong oe sonhaeng chakopdul goa Chungguk oe kukka chonryak* (Seoul: Simin oe sonmun, 2004).

conservative academic establishment took keen interest in this pursuit. At the time of the patriotic education movement of the 1990s, as uncertainty peaked about the degree to which South Korean influence might spread to Jilin's Yanbian Koreans and the North Korean regime might collapse, some sought assurance in the belief that Koguryo (Gaoguoli) had actually been a subordinate state of successive Chinese dynasties. Given the goal of preventing Taiwan's de jure independence and the recent tightening of control over Tibet and Xinjiang, central authorities pressed provincial and central academies of social science to make such historical claims. Advocates of Koguryo's Chineseness did not at first broadcast their views widely but were emboldened. As in the case of Tibet, there is no professional academic community capable of refuting these historical claims.

The South Korean predilection to cling tightly to narratives of an early history of proud resistance to foreign dependency and obscure Chinese moves to reinforce historical claims to border areas did not appear likely to arouse tensions. Unlike territorial disputes elsewhere, neither state claims land that is held by the other, and Sino–South Korean ties were advancing well, led by burgeoning trade and investment. In the face of North Korean assertiveness, higher-priority matters took the spotlight. From the U.S. standpoint, there was no rationale to put emphasis on diverging publications about a state from the days of the Roman Empire, and the dispute over Koguryo was met with disbelief and indifference.

China's treatment of its neighbors, however, is a U.S. concern. Whether in border disputes with Vietnam, India, or Japan or on the Taiwan issue, it has a stake in China not throwing its weight around, but instead adopting conciliatory tactics that keep the region in equilibrium. The same holds true on the Korean peninsula. Any suggestion that China may seek territory from a neighbor or even justify a sphere of influence through historical arguments could be seen as a step toward expansionism. It could cause U.S. identification with a democratic ally in opposition to a communist-led potential threat, consistent with lingering U.S. self-identity as the defender of the "free world" and with renewed attention to the moral obligation to champion democracy. Along with other values issues, history raises the need for U.S. reassurances contributing to long-term regional stability.

The United States and Past Sino–South Korean Relations

Before 2003, the U.S.–Sino–South Korean triangle was of little significance, and Washington had little reason to think about historical memory as a factor in Sino–South Korean relations apart from the legacy of the Korean War. U.S. support for South Korean territorial integrity was assumed, and North Korean territory seemed far removed from the agenda at hand. U.S. power was so much greater than that of South Korea, it gave little thought to independent views in that country on a significant great-power matter such as Sino-U.S. relations. China continued to insist on a role for North Korea, refusing on political matters to work within the framework of this triangle. Boldly pursuing the sunshine policy, Kim Dae-jung took care to cultivate ties to the Clinton administration that would not give it any cause to be concerned about his reliance on China to persuade Kim Jong-il. Even after his unsuccessful meeting with George W. Bush in March 2001, Kim Dae-jung could not turn to China. Talk of balancing powers or seeking equidistance seemed far removed from the reality of the first decade after normalization of relations between Seoul and Beijing. Having waited long for this breakthrough, Seoul was averse to either challenging Beijing or damaging its sole alliance. The situation changed in late 2002 with the nuclear crisis and the election of Roh and again in 2007 with Lee's election.

For a time, Sino–South Korean ties remained primarily economic, limited in ways consistent with U.S. expectations for an ally and the lack of multilateral diplomacy over North Korea. Yet, given South Korea's longstanding eagerness for normalization and sensitivity about keeping ties on an upward course, this relationship acquired a special character. It clearly ranked second only to U.S. alliance ties and, to a degree, was both independent of those ties and served as a balance. With an agenda expanding to include security and the emergence of tensions over trade in the summer of 2000, there was a notable rise in triangularity. The former resulted from the scope of the inter-Korean summit, and the latter from a trade war known as the garlic battle. In this dispute over tariffs and protectionism, China showed through its sharp escalation from garlic to vital industrial products in comparison to the retaliatory measures used against Japan in a similar agricultural case that it was in the stronger position and would tolerate no such behavior. Yet, since Seoul had miscalculated by ignoring Chinese warnings and defying the logic of its huge trade surpluses with China,[7] this response to the use of its safeguard measures was not widely interpreted as abuse of power and did not reverberate in the United States. The rapid rise in Sino–South Korean trade seemed strictly a matter of economics.

[7] Jae Ho Chung, "From a Special Relationship to Normal Partnership? Interpreting the 'Garlic Battle' in Sino-South Korean Relations," *Pacific Affairs*, Vol. 76, No. 4 (Winter 2003–4), pp. 549–68.

In the Six-Party Talks, especially from 2005, the U.S.–Sino–South Korean triangle acquired unprecedented significance. With Japan marginalized in its obsession with the abductions issue and Russia peripheral as it focused on ties with North Korea as a means to be taken seriously, the other three states faced the challenge of coordination. This intensified from the end of 2004 as Roh made clear his frustration with Bush's hard-line approach, acquiring importance in the summer of 2005 when Roh was able briefly to take the initiative in dealing with Pyongyang, then Hu Jintao shepherded the September 19 Joint Statement, and then Roh rushed to boost economic ties with Pyongyang even as Bush imposed financial sanctions. Following the nuclear test, Sino-U.S. cooperation led to the Joint Agreement of February 13, 2007, while Roh pledged to restrain his overtures to Kim Jong-il in order to achieve denuclearization. Later, as Roh planned an inter-Korean summit that would boost economic assistance and promote a peace regime replacing the longstanding armistice on the peninsula, Bush urged that its foremost objective be denuclearization. As a party to expected four-way talks on a peace regime and organizer of the Six-Party Talks, China remained rather aloof from these squabbles.

In 2004–7, the alliance struggled due to lack of agreement between Bush and Roh on strategic questions related to the nuclear crisis or overall regional policy. At the same time, U.S. ties with China had overcome differences over military buildups and Taiwan by finding common cause in addressing the North Korean issue and other matters. Given the delicate nature of both bilateral relations, U.S. policy makers were reluctant to become entangled in matters that lack high urgency. Knowing little about the significance of the Koguryo issue, few put it into the wider context of regional strategic thinking.

After Lee's election, there was renewed attention to strengthening the alliance, including emphasis on values that bolster bilateral ties. This had implications for raising human rights concerns or reciprocity in North Korean ties, while tilting the balance away from ties with China based solely on realist and economic concerns. As universal values reemerged as a theme in Seoul, Beijing took a dim view, restraining pressure against the North while increasing economic ties as its indispensable partner.

The Chronology of the Dispute

Koguryo (37 BC to 667 AD) was one of three states dominated by the divided Korean nation, situated not far from the borders of Han, Sui, and Tang China as well as of the divided Chinese states during the interval from Han to Sui. Dynastic historians of China have not included it as a Chinese dynasty, while the historiography of Korea leaves no doubt about its critical role in that country's evolution. Even as modern nationalism has shown increasing interest in affirming past claims to the inland borders of today's People's Republic of China, South Koreans were unaware of any intention to consider Koguryo within the Chinese state. This changed with assertions by provincial academic groups that it is, indeed, part of their state's history, and the fierce reactions in South Korea that this strikes at the very heart of Korean national identity, as Koreans view it as one of three coexisting Korean kingdoms that were combined into a single, unified Koryo state. The fact that the Chinese government echoes these assertions and no countervailing publications suggest an interest in correcting them leaves no doubt in a state such as China, where censorship operates, that national leaders are behind this claim.

The recent controversy relates to a 2001 North Korean application to UNESCO to include on the World Cultural Heritage list mural paintings that survived from the time of the Koguryo state. Then, in 2002, Chinese authorities gave Jilin province and its academy of social sciences the task of conducting a multiyear project on Northeast Asian history, which would draw attention to the cultural heritage of that state, much of which could be traced to locations now within this province.[8] The scene was set for Jilin representatives to insist that a state once present on their territory had in fact been Chinese under strong influence from Chinese culture and language. That argument is buttressed by evidence that this was an era of considerable borrowing of China's high culture, but, rather than stop there, the nationalist rhetoric carries Chinese claims much further.

The dispute intensified in 2003, when North Korea's attempt to register heritage sites was directly countered by appeals from Liaoning and Jilin provinces. Then, in 2004, South Koreans were enraged when they became acquainted with the framework devised by the Northeast Project in Jilin for treating Koguryo history as part of China's local history. The fact that the Ministry of Foreign Affairs deleted Koguryo from the website on Korea indicated that the central government endorsed the framework, and the Chinese Academy of Social Sciences in Beijing gave no reason for concluding it was not privy to the same reasoning. China stopped

[8] Samuel S. Kim, "Nationalism and Globalization in South Korea's Foreign Policy," unpublished paper, 2007.

sending scholars to seminars in Seoul on ancient history, while through 2004 NGOs in South Korea gathered more than 1 million signatures as part of a protest movement. Titles issued by the Northeast Project were now closely followed and found to cover part of Korea's heritage, raising concerns about the borders in the region. South Koreans perceived these affronts as "historical aggression." The Korean media was filled with outraged reactions against China's "attempt to claim part of Korean history as its own."[9] If the issue was minimized in the Chinese press, its impact was huge in South Korean newspapers, with sobering effects on public opinion toward China.

A visit by Foreign Ministry official Wu Dawei diffused the tensions for a time.[10] The Roh administration was eager to avoid any row and accepted explanations that China considered this to be an insignificant matter confined essentially to the provincial level. An understanding was reached not to politicize the issue or allow it to influence bilateral relations. Thus, the issue was considered settled until it resurfaced in September 2006, when South Koreans discovered on the website of the Center on China's Borderland History and Geographical Research new assertions that Koguryo was a provincial vassal kingdom under Chinese authority, not an independent Korean state.[11] The resulting fury on the Internet and in the media focused on how the state-financed rewriting of border histories casts doubt on China's motives in dealing with Korean reunification. This time, the South Korean government did not raise the issue and China did not indicate that it took the revival seriously; both sides assumed that their quiet understanding of 2004 still held. In this second outburst, some Chinese gave assurances that there exists no central policy to arouse sentiments over this issue, and a scholar wrote a reassuring history that showed Koguryo was Korean.[12] Meanwhile, the Chinese dismissed the cause of the furor as either trivial – some historians in peripheral locations in the Northeast saw an opportunity to win grants to gather and display Koguryo artifacts – or sensationalist – Korean media looking for themes to attract readers. Yet, some Chinese took a hard line, charging that a fuss was being made because nationalists looking to reunification were

---

[9] Kim Seok-hwan, "Cooperation a Must in Region," *JoongAng Daily*, December 24, 2004.

[10] Honda Yoshihiko, "Chuchokan o yusaburu kodai kokka no genei," *Sekai shuho*, November 9, 2004, pp. 26–9.

[11] Choe Sang-Hun, "Tussle over a Vanished Kingdom," *International Herald Tribune*, October 12, 2006.

[12] Interview with Ambassador Moon Chung-in, October 12, 2007.

using this pretext to express Korean territorial pretensions toward Jilin and Liaoning provinces.

Publication in June 2007 of a Korean translation of a Chinese 2001 book exposed the ambitious range of Chinese historical revisionism. This book claimed all three of the kingdoms in Korean history, including Shilla and Baekje, as part of China's history. With arguments that they were founded by exiles from a Chinese dynasty or a Chinese ethnic minority, had vassal ties to China, or even were directly ruled by it, these unprecedented claims shocked Koreans.[13] Academics eager to provide the widest possible justification for China's current boundaries were encroaching on the historical terrain considered vital to the emergence of the Korean nation; their views had gone unnoticed for a time, but no longer would this happen, as South Koreans became sensitized to the linkage between the historical controversy and China's assertive posture in using North Korea for its purposes.

Carefully reviewing the controversy in 2009, Jae Ho Chung explains the rationale for China regarding Koguryo as local history as due to the fact its capital for 470 years before it moved to Pyongyang was in territory now part of China and up to three-quarters of the population (including Han, Manchus, Mongols, and Jurchens) were not Korean. He adds that increasingly the Chinese are insisting that this kingdom was solely part of China, excluding it from Korean history, and claiming it even after Pyongyang was chosen as the capital. His research made clear that the historians enlisted in the Northeast Project were given indisputable official backing by the Chinese Academy of Social Sciences.[14]

The Significance of This Dispute

History issues gain salience in circumstances where nations are struggling over far-reaching questions of identity. In South Korea, great uncertainties abound related to domestic clashes between conservatives and progressives, inter-Korean contacts with uncertain consequences, and even the growing rivalry of great powers, including the sole ally of the past sixty years, the United States. With the Six-Party Talks advancing and the second inter-Korean summit causing more divisiveness in 2007, Koguryo entered the picture along with Japanese colonialism as a theme that could take center stage. Japan's repentance/compensation for its colonial reign

---

[13] *Chosun ilbo*, June 4, 2007.
[14] Chung, "China's 'Soft' Clash with South Korea," pp. 468–83.

in Korea is an acknowledged part of the normalization process with North Korea and draws repeated attention in South Korea that shows no sign of subsiding. Rather than seeing China's claim to Koguryo as a narrow academic argument, hurtful to Koreans but of only symbolic significance, it loomed as an early indication of China's nefarious interests, even for conservatives overshadowing the Japanese dispute since it was directly linked to management of the security threat from North Korea and to the rapid rise of a power already far more consequential than Japan.

One background factor was South Korean attitudes toward the United States and their implications for relations with China. In 2002 through 2003, images of anti-Americanism raised doubts about South Korean dependability. In 2004, the electoral sweep by the Uri Party, including many votes from young people expressing preference for China, was another eye-opener. When in the first half of 2005 and again from that fall, tensions between Roh and Bush came more into the open, U.S. expectations for bilateral relations were limited, and Americans paid little attention to the fallout from the 2004 dispute over Koguryo. Yet, from mid-2006 North Korea's missile launchings and nuclear test changed the terms of debate in the United States and South Korea. Many awakened to South Korean misgivings over Roh's foreign policy and dependence on China on peninsular matters. In one article of August 2007, the *Christian Science Monitor* reported that 82 percent of South Koreans regarded China's claims that Koguryo had been a Chinese province as a sign of territorial ambitions. Similar numbers saw China's rise posing a threat to South Korean national interests and as many as 74 percent of respondents also saw China propping up the North Korean regime to exert influence over reunification. With such distrust toward China, it could not have been surprising that four times as many favored close ties to the United States and twice as many, following the U.S. shift in February 2007, agreed that the United States was taking South Korean interests into account in dealing with the North Korean nuclear issue.[15] Koguryo's impact reassured Americans even before Lee's December election.

Another factor is what to make of China's rapid rise and South Korea's growing economic dependence on it. Whether South Koreans regard the response to Koguryo as the legacy of a communist party dictatorship inclined to chauvinism or as a harbinger of an emerging hegemonic power

---

[15] Haesook Chae and Steven Kim, "Not the South Korea We Thought We Knew," *Christian Science Monitor*, August 13, 2007.

asserting historic rationalizations for expansionism, they are inclined to treat it as more than an arcane academic discussion.

The debate on the rise of China was truncated because South Koreans were: anxious to achieve normalization and then to sustain it; intent on obtaining assistance in dealing with North Korea; alert to Chinese sensitivities about criticism, especially from a state long treated as client; and energized by the ever-greater economic interdependence. Fear of China's rise as a political power prone to sinocentrism and as an economic power that could overtake the South in its limited number of internationally competitive industries was suppressed. When the Koguryo issue arose, the floodgates to criticizing China were partly opened.

With Bush's unilateral and divisive policies, as seen from Seoul, the tendency grew during his first term to credit Beijing more than Washington with being helpful for Korean reunification. This was visible in the early euphoria after the inter-Korean summit, and Jae Ho Chung pointed to the ambivalence of South Koreans.[16] The Koguryo issue as well as the deepening rifts apparent in the nuclear crisis changed this pattern. By the end of 2007, concern over "anti-Americanism" and "leaning toward China" had waned, as the focus was shifting to the state of ties between North and South Korea and, it followed, to the two states perceived as exerting the most impact on this.

With a conservative South Korean president taking office in February 2008, U.S. concerns faded about a special Sino–South Korean relationship emerging. Indeed, China was now concerned about Lee's priority to U.S. and even Japanese relations. In four meetings in four months, Lee and Hu Jintao tried to overcome this, upgrading ties to a "strategic, cooperative partnership," agreeing to boost trade from $145 billion to $200 billion in 2010, and pledging more intensive efforts to get North Korea to fulfill the terms of the Joint Agreement. With the United States active in bilateral diplomacy with the North, China and South Korea had more reason to cooperate. Economically tougher times also raised the stakes for increasing trade and exploring establishment of an FTA. Yet, in the background, values differences lingered. In the summer of 2008, as summits proceeded, Koreans grew concerned about Chinese territorial claims for Ieodo island (although these concerns were later quieted) and about Chinese Internet rumors that South Koreans regarded the Sichuan

[16] Jae Ho Chung, "South Korea between Eagle and Dragon: Perceptual Ambivalence and Strategic Dilemma," *Asian Survey*, Vol. 41, No. 5 (September/October 2001), pp. 777–96.

earthquake as "God's punishment to China," as one blogger had written. Chinese gave little leeway to freedom of expression in the South that did not show respect, as many in the South grew more fearful of dependency. History loomed in the background for the two states, one allied to the United States and the other insistent on balance with North Korea.

After long being preoccupied with Japan's challenge to Korean national identity, South Koreans awakened to the possibility of a challenge from China. As nervousness about China's rapid rise was spreading; South Koreans, who had been conditioned since normalization to avoid sensitive remarks that could damage relations, suddenly found a safe outlet in a traditional East Asian manner of arguing through references to history. If the dispute did not rise to the level of new diplomatic exchanges, it simmered in a way that contributed to rising tensions over other bilateral issues in 2008–9: signs of mutual snubbing as Lee took power and Hu reacted to his new foreign policy priorities; South Korean anger at brazen Chinese conduct during the "sacred torch" parade in Seoul prior to the Olympics; Chinese Internet postings targeting supposed South Korean slurs followed by booing of South Korean teams at the Beijing Olympics; renewed trade tensions in the financial crisis; and clashing approaches to assisting North Korea against the backdrop of UN sanctions.

Putting the Koguryo Dispute in Context

For foreign academics, interconnections among historical memories, national identities, and strategic thinking about the future of Northeast Asia deserve new attention in awareness of two separate components: (1) the legacy of Japan's defeat in 1945, which is still characterized by incomplete normalization; and (2) the legacy of sinocentrism after one-and-one-half centuries of Chinese weakness in exerting influence as a rising power. The Korean peninsula is on the frontline in both respects. In the search for reunification, rethinking of national identity is inevitable, raising anxieties and focusing attention on rival historical interpretations. Disconnected bilateral discussions may become part of a regional process, in which values cannot be ignored. The U.S. tendency to make universal values a precondition for international organizations and regional agreements means that it has to be prepared to discuss other notions of the values that matter in a region. In 2007, the United States took the lead in raising the subject of norms and principles in the Six-Party Talks working group on a multilateral security framework. While in these official settings such discussions proceed narrowly and slowly, academics can be expected to respond with more comprehensive approaches to values and the importance of historical memories in the competition to shape the values debate.

The end of the cold war changed the context of two blocs of states clashing over values as well as security, while raising new doubts about the role of values in U.S. ties with other nations. In this context, China's turn to political repression from June 4, 1989, and the Soviet Union's shift toward political openness and international cooperation with dramatic breakthroughs in 1989–91 raised the salience of synchronizing the responses of Washington, Tokyo, and Seoul in order to provide a roadmap for regional integration with values in the forefront. Urging at times restraint and at times urgency on Tokyo in its overtures to Moscow and at times seeking more restraint from Seoul in its *nordpolitik* and from Tokyo in its post-Tiananmen engagement of China, Washington faced more complex triangularity than at any other time since 1945. Yet, its brief ad hoc responses revealed continued discomfort with this configuration, and it refocused on bilateralism. Finally, North Korea's challenges to the security status quo raised a series of triangular dilemmas that proved more continuous and involved more states than anything that had preceded it. Could the United States solidify the alliance triangle both to deal with the first and second nuclear crises and to coordinate handling of the sunshine policy in 1998–2002 and the Joint Agreement in 2007? Even more critical, could it manage the triangle as a factor in responding to China's rise on matters of globalization and regionalism?

Japan is not well positioned to make its views known on the Koguryo issue, but there can be no doubt about them. After all, its histories are filled with references to the independence of Korea from China, and recent Chinese treatment of Korean history draws parallels to Chinese claims elsewhere in Asia, perhaps extending to Okinawa as well Taiwan, which run contrary to Japanese interpretations. Since any sign of interest by Japan would provoke a brusque response from China's Foreign Ministry and tar South Koreans with negative association with this questionable source on historical matters, it must react cautiously. Historical wounds are too raw for the Japanese to assume, as some did at the peak of the 2004 Koguryo dispute, that declining emotionalism toward their country as the "Korean wave" narrowed the cultural gap meant that rising resentment toward China – fueled by the Koguryo issue as well as China's violations of human rights for refugees forcibly sent back to North Korea – would spare Japan from further criticism.[17] Triangularity with the United States and South Korea offers Japan its best chance to make its views heard.

Japanese progressive sources echo the Korean view that the Northeast Project is filled with historical distortions, such as that when the Sui/Tang dynasties sent forces to Koguryo, this was a war of Chinese unification. They raise the possibility that this project is part of a strategy to deal with border questions by building a national state uniting fifty-six official minorities and overcoming separatism. Yet, their idealistic response is to strive for a new shared historical consciousness of the East Asian region, as if China is ready to change course.[18] Such idealism was rekindled by the DPJ with its joint history plans and talk of an East Asian community. If China is unyielding on Koguryo, far removed from the most sensitive historical issues, it is hardly prepared to find common ground.

The 2004 flare-up, although quieted through joint political efforts, testifies to the considerable sensitivity, even explosiveness, of clashing historical narratives in Northeast Asia. Sino-Russian, Sino-Japanese, and Russo-Japanese differences have drawn much of the past attention, but a divided Korea groping for new shared nationalism has lately had more intense differences with Japan as well as China. The problem with China extends to the sea, as Ieodo (Socotra rock) in the East China Sea is also disputed, even though it is not given international recognition as an island.[19] Yet, Koguryo is the center of controversy.

China's nervousness about dismemberment and ethnic separatism has a long history.[20] In the first decades of the twentieth century after the loss of Taiwan, concerns mounted accompanied by frenzied discussions of who is part of the Chinese nation. In the 1950s through the 1970s, anger centered on the United States over Taiwan, India over Tibet, and the USSR over Xinjiang kept these concerns alive. Reforms in the 1980s revived fears that relaxation of coercion would fuel separatism, and the collapse of the Soviet Union made such fears more palpable. Thus, the Northeast Project has a lengthy pedigree well rooted in a state-centered worldview that gives little merit to ethnic sentiments or human rights.

China may expect reassurances of its own. Reports that Korean maps exist that show areas in Northeast China to belong to Korea during

---

[17] *Asahi shimbun*, evening edition, August 11, 2004, p. 3.

[18] *Asahi shimbun*, December 11, 2004, p. 16.

[19] Hiramatsu Shigeo, "Chuhan ryoyuken arasoi kara Nihon ga manabu koto," *Seiron*, July 2007, pp. 264–71.

[20] Yu Yongtae, *Kansei no naka no keisho: Higashi Ajia no rekishi ninshiki to rekishi kyoiku no seisatsu* (Tokyo: Akashi shoten, 2009), pp. 138–59.

the Joseon era do not reassure it.[21] Prickly nationalist behavior that in the past has irritated diplomats from other states does not serve South Korea's prospects of becoming a facilitator of regional cooperation. Standing on principle against Japanese revisionism, U.S. unilateralism, and Chinese signs of returning to sinocentrism is appropriate, but this may become more effective by toning down nationalist overtones unnecessary to defend the country's fundamental interests. Lee's approach is devoid of Roh's emotionalism, but that does not satisfy China.

Varied interpretations of China's motives in raising the Koguryo issue deserve to be further tested. The least worrisome would be if it were sending a message primarily to North Korea, which is most closely identified with the Koguryo state and is not trusted in its nationalist challenges toward China. In 2004, 2006, and 2009, China was frustrated by the North's defiant and belligerent tone as well as lack of respect for China's efforts to find a stable compromise solution to the nuclear crisis, and the Koguryo theme was one way to register dissatisfaction – a kind of wake-up call that asserts China's stake in the peninsula dating back over two thousand years and that its interests should not be ignored. After all, as Jin Linbo explains, attempts by China to prepare a joint presentation covering the artifacts of the Koguryo kingdom were rejected by North Korea, arousing suspicions in China and driving it to develop an independent proposal that set the rivalry in motion.

A reassuring possibility would be if China were preemptively dealing with a possible territorial claim by a united Korea likely to be newly aroused by nationalism. With a Korean minority area on the border and South Koreans alert to old maps with boundaries different from present ones, some Chinese are suspicious that longstanding high levels of nationalism on both sides of the Korean peninsula will coalesce into a movement with territorial pretensions. In the coverage of Jin Linbo, we find ample evidence of suspicions of nationalism among South Korean politicians and academics, fueling distrust in China.

Increasingly, however, the evidence suggests a more sinister motivation linked to a view of history disrespectful of its neighbors and ominous for the rise of sinocentrism. It is this prospect that poses the need for an alternate history reinforced by South Korean shared thinking with the United States and, if possible, Japan. This should not vilify the past China-centered order even as it draws the line against glorifying it and,

---

[21] "Old Maps Highlight Current Chinese Territory as Ancient Korea: 'Study,'" *Yonhap*, November 20, 2007.

in that way, challenging current principles of international relations and of mutual respect.

As Chinese economic linkages to North Korea expanded while inter-Korean ties were blocked by the North, the prospect grew of the isolated leadership in Pyongyang falling under China's sway. Chinese historical thinking increasingly gave ammunition for the re-creation of a divided state. In 2010, Kim Jong-il's belligerence toward others appeared to serve China's interest in shaping reunification moves.

Conclusion

Korean history raises far-reaching concerns about clashing worldviews. Koreans look back at the long history of the tribute system as quasi-imperialism, while Chinese view it as a model of harmonious international relations. Korea's voice was muffled, even if China rarely sent troops except at Korea's invitation to quell Japan's invasion in the 1590s. Given contemporary China's great sensitivity to criticism and its suspect maneuvering to broker any preparations for reunification on the peninsula, the South Koreans are reminded of China's past hegemony. South Koreans also regard the Korean War as aggression backed by China, which was not stopped even as North Korea kept up terrorism and assassination attempts to the late 1980s. Chinese writings about the history of socialism and the struggle against U.S. hegemonism differ from these views, and as China's power grows, China is becoming more assertive about the struggle against enemies of socialism rather than converging with U.S. or South Korean views of the cold war.

For China and Japan, clashing views of the history of Taiwan cannot be divorced from the overall history issue. The way the Taiwan issue is handled by Beijing may cause other history differences to widen. Just as the Koguryo question enflamed concerns over sinocentrism in Seoul with linkages to security concerns about the fate of North Korea, a tough posture toward Taiwan, ignoring its history of separation from the mainland, could arouse fears of sinocentrism in Tokyo with linkages to security fears about the sea lanes. In India, Russia, and parts of Southeast and Central Asia, historical controversies could also fuel concern about Chinese intentions. Nor should the United States assume that it is immune just because it has no direct territorial dispute with China. What is at stake are clashing perceptions of the regional and international order. In the period before 1840, the failure to resolve such a clash stymied relations, leading to the Opium War. In the period 1949 to 1971, the intensification of this divergence led Washington and Beijing to oppose each other in the Korean War and then in the buildup to the Vietnam War. Failure to reach some shared understanding of history poses the danger of a repeat of tensions that could divide China and some of its neighbors as well as the United States.

There is reason for the United States to welcome awareness by the South Korean people of potentially destabilizing effects from China's rapid rise as a political and military power. Romanticism about China accompanied by excessive negativism toward Japan and a lack of caution in responding to proposals that could lead to exclusive regionalism or Chinese domination in Asia is not in the U.S. interest. Signs of gullibility toward China as well as anti-Americanism in polls in 2002–4, even including Uri Party politicians who swept to power in the April 2004 National Assembly elections, left many Americans wondering whether South Koreans were switching their allegiance. Thus, when the backlash against China followed later in 2004, it is understandable that some breathed a sigh of relief. Yet, with coordination to meet the challenge of North Korea's nuclear program taking precedence, there was little interest in Koguryo evolving into another obstacle to mutual trust. Some were also concerned about excessive exuberance over Korean nationalism and do not want additional issues to arise, even ones targeting China. Above all, respect for Korean sovereignty and territorial integrity is a central value that the United States has reason to articulate, while it also supports balanced assessments of national interests.

Overcoming the history divide is not a one-way street, but China's insensitivity to South Korea suggests that the primary challenge emanates from a country defensive of a past based on a hierarchical order it had forged and defensive of a communist party that distorts its evolution and demonizes the history of its past enemies. As seen in the dispute between Japan and South Korea, China can take advantage of other historical divides. If U.S.-Japanese or U.S.–South Korean relations are rocked by clashes over history, this would be another distraction from the primacy of sinocentrism as a threat to trust. Rather than face that outcome, U.S., Japanese, and South Korean officials and academics would do well to strive for greater historical understanding within this triangle and a long-term perspective supportive of the emergence of an Asian-Pacific community. While China is encouraged within the scope of the emerging East Asian community to limit sinocentrism in order to construct a shared regional history, it also can be welcomed into a larger community, whose history tests its interest in shaping the global order from within rather than tearing it asunder from without, drawing on imperial and Maoist legacies.

There is reason to think that Chinese willingness to broach nationalist views on the history of Koguryo is intended to send a message to Koreans in the North and the South. It could be a preemptive strike against an upsurge of nationalism directed against China as well as against territorial claims on land situated inside Northeast China. Also, it could be an assertion of the continuing right of China to play a large role in influencing the fate of North Korea and the peninsula as a whole, as it did during the Koguryo era. At a minimum, China is stressing the inviolability of its current borders. Yet, some wonder whether more ambitious goals could make it impervious to negative reactions in South Korea and emboldened to expound a sinocentric worldview in which history becomes an integral part of assertive regional and global claims.

The Korean peninsula has become the centerpiece in maneuvering over historical memory. Naoto Kan was preparing a statement for August 29, 2010, to mark the one hundredth anniversary of the Korean annexation. North Korea sought to shift the focus from the Six-Party Talks to negotiations for a peace regime to replace the armistice that ended the Korean War, insisting on massive funds to cover historical damages from the United States as well as Japan. Above all, China, with its eyes on reunification with Taiwan and restoration of features of its sinocentric regional order in place of the U.S.-centered order characteristic of the cold war, was growing more forthright in challenging the status quo and the historical worldview behind it. Gaining more influence over the process of dealing with North Korea, China was positioning itself in the triangle with the United States to play a role in recasting the struggle from denuclearization to historical justice. Whereas Japanese imperialism had been the main historical theme, it was now being replaced with Western imperialism and hegemonism during the cold war and their legacy. Given the divisions in Tokyo, Seoul, and Washington in thinking about history, coordination would be difficult in the face of this new challenge.

Index

Abduction issue, 38, 90, 100, 113, 132–3, 137, 155–60, 163, 214; emergence of, 23, 153

Abe Shinzo, 2, 8, 134, 146, 150–8; and comfort women, 18, 27, 85, 105, 110, 116–17, 135, 140; and constitutional change, 23, 106; and revisionism, 5, 13, 90; and Yasukuni, 27, 135–6

Accidental deaths of schoolgirls in 2002, 58, 69–70, 99, 132

Afghanistan, 69, 79, 82, 92, 109, 155

Agreed Framework, 67

Ahn, Yonson, 186

Anti-Americanism, 11, 59, 66, 89, 99, 132, 148, 157; and candlelight vigils, 69, 160; impact of, 72, 136, 218–19, 225; shift toward, 7, 46, 50–2, 70, 140, 145

Anticommunism, 2, 4, 45, 48, 124; shift from, 54, 56, 75, 89

Anti-imperialism, 2–3, 6, 36, 81, 89–90; and sinocentrism, 13; and U.S. open door policy, 33

Apelovitz, Gar, 41

Arc of freedom and prosperity, 8, 156

Armitage, Richard, 133–4

Asada Sudao, 41

ASEAN (Association of Southeast Asian Nations), 3, 26, 131, 158

ASEAN Regional Forum (ARF), 102

Asia-Pacific community, 14, 74, 79, 147, 225

Asian Americans, 116, 153–4

Asian financial crisis, 7, 102

Asianism, 7, 12, 35–6, 39, 72, 162, 165–7

Asian-Pacific Economic Cooperation (APEC), 102, 152, 155

Asian values, 7, 85, 93, 145, 156

Asian Winter Games, 192

Asian Women's Fund, 110, 118

Aso Taro, 8, 23, 27, 87, 109, 117, 137, 156, 164

Atomic bombs, 6, 12, 29, 39–44, 74, 90, 94, 148, 152

Australia, 43, 155

Axis of evil, 8, 10, 14, 68, 84, 145, 148, 150

Baekdu (Changbai) mountain, 192

Balancer, 65, 100, 163, 213

Ban Ki-moon, 181

Beef imports, 69, 138, 160

Beijing Olympics, 5, 10, 173, 205, 220

Bernstein, Burton, 41

Bianzhong, 176

Bosworth, Stephen, 147

Brezhnev, Leonid, 81

Bush, George H. W., 76

Bush, George W., and apology, 59; and Bill Clinton, 9–10, 67; and Japan–South Korean ties, 18, 134, 152, 154, 160, 213; and North Korea, 77, 148, 219; and values, 5, 11, 14, 75–8, 82–4, 145–6, 150; views of, 8, 77–8, 89, 155, 157, 159

Butow, Robert, 40–1

Camp Zama, 99
Canada, 110, 116
Carpet bombing, 29
Carter, Jimmy, 77, 148, 150
Central Asia, 224
Cha, Victor, 68, 124
Chang, Iris, 127
Cheju Island massacre, 54
Cheney, Richard, 134
Cheonan, 12, 74, 80
Chiang Kai-shek, 33–4
China, image of, 81, 134, 150, 221; sixtieth
    anniversary, 5, 147; smile diplomacy of,
    126, 136; strategic competitor, 148
Chinese Communist Party, 1; legitimacy of,
    13, 209, 225
Choi Kwang-sik, 183–4, 191, 201–2
Chun Doo-hwan, 25, 50–3, 149–50
Chun Jin-sung, 172
Chung, Jae Ho, 209–10, 217, 219
Civilian killings by U.S. in Korean War,
    45–6, 54–62, 70, 149
Clark, Mark, 113
Climate change, 3, 7, 11, 79, 147
Clinton, Bill, 40, 67, 76, 83; and apology,
    46, 57–8, 63, 70; and North Korea, 77,
    101, 112, 150; and values, 9–10, 144
Clinton, Hillary, 101
Cold war, end of, 25, 54, 63, 70, 88–9, 99,
    211, 221; end of and history, 4, 6–7, 94,
    105, 125; impact of, 22, 75, 81–2, 129,
    145, 171; positive outcome of, 14; views
    of, 86, 151, 162, 165, 224, 226
Collaborators, 91, 125, 129–30
Colored revolution, 11
Comfort women, 25–6, 42, 105, 109–10,
    113, 125, 127–8, 141, 156; issue in
    2007, 8, 18, 85, 116–17, 135
Commodore Perry, 36
Comprehensive, verifiable, irreversible,
    denuclearization (CVID), 100
Confucianism, 1, 6, 208, 211
Constitution, of U.S., 4; of Japan, 13, 20,
    23, 90, 158
Cultural genocide and Japanization, 86,
    94, 98, 103, 114
Cultural opening, 158–9, 166

Daejoyoung, 195, 197, 199–200
Dalai Lama, 10
Defense guidelines, 23, 92, 99

Democracy, acceptance of, 19–20, 75, 77,
    81–2; and alliances, 4, 47, 68, 72–3,
    97–8, 125, 141; and the future, 1, 11;
    maturity of, 7, 102, 157; principles of, 8,
    101, 149; values and identity, 17–18, 28,
    70, 144, 211–12
Democratic Party of Japan (DP or
    Minshuto), 5, 12, 137, 160–7, 222; and
    the U.S., 8, 75, 99, 155
Democratization movement, 50–3, 167
Democrats and Republicans, 12, 76–9
Deng Xiaoping, 2, 177
Devil's Gluttony, The, 25
Dictatorship, 4, 46, 77, 145; U.S. support
    for, 50–1, 82, 87
Dokdo/Takeshima, and history, 5, 121–2,
    130; and U.S. Board on Geographic
    Names, 18, 160–1; designation of
    Takeshima Day, 105, 107, 133; disputes
    over, 27, 90, 108–9, 111–12, 134,
    138–9, 149, 155
Dower, John, 28

East Asian community, 3, 6, 14, 163–4,
    208; advocacy of, 8, 12, 79, 92, 137,
    147, 167, 222
East Asian Summit (EAS), 102, 151, 158
Economic protectionism, 76, 79, 83, 93
Eda Kanji, 37
Electricity, 100
Emperor, 20, 29, 105, 166; Hirohito, 4;
    visit of Akihito to China, 25; visit to
    South Korea, 164–5, 167
Enola Gay, 40, 149
Ethnic Koreans, in China, 179–80, 183,
    192–3, 202, 211–12, 223
Europe, 11, 78, 84–5
European Union (EU), 110, 116

Fishing, 111, 131
Five People's Harmony, 37
Flying geese formation, 102
Forced labor, 113
France, 90
Fraternity, 163–4
Free market economies, 80, 82–3, 98
Free trade agreements (FTAs), 48, 69, 79,
    92, 107–9, 131, 152, 188, 219; and the
    U.S., 12
Free world, and values, 4–5, 98, 145, 209,
    212

Friendship relations, 2, 4
Fujisaki Ichiro, 43
Fukuda Yasuo, 23, 90, 100, 126, 135–7, 156–60; and Yasukuni, 27
Fusosha, 110–11, 132

G-2, 163
G-8, 137, 160
G-20, 74, 79
Garlic trade war, 213
Georgia, 10–11
Gleysteen, Bill, 53
Globalization, 7, 11, 72, 78–9, 144, 208, 221
Gorbachev, Mikhail, 76, 88
Great Britain, 32–3, 37–8, 43, 80, 90, 155; and Anglo-Japanese alliance, 118–21
Great East Asia Ministry, 33
Greater East Asia Co-Prosperity Sphere, 34, 36
Green, Mike, 117, 133–4
Gries, Peter Hayes, 172, 183, 210
Gulf War, 23, 99, 125–8

Hasegawa Tsuyoshi, 40–1, 152–3
Hashimoto Ryutaro, 26, 37, 87
Hatoyama Yukio, 73–4, 78–80, 137–8, 143, 146–7, 161–7; and history, 2, 13
Hayashi Fusao, 36–7
Helsinki accords, 84–5
Henderson, Gregory, 50
Hideyoshi, Toyotomi, 18
Hill, Chris, 84, 134, 157
Hinomaru, 24
Hiroshima, bombing of, 6, 39–44, 87, 148; visit to, 3, 12, 42, 74, 150, 166–7
History and values, 3, 8–9, 13, 72, 76, 147–8
History card and China, 38, 86, 145
History projects in China, 5, 209
Hitler, Adolf, 4, 5, 86; and Nazism, 80
Honda, Mike, 116, 135, 140, 153–4
Hong Kong, 102
House of Representatives, 18, 85, 110, 116–17, 122, 135, 140, 149, 153–4
Hsu, Norman, 154
Hu Jintao, 2, 136, 174, 181, 188, 205, 208, 214, 219–20; and Japan, 27, 152; and sinocentrism, 13

Hu Yaobang, 25
Hubbard, Thomas, 120
Human rights, 8, 11; and China, 3, 222; and Japan, 20, 41, 101, 164; and North Korea, 10; and South Korea, 47, 73, 173, 205, 214; and United States, 50, 68, 144, 148, 150

Ienaga Saburo, 25, 33, 41
Ieodo island (Socotra rock), 219, 222
Imperial system, 19
India, 33, 119, 212, 222, 224
Indian Ocean refueling, 79, 99, 155
International Military Tribunal of the Far East (IMTFE), see Tokyo Tribunal
International People's Tribunal on the Dropping of Atomic Bombs, 42
Iran, 79, 147
Iraq War, 8, 39, 69, 75, 84–5, 88, 92, 99, 154–5
Ishihara Kanji, 37
Ishihara Shintaro, 38

Japan, apologies of, 86–7, 105–6, 110, 113–18, 127, 152, 164; apology to, 156–7; colonialism of, 1, 7, 60, 97, 102–4, 122, 167, 217, 226; militarism of, 8, 20–1, 80, 143; revisionism of, 1–2, 4, 125, 128, 160–1, 164, 223; romanticized, 81; spiritual vacuum of, 20–2, 30; war conduct of, 82, 86
Japan Sea vs. East Sea, 156
Jia Qinglin, 187
Jiang Zemin, 2, 26
Johnson, Lyndon, 148
Joint Agreement of 2007, 10, 84, 100–1, 152, 214, 219, 221
Joint Statement of 2005, 10, 84, 134, 214
Jucheism, 129
Jumong, 194–8, 202–3

Kaifu Toshiki, 105
Kamikaze, 18, 82, 87
Kan Naoto, 74, 80, 226
Kando Convention, 182
Kanemaru Shin, 163
Kang Jun-yong, 182–3
Katsura Taro, and Katsura-Taft, 119–21
Kellogg-Briand Treaty, 29
Khrushchev, Nikita, 81

Kim Dae-jung, 7, 102, 158; and Bush, 64, 67, 132, 159, 213; and visit to Japan, 26, 98, 105, 109, 129, 131, 152; and visit to Pyongyang, 64, 112, 129; kidnapping of, 156–7; views of, 47, 58, 69, 99, 213
Kim Hyun-hee, 137
Kim Jong-il, 147, 152, 213–14, 224; views of, 64, 101
Kim Moon-so, 183
Kim Tong-choon, 60
Kim Woo-jun, 183
Kim Young-sam, 105, 109
Kimigayo, 24
Kitaoka Shinichi, 6
Kobayashi Yoshinori, 38–9, 127
Koguryo, impact of, 5, 130, 172–4, 178–84, 205–7, 215–19
Koizumi Ichiro, 87, 106–7, 146, 152, 155; and realism, 23, 162; and Yasukuni, 2, 18, 27, 38, 90, 105, 109, 129, 132–4, 140, 149; visit to Pyongyang, 132
Kono Yohei, 26–7, 105, 110, 116–18, 153
Korea, annexation of, 24, 94, 97–8, 102–3, 111, 118–21, 133, 151, 161, 167; annexation and the U.S., 12; annexation centennial, 159, 166, 226; division of, 6, 46, 51, 75, 82, 87, 149, 185; modernization of, 87, 102–3, 149
Korean Airline (KAL) bombing in 1983, 137
Korean Peninsula Energy Development Organization (KEDO), 112
Korean War, 1, 8, 47, 51, 55–7, 60, 75, 99, 171; and North Korean aggression, 4, 82, 102; anniversary of, 74; views of, 86–7, 153, 213, 224–5
Koryo, 176, 211
Kubota Kanichiro, 104
Kuroda Katsuhiro, 106
Kwangju massacre, 46, 50–4, 59, 70–1, 99, 130, 149
Kyuma, Fumio, 41, 152–3

Lee Hoi-chan, 59
Lee Myung-bak, 2, 69, 109, 111, 113, 136–7, 143, 157–61, 164–7; and China, 174, 187–8, 205, 219–20; and history, 5, 27, 63, 78, 108, 126; and U.S. ties, 12, 47, 68, 71, 79–80, 92, 100, 146, 214; and values, 85, 150, 156
Lefkowitz, Jay, 85
Legend of Xue Rengui, 203

Lenin, Vladimir, 13
Liberal Democratic Party (LDP), 5, 21, 76–7, 137; conservatives of, 8, 83, 160

Ma Dezheng, 177, 209
Ma Ying-jeou, 3
Macao Banco Delta Asia sanctions, 10, 134, 214
MacArthur, Douglas, 30
Manchuko, 32, 36–7
Mao Zedong, 2, 4, 13
March 1 movement, 103
Marine Self-Defense Force (MSDF), 23
Maruyama Masao, 28
Marx, Karl, 13
Marxist historiography, 21, 77
Matsuo Fumio, 42
McCain, John, 11, 78
Media coverage survey, 48–9, 52, 56, 61
Middle East, 89
Minear, Richard R., 30
Minjung history, 54
Missiles, 101, 112, 218
Miyazawa Kiichi, 25
Mondale, Walter, 149
Mongolia, 155, 182
Mori Yoshiro, 87, 129
Multilateralism, 3, 14, 84–5
Mun, Pu-sik, 51
Murayama Tomiichi, 26–7, 37, 105, 112, 128, 137

Nagasaki, 6, 12, 39–42, 44, 74, 87, 148
Nakanishi Tsutomu, 32
Nakasone Yasuhiro, 25, 85, 105
Nanjing massacre, 24, 26, 29, 41, 127–8
National Guidance Alliance, 62
National Human Rights Commission, 54
National identities, 69–71, 75, 83, 145–6; and history, 5–6, 47, 72, 74, 86, 182–3, 191–2, 211, 217, 220; and Japan, 20, 166; and North Korea, 64, 66, 129; and U.S., 4
National museum's demolition, 26
NATO, 92, 148, 155; expansion of, 11
Negroponte, John, 84, 117
Neighbor clause, 104–5, 111
Neoconservatives, 83–5, 88, 134
Netherlands, 32, 37–8, 43, 110, 116
newly industrialized economies (NIES), 102
Nihonjinron, 166

Ning Fuqui, 173
Nixon, Richard, 77, 148, 160
Nobel Prize, 11
No-gun Ri, 46, 55–8, 70–1
Nordpolitik, 221
Normalization of Japanese–South Korean
   relations, 24, 113, 130, 165–6; and
   history, 2, 104, 151, 220
Normalization of Sino-U.S. relations and
   Joint Communique, 24
Normalization of South Korean–Chinese
   relations, 171, 179, 185, 202, 206, 213,
   219–20
North Atlantic Treaty Organization, *see*
   NATO
North Korea, demonization of, 81;
   historical grievances of, 5, 155–6
Northeast Asian Peace and Security
   Mechanism, 84
Northeast Project, 174–80, 183, 190–1,
   198–9, 202, 206, 209–11, 215–17,
   222
Northern Territories, 160–1
Nuclear weapons abolition, 11, 43
Nuclear weapons of North Korea, tests
   of, 10, 64, 101, 218; threat of, 38, 63,
   65–6, 89, 93, 99, 144; views of, 3,
   79
Nye, Joseph, 166

Obama Barack, 2–3, 43, 68, 74, 97–8,
   146–7, 164, 166–7; and North Korea,
   101; and values, 5, 11, 14, 78–9, 85,
   123, 150
Obuchi Keizo, 26, 87, 98, 105, 129, 131,
   152
Ogura Kazuo, 90
Okawa Shumei, 32–3
Okazaki Hisahiko, 34, 38, 154
Okinawa, 221; and U.S. bases, 73–4, 79,
   99
Opium War, 224
Organization for Economic Cooperation
   and Development (OECD), 102
Owada Hisashi, 19, 22
Ozawa Ichiro, 92, 163–5

Facific Economic Cooperation Council
   (PEEC), 102
Pacifism, 22–3, 40, 77–8, 81, 125–8,
   158
Pakistan, 79

Pal, Radhabinod, 29–30
Park Chung-hee, 2, 50–1, 91, 113, 130,
   211
Park, Doo-Bok, 187
Park Geun-hye, 188
Park Yu-ha, 106
Passing and entrapment, 162
Peace Friendship Exchange Program,
   43
Peace regime, 226
Peacekeeping operations (PKO), 128
Pearl Harbor, 4, 33, 36, 42, 87, 94, 148,
   167
Perry process, 112
Philippines, 12, 80, 86, 119
Portsmouth Treaty, 118
Presidential Truth Commission on
   Suspicious Deaths, 54
Prisoners of war, 43–4, 82
Putin, Vladimir, 151

Reagan, Ronald, 50, 76–7, 82, 85, 88, 148,
   150, 160
Realism, and alliance ties, 10, 90–3, 107,
   146–8, 157, 165; and China ties, 214;
   and history, 3, 154, 158; and U.S. shift,
   22
Refugees, 205, 221
Regime change, 64, 75, 94
Regional security framework, 11
Regionalism, 65–6, 72, 78, 94, 102, 221;
   and exclusivity, 3, 6, 225
Religious fundamentalism, 9
Reparations, 24
Reunification, 13, 99, 185; and identity,
   72, 75, 78, 91, 156
Revolution, in China, 8, 13, 90; in Russia,
   90
Rhee, Syngman, 50, 75, 77, 102, 113
Ri Ui Ha, 184
Rice, Condoleezza, 134
Roh Moo-hyun, 1–2, 7, 60, 86, 102, 107,
   132; advisers to, 66, 130; and Bush, 10,
   59, 64, 68, 152, 214; and China, 172,
   189, 216; and Japan, 109, 133, 135–6,
   146, 155, 157–61; and progressive
   views, 5, 46–7, 73, 99, 163; and
   reunification, 13, 91, 129; visit to
   Pyongyang, 156, 214, 217
Roh Tae-woo, 53
Rumsfeld, Donald, 134
Rusk, Dean, 121–2

Russia, 5, 10, 89, 94, 214, 224; and
    normalization, 129, 160
Russo-Japanese War, 86, 90, 118, 149

Sakurai Yoshiko, 38, 115
San Francisco Peace Treaty, 1, 24, 31, 35,
    113, 122, 153
Seoul Olympics, 99
September 11, 2001, 23, 67, 82, 89, 94,
    99, 132
Shigemitsu Mamoru, 32–4, 36
Shorrock, Tim, 51
Sigur, Gaston, 53
Singapore, 102, 158
Sino-Japanese War, 86, 185
Sino-Soviet split, 86, 88
Sinocentrism, 2–3, 12, 164, 208–9, 224–6;
    and Koguryo, 4, 173–5, 182, 219–20;
    and order, 98, 103, 223, 226; and U.S.,
    7–8, 13–14
Six-Party Talks, 100–1, 112–13, 148, 159,
    185, 189, 214, 217, 220, 226; and
    agreements, 10, 152; purpose of, 84
South Africa 60
South Asia, 7
Southeast Asia, 34, 89, 224
Southwest Asia, 7, 89
Sovereignty, 3, 11, 65, 73, 80–1, 94,
    156–7, 160, 209; and article 9, 20; and
    self-determination, 80, 83
Soviet Union, and World War II, 29, 40–1;
    collapse of, 4, 88, 211, 221; military
    buildup of, 8, 93; victimization by, 76,
    222
Spanish-American War, 86
Stalin, Josef, 4, 81; worldview of, 5, 13
State-centered values, 76, 222
Status of Forces Agreement (SOFA), 58
Stimson, Henry, 40
Straub, David, 53–4, 59
Suh, J. J., 66
Sun Jianzheng, 179
Sunshine policy, 64, 185; and U.S., 67,
    163, 213, 221

Taewang Sasingi, 195, 203
Taft, William, 119–20
Taiwan, 3, 90, 102, 161–2, 212, 214,
    221–2, 224, 226; and U.S., 150; missile
    crisis of, 23; peace treaty with, 24
Takeuchi Yoshimi, 35

Tamogami Toshio, 39
Tanaka Akihiko, 156
Tanaka Yuki, 42
Territorial disputes, 74, 90, 160, 210, 212,
    217
Terror-sponsoring states, 159
Terrorism, 23, 49, 63, 67, 69, 86, 224
Testuya Takahashi, 134
Textbooks, 6, 25–6, 90, 105, 108, 110–11,
    132, 138–9, 158; and Japan Teachers'
    Union, 24–5, 127–8; in China, 177–8,
    183
386 generation, 46
Three non-nuclear principles, 40, 162
Tibet, 3, 10, 182, 205, 212, 222
Togo Shigenori, 33
Tojo Hideki, 33–4
Tokyo Olympics, 24
Tokyo Tribunal, 21, 27–34, 41, 44, 86, 94,
    140, 153, 156; revelations at, 24; viewed
    as abnormal, 75, 127, 148
Tourism, 158, 205; to Mount Kumgang,
    64
Triangular alliance, 4, 10, 74, 100, 107,
    112–15, 142, 145–8, 151–3, 167, 221–2
Triangular analysis, 151–3
Triangular Coordination and Oversight
    Group (TCOG), 112, 159
Trilateral summit, 6, 92, 151, 164; and
    joint history, 6, 208, 222
Triumphalism, 7, 77, 85
Truman, Harry, 41, 153
Truth and Reconciliation Commission
    (TRC), 46, 60–3, 70, 129–30
Tsukurukai, 26, 110–11, 128
Turkey, 149, 154

U Silha, 210
Unit 731 and biological human
    experiments, 25, 42
United Nations Educational, Scientific, and
    Cultural Organization (UNESCO),
    178–9, 190, 201, 215
United Nations Security Council, 11, 40,
    133–4; resolutions and sanctions of,
    101, 147, 220
Universal values, 79, 93, 141, 156, 164–5,
    208, 214, 220; and America's mission, 7,
    10, 150; as smokescreen, 11
U.S., and Japan's colonialism, 118–19,
    149; leadership and values, 7–10, 81, 88,

144–7, 220–1; marginalization of history, 3, 7, 72, 74, 113–14, 122, 131, 138–9, 143, 153–4; unilateralism of, 73, 75, 77, 84, 163, 223
U.S. Forces Korea (USFK), 58, 69
U.S.-Japan Security Treaty, 74, 99, 162
U.S. occupation, of Japan, 19–20, 75, 80, 101, 147, 153; of South Korea, 51, 75, 80

Vietnam, 90, 182
Vietnam War, 48, 58, 86, 88, 90, 148, 225

Wakamiya Yoshibumi, 134
Wan Yi, 187, 212
Wang Qing-wei, 34
War criminals, 25, 29; class A, 21, 27–8, 32–3
Wartime operational control, 69, 100
Watanabe Tsuneo, 134
Weapons of mass destruction (WMD), proliferation of, 63, 68, 79; views on, 47, 67, 145, 189
Wen Jiabao, 27, 136, 181
Wickham, John, 53
World Cup, 132

World financial crisis, 7, 23, 79, 108–9, 220
World order, justness of, 3, 224
World War II, 3–4, 8, 12, 80, 86, 153; and Japanese national identity, 17–18, 21; as struggle among imperialists, 81, 86–7
Wu Dawei, 181, 216

Xi Jinping, 92, 165
Xinjiang, 3, 212, 222

Yachi Shotaro, 142
Yagi Hidetsugu, 110
Yanagida Kensuke, 113
Yanbian, 192–3, 212
Yang, Jai-Hoon, 118–22
Yasukuni Shrine, 2, 18, 25, 75, 109–10, 134, 156–7; suspension of visits to, 5, 27, 78, 90, 105
Yellow peril, 90
Yeongae Somun, 194–200
Yongbyon reactor, 10, 100
Yoshida Doctrine, 2, 22, 72, 166
Yoshida Shigeru, 113

Zainichi Koreans, 161, 164
Zoellick, Robert, 115, 134, 149